5/92.

Shakespeare's *Edward III*

Shakespeare's
EDWARD III

Edited by Eric Sams

Yale University Press
New Haven and London

Set in Garamond by Best-set Typesetter Ltd., Hong Kong
Printed and bound in Great Britain by Martins, Berwick upon Tweed

Library of Congress Cataloging-in-Publication Data

Sams, Eric.
    Shakespeare's Edward III/Eric Sams.
    Includes bibliographical references and index.
    ISBN 0-300-06626-0
    1. Edward III (Drama) – Authorship.   2. Shakespeare, William,
1564–1616 – Authorship.   3. Edward III, King of England, 1312–1377 – In
literature.   I. Edward III (Drama).   II. Title.
PR2859.S26   1996   96–7371
822.3'3—dc20   CIP

A catalogue record for this book is available from the British Library.

10   9   8   7   6   5   4   3   2   1

tertio ad manes fratrum

Contents

Acknowledgements

I am grateful to my family and friends for all their timely assistance and encouragement. Clifford Broadbent, Charles Hobday and Jon Mills were especially generous with their time and helpful with their comments. So was the late Eliot Slater, who started me on this quest in 1982. A special word of thanks is due to Karl Wentersdorf for a long loan of his magisterial 1960 dissertation on *Edward III*, which would surely have settled the authorship question decades ago, had it been published. I am again much obliged to Yale University Press; and the holdings and services of the London Library were, as ever, indispensable.

I

Introduction

Over a decade ago (Sams 1985d, 1986d) I published a 400-page edition of *Edmund Ironside c.* 1588 which assigned that play to Shakespeare for reasons including hundreds of close and clear parallels. That attribution, first advanced in 1954 by the American scholar E.B. Everitt, has found favour with few specialist Shakespeareans, despite the copious evidence and the absence of counter-arguments. This time, however, the profession may prove more persuadable. Over the last 200 years, *Edward III* scholars have been confidently announcing the Shakespearean credentials of the play, which are now generally accepted by literary Academia. But such acquiescence is by definition theoretical, not practical, and passive, not active. On its own, it can never overcome such obstacles as exclusion from the Oxford *Complete Works* (Wells 1986c, xxi) and *Textual Companion* (Taylor 1988, 136–7). Those editors themselves later expressed regret for the omission (Taylor 1990; Wells 1990); but this unobtrusive recantation, reported from a literary conference, has made no detectable impact on the profession or the public. Further effort is still needed to restore *Edward III* to the canon, for the first time in 400 years, and thus celebrate the quatercentenary of its original publication in 1596. Hence this edition.

To admit an entire new play, however, is to admit previous prejudice. In Academia, furthermore, what is not known is not knowledge. Under cover of this darkness, the notion of 'collaboration' (Muir 1953, 1960 and Kerrigan 1986b, 1990) has crept in and gained ground. It purports to explain the presence in *Edward III* of a style unfamiliar to many an expert eye. The modern professional mind-set still views every variant version of any Shakespeare play, or any unfamiliar style, as the work of anyone but Shakespeare himself. He cannot possibly have written thus, at any stage of his career; so the explanation must be some unknown person or persons 'collaborating' with him (Taylor 1988, 217, on *1 Henry VI*), or 'imitating' or 'plagiarising' him (Proudfoot 1982, 1986b and Bate 1995a, 1995b, 81n, on *Ironside*), or 'memorially reconstructing' him (in almost every modern edition of every two-text play); and so forth. This preserves him as a 'late-developing' dramatist, free from the least taint of inferiority. But the unanswerable point has been made (most recently in Sams 1995a) that all these conjectures are just literary inventions emanating from the élitist attitudes of 1920s Oxbridge that still dominate orthodox scholarship world-wide. Before then, no such notions had ever existed. Shakespeare's early start and conscientious revision, conversely, have always been as well documented as they are economical and sensible; and their natural corollary is the existence and recycling of very early Shakespeare plays which, though popular and profitable, and hence published as well as acted, were for good reasons neither acknowledged nor collected. So they might well exhibit internal stylistic variety, which would be much more obvious to later critics than to earlier audiences or readers, or indeed to their author.

The tide of current orthodoxy is sluggishly on the turn. At least one professional (Honigmann 1982, 90; 1985, 126) has cogently contended that Shakespeare wrote his first plays long before the accepted date of *c.* 1590, his twenty-sixth year. It is generally agreed that he was on occasion an assiduous reviser (Wells 1986c, 1025; Honigmann 1989; 188–221). Furthermore, some of the possible early plays have been officially identified, such as *The Taming of a Shrew* (Wells and Taylor, in Taylor 1988, 169). Before long, all the modern 'collaborators', 'plagiarists' and 'memorial reconstructors' will be seen as the unevidenced and unnecessary entities they are. One single hand is enough explanation. Of course it grew in strength and cunning over the years – a development readily traceable by the factual title-page datings due to be adopted by the *Oxford English Dictionary* in its 2005 third edition (Simpson 1993), and perhaps also, in due course, by the text-editors of all future Shakespeare volumes and series (Sams 1992a, 1995a). Meanwhile, general readers can judge for themselves the strength of the internal *Edward III* evidence for authenticity and unity. This is summarised under separate headings in Section VII, after chapters on early commentary up to 1760 and the subsequent evolution of the current consensus. Two appendices draw inferences from (a) *Edward III* and (b) Hand D in *Sir Thomas More* about the authorship of *Edmund Ironside*. But first and foremost, the play's the thing; so its text and detailed notes, preceded by an uncomplicated synopsis of its action, now follow.

II

Synopsis

The Reign of King Edward III (1596)* is about that monarch's successful invasion of France (1–175, 1043–2600) and his unsuccessful assault on the Countess of Salisbury's virtue (135–40, 178–1037, 1477–9). An observer calls the latter campaign 'a lingering English siege of peevish love' (372); a participant in the former woos death with a smile (2304); thus the two main threads of love and war are interwoven. They were drawn from separate sources: war from the chronicles (Froissart and Holinshed), love from a novel (in Painter's *Palace of Pleasure*). Their contrasts provide large-scale structure, their interlinkages create phrases and imagery. Further, each is adroitly aligned as a separate aspect of one single unifying topic, namely the rights and wrongs of vows and promises, and hence the complex nature of political or social duties and responsibilities including due observance of the law. Edward already has his own queen and his own realm; what will result from his attempts at further conquests?

Here is the story. First (I.i), Edward's own parents (King Edward II and the French princess Isabel, daughter of Philippe le Beau) are presented as solemn sureties of sovereignty over both realms, recently violated by the false pretence of 'rebellious minds' that only descent through the male line is valid. Such a doctrine would be anathema to loyal subjects of any queen, even the virgin Elizabeth I. The character who announces it is himself a Frenchman, the Count of Artois, who devotes a long speech (14–44) to the conflict between his natural loyalty and his equally inborn love of truth. Next, the Duke of Lorraine arrives and requires Edward to pay personal homage to the King of France within forty days; this summons too is deliberately couched (60–70) in terms of duty and responsibility. Thus each monarch seeks to upstage and downgrade the other; and as a further irony Edward notes that he has no sooner decided to invade France than he is summoned there by its sovereign (71–3). Some aspects of this exposition seem mismanaged; thus Edward is made to enquire into matters with which he must have been perfectly familiar. But the scene as a whole is dextrously designed to run the gamut from loyalty to treachery, tuned by contrast and paradox to the utmost

* That text, as usual in the 1590s, had no act or scene divisions; these have been inserted from later editions for convenience of reference.

pitch of intensity heard in such antitheses as 'that is most false should most
of all be true', as Lorraine says of his countryman Artois (122). A further
episode introduces Sir William Montague with news of invasion from the
north; David, King of Scotland, is 'straight forgetting of his former oath'
(133). Even the young Prince of Wales, better remembered as the Black
Prince, is portrayed as divided between two loyalties: 'thou must begin/now
to forget thy study and thy books/and ure thy shoulders to an armour's
weight' (163–5). Everyone marches off to the wars.

Thus the exposition is completed. But the scene is now set for a modula-
tion from war to love, and the introduction of a new subject. Edward's
reaction to the news of invasion is intentionally surprising. He appears
unmoved by the loss of his border towns. His first thought is for the Countess
of Salisbury, besieged in her castle by the Scots in her husband's absence. In
a studied aside, Edward calls upon a character who will play no significant
part until much later in the action. This seems to be an authorial after-
thought. The text thus far has offered no reason for the Earl of Warwick's
presence, and made no provision for his entrance. His sole function is to reply
'It is, my lord' to Edward's question about the Countess: 'That is thy
daughter, Warwick, is it not?' (138, 141). The King knows it is; and he
knows her. The audience will rightly infer that his plans are more personal
than strategic; he marches north as if pulled by a magnetic pole. He is less
concerned with repelling the Scots than with being attracted by and to the
Countess.

The change of scene (I.ii) begins with another deliberate linkage. We know
that the King is turning north towards the Countess. Just as literally, she is
first seen facing south: 'in vain my poor eyes gaze/for succour that my
sovereign should send' (178–9). Thus her first thoughts are of him, as his
were of her. We then learn that Montague, who had reported the Scottish
invasion, was her envoy and emissary, charged to request help. She fears that
he has failed to plead her cause with sufficient fervour. This too is dramatic
irony; we know he had no need to; the King had vaulted into the saddle and
galloped to her rescue at the mere mention of her name.

She first appears alone on an upper stage, symbolic of her isolation and her
exalted merits. She is characterised as queenly in her resentment and spirited
in her defiance of intruders. Soon her chastity will be proclaimed and lauded.
The Tudor public could hardly fail to recognise certain qualities of their own
queen, who not long before had delivered her famous speech at Tilbury in
defiance of an entire invading Armada: 'I know I have the body of a weak and
feeble woman, but I have the heart and stomach of a King'. Her thoughts of
'foul scorn' that 'any prince of Europe should dare to invade the borders of
my realms' are fully shared by the Countess. Indeed, Elizabeth's actual phrase
'tyrants fear' is applied to the Countess (278); in a different sense, and
perhaps inadvertently, but the link is there.

Next, the Countess is made to overhear two revealing colloquies, full of
further ironies. First, the French Ambassador makes a brief reappearance. In

an era when roles were economically doubled, clear labelling was essential. We now understand why the Duke of Lorraine's name was woodenly repeated on his first entry (56, 59). He is to be recognised, with a shock of revulsion, as the 'Lord of Lorraine' addressed by King David, thus confirming the Tudor audience's worst fears about a treacherous clandestine league between France and Scotland. That point made, he departs. King David has already presented himself, by his blank verse style, as a Pistol or Parolles type of *miles gloriosus* or braggart soldier, whose rhetoric is tricked out in such tartan stuff as 'bonny' or 'whinyard'. The accession of the actual king of Scotland as James I of England in 1603 could not have been foreseen. He ruled both realms until his death in 1625; and he would not have relished hearing his native land derided as bleak and barren (191), its denizens as uncivilised (189), its diction as uncouth patois (185) or his own predecessor as a comical coward who takes to his heels as soon as the English army's approach is announced ('upon the bare report and name of arms', as the hostage Countess is incautiously quick to comment, in line 260), soon after a long speech (196–215) of inflexible dedication to the fight against England.

This is yet another motif of the broken vow. Meanwhile the Countess's spiritedness, her desirability and her riches have already been established (178–95, 220–2); and her transition from helpless prisoner to gracious and grateful hostess prepares the ground for King Edward's violent craving for her, in defiance of his own marriage-vows.

Here is a rich field for dramatic characterisation, much cultivated even in minor roles. Thus King David's henchman Sir William Douglas speaks only four lines (220, 223, 236, 238), each with a revealing parenthesis; 'my liege' thrice and 'my man' once. Thus we know that he fawns on his master and condescends to his servant. The hero-king Edward's nature is depicted and developed in subtle detail. On his arrival he scorns and dismisses the departed Scots as stealing (in every sense) foxes. Having thus seen himself as hunter and pursuer, he instantly falls prey to the Countess's beauty. Neither it nor she is unknown to him; but he dissembles with a deliberate echo of his earlier question to her father: 'This is the Countess, Warwick, is it not?' (276). And again: 'Hath she been fairer, Warwick, than she is?' (281). The interest is heard turning to obsession.

From now on, the main themes of love and war will be further intertwined by the presentation of each in terms of the other. The King will besiege a prospective mistress, yet woo France like a bride; 'how gently had we thought to touch thy breast' (1349) is addressed to that country, not the Countess. Both compounds contain new elements, each to be separately isolated, of swearing and forswearing. What now follows is an ornamented baroque duet between the lovesick King and the object of his infatuation. For this purpose the poetic style is deliberately retuned to a heightened key of language and imagery, culminating in a set-piece speech from the Countess (324–44) contrasting the outward austerity of her surroundings with the inward

warmth of her hospitality. Such florid comparisons, in the imagery of plant
life, come naturally to her. Edward is readily persuaded to stay for a night or
two. We are to infer that the Countess, for all her sophistication of utterance,
is emotionally naive as well as personally modest. She has implored her royal
admirer to enter her castle, even though he has already declared his feelings
and intentions plainly enough. He should pursue the Scots, 'Lest yielding
here I pine in shameful love' (300); and he is well aware, as we learned in an
earlier scene (139–40), that the Earl is safely far away in France.

Now the poetic language is still further enhanced by conscious craftsman-
ship, in the manner and often in the language of Shakespeare's published
poems and the still unpublished sonnets. In the ensuing scene (II.i), the
King's secretary Lodowick muses on his master's infatuation and lends a hand
with love poetry. For his pains, he was denounced by Swinburne (1880, 245)
as a pimp. But this misses the moral by miles. The secretary is presented as a
born stylist whose natural speech is artistry itself, all colour-painting and
balanced periods. The virtuoso vocabulary of his opening lines (350–73)
contrasts white and red, with a connoisseur's fine discrimination among five
different shades of the latter (cherry, scarlet, oriental, brick and coral). His
master Edward later addresses him as a gifted poet, who can 'beguile and
ravish soft and human minds' (430); so Lodowick's diction has to be heightened from the first, as dramatic realism requires. His deliberately slow and
laborious composition of the requested love lyric (410–526), with its wilfully
inept opening lines that compare the Countess first to the virgin goddess
Diana (492) and then to the decapitating heroine Judith (522), is therefore
intended ironically. It radiates a gentle good humour designed to offset and
if possible palliate Edward's serious satyriasis. His own royal ironies, such as
'thinkest thou I did bid thee praise a horse?' (450) and 'rather have her chased
than chaste' (505) respond well to this tender teasing. Master and secretary
are clearly on affectionate terms.

The most elevated style of all however is reserved for the Countess herself.
As she at last recognises that her virtue is under siege, her blank verse (584ff.)
takes on a new tone of thoughtfulness and dignity. Her metaphor for her
beauty, as the King sees it, has a beauty of its own: 'like an humble shadow/
it haunts the sunshine of my summer's life' (587–8). This makes an apt
prologue to her homily (604–31) on the marriage bond that binds them both
to others; the main theme of oath-taking is restated in a new mode.

It is then further developed in a separate sub-scene (651–768) where the
Earl of Warwick is cunningly enmeshed in self-violating vows and suborned
as an accomplice in the seduction of his own daughter. A loyal offer of aid is
perverted into sheer satanism. The paradox is explicitly avowed: '[Edward]
hath sworn me by the name of God/to break a vow made by the name of
God' (705–6). There must be something amiss with the premises of such
syllogisms. Artfully dissolved into the play's action, this poison crystallises
out into two Warwicks, one 'an attorney from the court of hell', briefed to
'seduce his child' (732, 738) and the other himself again when, to his joyous

relief, the Countess has successfully defended herself and been found innocent. Her threat of suicide restores her sovereign's sanity; as he contritely
exclaims, 'I am awaked from this idle dream' (1025).

Meanwhile Edward's mettle is further tested in a martial interlude (II.ii).
The Earl of Derby, though on stage in the first scene, had nothing to say. His
sole function was to recruit allies for the fight against France, especially the
emperor of Germany. He now returns and reports success (826–30). Lord
Audley's voice has already been heard, but only to announce the French
ambassador (56–7). His charge was to recruit foot-soldiers; he has now
brought his levies for inspection. Expectation is aroused, only to be dashed.
Edward's thoughts are elsewhere, a point dramatically reinforced by a
modern-sounding Freudian slip; he is made to say 'Countess' when he means
'Emperor' (854–6, 860). The King has become her subject, indeed slave.
Germany is brushed aside; the infantrymen are dismissed with a trivial quip
(852). Every phrase serves to heighten the continual resemblances and contrasts between love and war; thus the symbol of the drum is introduced only
to be toned down and retuned to a serenade (869–80). The drum has to
belong to the Black Prince, so that his face can remind his father of neglected
ties and duties, and thus constrain the King to correct his 'strayed desire'
(900). This further vow, by yet another device of contrast, is then used to
make Edward's imminent renunciation of his wife, and his acquiescence in
her death, all the more outrageously wicked. Here is a carefully crafted crux:
'I go to conquer kings and shall I not then/subdue myself . . . ?' (921–2). The
audience is made to feel that Edward's eventual renunciation of evil, however
belated, is redemptive; within the developing drama, his conquest of France
begins with his victory over himself.

Meanwhile, at the mere mention of an off-stage smile (926, 928), all the
fine words are forgotten again; Edward's Queen Philippa is insulted and the
rightful crusade abandoned. No wonder the Countess was earlier compared
to Cleopatra (865). Soon she will be likened to Lucrece (1021–2). This
deliberate cross-reference reveals a new and compelling aspect of her character. We have seen her beauty, wit, charm, humour, courage, hospitality,
impulsiveness, loyalty and affection (her first thought on inviting the King to
stay was how proud her husband would be, 304–5). Now all this is raised
to a still higher power. Once again the motive force is a rash promise which
is turned against its maker; by another ingenious counterpoint, the King is
finally outwitted by his own device, now adapted to good instead of evil
ends. The Countess is Lucretian in her accoutrements and imagery as well
as her soul, and as much a Roman dame as an English lady in being resolute
for death rather than dishonour. Hers is the brightest portrait in the entire
play.

Thus the dramatic tension has been tightened from Lodowick's detached
humour through Edward's mounting passion to an evil climax, his willing-
ness to murder the Countess's husband and his own wife for the sake of his
own obsession. With the Countess's outraged rebuttal the breaking-point is

reached, and Edward is himself again. The warrior-hero is exposed as an anti-hero. But his martial exploits will redeem him for his Tudor audience, which will applaud him for making war, not love.

Now the scene shifts to the French court (III.i). So far, King John has been heard only as a minatory voice off-stage (60), summoning Edward to do him homage. Now we see him in person, with his two sons. The Duke of Lorraine reappears, back home after encounters with the English enemy and the Scots ally; thus the action is again adroitly interlinked. The princes are presented as vacuously belligerent; their father is more astute and apprehensive, asking for crucial information about the enemy's strength and receiving cold comfort in reply. In palliation, division and disloyalty are expected within England itself (1055–60); these are surely anachronistic topical references to Tudor times. Each side's allies are mustered for comparison, and John's arrive in person.

A mariner announces (1108–26, 1132–6) the arrival of Edward's invasion fleet, again in topical terms designed to recall the Spanish Armada of 1588. The French king is shown as a skilled strategist disposing his forces effectively and with dispatch. All the dramatist's skills are now deployed to paint a sea battle on stage; the verbal backcloth drapes a purple patch of blood and thunder across the whole horizon. Thus the naval battle of Sluys in 1340 is fought and won again by the heroic English, whose skill and daring at sea are fresh in the audience's collective memory.

Next (III.ii) comes a brilliant vignette of undermined morale in a nation at war, riven by rumour and disquiet. Three wretched refugees have taken to the roads with their children and baggage. They are sharply characterised in a line or two each; One is dauntless, Two fearful, Three defeatist. A Frenchwoman is obsessed with absurd prophecies. Another set-piece speech (1286–316) presents a panorama of lost battle, defeat, despair. From the vantage point of imagination, five cities can be seen on fire, with casualties on a scale to match the slaughter at sea.

The play proceeds with further episodes selected from the chronicle sources to illustrate the main contrasting themes of loyalty and betrayal. Another Frenchman, Gobin de Grey, is shown (III.iii) as a willing convert to the English cause, which must accordingly be just; like Robert of Artois, he bears a noble-sounding name, and he is handsomely rewarded with 'five hundred marks in gold' (1328). The Black Prince too is characterised as clement, within reason; 'those that would submit we kindly pardoned' (1344), while others were sensibly slaughtered. History is briskly compressed to provide added springs of action. The battles of Sluys, Crécy and Poitiers are staged 'apparently in the course of a week or so' (Armstrong 1965, 197) though their historical dates were 1346, 1356 and 1340 respectively. Crécy is now already imminent, and the massive strength of the French forces is stressed, to enhance the coming victory. An eve-of-battle confrontation is arranged between warring monarchs, whose persons are presumably protected by the laws of chivalry. The French king makes a speech of defiance tempered with attempted bribery. Edward has 'broke league and solemn covenant' (1381); but might he be bought off with 'exceeding store of treasure, pearl and coin' (1389)? Never; he vows to have the crown of France, 'or one of us shall fall into the grave' (1418). Then King John proves to be embarrassingly well informed about his English enemy's love-life. The most evident source of this intelligence is the playwright himself, in his tireless search for dramatic unity. The French further scorn the English soldiers for their fondness for beef and enfeeblement from the lack of it.

Now comes a new interlude of solemn ceremony. As a prelude to the grant of knighthood won and conferred on the field of battle, the Black Prince is invested, piece by piece, with the ominously sombre armour that gives him his name. Breastplate, helmet, lance and shield are each the subject of a six- or seven-line invocation from his father the King and the court nobility; 'fight and be valiant, conquer where thou comst' (1508f.) recurs like a litany. Thus awe is to be instilled into the audience by evoking a quasi-religious ritual.

In immediate contrast, as if divine intervention had already been granted, comes a brief scene (III.iv.1555–68) depicting the desertion of French auxiliaries, with disastrous loss of life and advantage. Then Edward decrees a breathing-space upon a 'little hill', symbolising his detachment from the battle. Again the ironies of loyalty are explored. The King's apparently callous refusal to dispatch succour to his hard-pressed son is extenuated by his larger loyalty to the laws of chivalry; reinforcement devalues doughty deeds. The tension thus generated between the King and his lords is resolved by the Prince's triumphant reappearance, the ceremonial award of knighthood on the battlefield, the strikingly disproportionate casualty lists and the thanks to God. In a further linkage of the two themes, love and war, the King himself now refers to his enemy's awareness of his infatuation (1676). In the ensuing parade of antique pageantry, still on the theme of parental duty, the Prince understandably takes an austere view of his father's failure to intervene (1686–90).

The continuity of vows and loyalty is reinforced by introducing the Earl of Salisbury and Lord Mountford, each by name (IV.i); they are thus recognisable as the Countess's husband and his protégé already mentioned in the opening scene (139–40). Their French prisoner Villiers is required to procure a passport from his friend Charles, Duke of Normandy, son of the French king. Villiers is released for this purpose, but promises to return into captivity if his mission is unsuccessful. 'Thus once I mean to try a Frenchman's faith,' says Salisbury (1736). The dramatist is determined to demonstrate, no doubt to the surprise and perhaps the dismay of his audience, that Frenchmen can behave nobly, just as English Edward can behave vilely. This rather thin material is stretched over two episodes; oath-taking has become an obscession.

The scene shifts (IV.ii) to Calais, where a year-long siege is being compressed into a few days. By a further invention, six sick Frenchmen are imagined as extruded from the town by their hard-hearted compatriots, 'that so expense of victuals may be saved' (1760). King Edward spares them, with a further flourish of royal largesse ('five crowns apiece'). But their appearance has given him an idea; when Calais sues for surrender, Edward demands six hostages who are to be anything but ill and hungry; indeed, 'the wealthiest merchants in the town' (1815). Again unhistorically, there is yet another conflict of loyalties. King David of Scotland has been captured by one John Copeland, who has sworn to deliver his prize to his sovereign in person, thus incurring the Queen's displeasure. All such threads will eventually be drawn together in complex patterns of reconciliation.

The safe-conduct theme resumes (IV.iii): Prince Charles of France is duly sued for a passport for Salisbury, in exchange for which Villiers will be given his freedom. But he has it already, as the Prince predictably points out, adding 'I wonder . . . thou shouldest importune me/for one that is our deadly enemy' (1828–9). But Villiers has vowed to return. By solemn argument he converts Charles to this idealistic viewpoint. Now comes the prophecy of doom already foreseen; perhaps 'one that was a friar once' (1278) is the same soothsayer as the present 'agéd hermit' (1895), again for the sake of continuity.

Similarly, the dramatic diction on the eve of Poitiers (IV.iv) is heightened to the same exalted level as the Countess scenes. During the colloquy on death between the young Black Prince and his mentor Audley, the lordly language even recapitulates the earlier ideas and associations; once again, for example, sunshine glints on serried armies as on silver plate, or on forest leaves (230–1, 1931, 1940). There are interventions from heralds bearing unacceptable terms and insulting gifts. The counterpoint of love described in terms of war is now inverted; 'danger woos me as a blushing maid' (2049). As the battle begins (IV.v), there are amazing signs and portents, as predicted. King John is again characterised as an alert and capable monarch, in his adroit explanation of why the ominous ravens are croaking, namely for English carcasses (2131f.). The safe-conduct theme returns with a final twist; Salisbury is about to be hanged. He has received, via Villiers, the desired passport duly endorsed by Prince Charles, but has now been captured *en route* for Calais. This compels yet another dissertation on oath-taking and -breaking. King John scores a further powerful point by explaining that Charles had no right to confer a safe-conduct upon his country's enemy. Charles's reply is mere petulance; his father is indulgent. Thus their dramatic characters are developed. But the Prince retaliates instantly, in accordance with the grand antithetical design, by charging the released Salisbury to tell King Edward that his own son the Black Prince has been slain, and that further retribution will follow.

But then we are instantly told (IV.vi) how the tables will be turned, by a stratagem. While the French are preoccupied with portents, the English bowmen are commanded to hurl flintstones instead of firing arrows, thus fulfilling the prophecy (IV.vii) that stones will 'rise and break the battle ray'

(1897, 1904). Meanwhile wise old Audley has been gravely wounded; and the Prince commiserates with his much-loved mentor, again in the linking language of love and war: 'thou wooest death with thy careless smile . . . as if thou wert enamoured on thine end' (2304–6).

Fresh strands now add new richness to the tapestry (V.i). Edward's queen intercedes for the burghers: 'kings approach the nearest unto God' by showing mercy (2391). There is still time for one more trick. The Black Prince is alive and well; but this news is prepared by a protracted and solemn announcement of his death, delivered by the newly arrived Salisbury. This prompts successive speeches of grief from his mother Queen Philippa and revenge from his father King Edward, typical alike in their characterisation and contrast. The play ends with two more set pieces; the King is allotted the standard lamentation for the fallen, while the Prince has a triumphant peroration about his own feats of arms and the fact that his realm is now a world power, not to be bullied by Spain or any other nation on earth (2589). Thus the patriotic fervour of Tudor times is anachronistically aroused and the play earns well-deserved applause. The audience is then treated to a culminating panorama symbolic of England's continuing greatness as she receives within her shores a ship proudly bearing 'three kings, two princes and a queen'. We are to understand that three of these, two kings and a prince, are enemy prisoners. King David has been unhistorically added just to swell their ranks; he has been brought to Calais in captivity, although in reality he was (as the playwright well knew) safely locked up in an English fortress.

This concludes a splendid theatrical entertainment, with action and character crafted on three levels. Chronicle history and romantic fiction have been combined for dramatic effect. This strong double foundation supports a wide-ranging arch of set-piece incidents and descriptions of love and art and war in all their aspects, ranging from the clash of nations in major battles to the character and relation of individuals, embellished with Tudor allusion and dissertations on such topics as the significance of death, the sanctity of wedlock and the power of poetry. The coping stones of these sturdy structures are composed of vows, oaths, divided loyalties, in a variety of legalistic formulation covering the entire drama and all its episodes and personae. Even its minor characters talk in such terms as 'heaven I call to record of my vows' (35), 'sworn true liegeman' (68), 'forgetting of his former oath' (133) and so forth.

Within this complex architecture the chief characters live their own lives, in their own separate quarters. The royal apartments preponderate. King Edward himself has more than 700 lines. His striving for conquest in love and war is the mainspring of the action; he is presented as the most manifold of monarchs, protean in his moods and aptitudes (including a detailed knowledge of Ovid) and Jovian in his power over life and death, for good or ill. His son the Black Prince and his enemy King John are next in the rankings, with some 300 lines apiece; but they both derive from Edward, whether in extension or opposition. The Countess alone is both independent

and integral; yet she is almost as many-faceted as her royal wooer. In particular she has the innate warmth and compassion that he lacks. She teaches
him decency. He also has to be taught humour by his secretary, tolerance by
his wife, remorse and chivalry by the sight and prowess of his son. He is
always an impulsive monarch, highly susceptible to influence and less obvi-
ously astute than his rival John.

There is an overriding moral; those who make passionate vows are taught
salutary lessons. Edward risks losing his queen, Warwick his daughter, John
his kingdom, Charles his dignity and Salisbury his life. The Black Prince is
transformed from a student into a national hero. Everyone is somewhat
changed, everyone learns from experience, including the Countess; yet she
remains serenely herself with a special Lucretian radiance conferred upon
her by her creator's poetic powers. Two other characters preserve their
individuality inviolate from first to last, the mentors and confidants of King
Edward and his son, namely the former's faithful secretary Lodowick and the
latter's faithful comrade Audley. Both love and war, we are instructed, have
their victories and their virtues.

But the play must speak for itself; ideally, to minds as open and receptive
as those of its own first audiences and readers. In the following text, the line
count derives from a successive numbering of the 1596 First Quarto, including its stage directions.* Its mislineation at 475–80 has inadvertently added
an extra line, here called 477a. In conformity with the latest edition of
Edmund Ironside (Sams 1985d, 1986d), each line here begins with a small
letter save at the start of a new train of thought as in that manuscript; this
gives an onward impetus to consecutive reading. For the same reasons,
punctuation has been reduced to a minimum. As before, stage directions (but
not speech-prefixes) have been consistently italicised. The many manifest
misprints in the 1596 first edition have been silently corrected, usually from
the second edition (1599) or the third (Capell 1760, to which all researchers
are indebted). Missing stage directions, like the traditional act and scene
divisions, have been supplied within square brackets. Once again the aim is
to present a modern-spelling text as plainly and directly as possible, for
purposes of study and comparison.

---

* In continuation of the system adopted by Dr Eliot Slater (1982, 1988) for his magisterial
work on *Edward III* vocabulary, thus facilitating line-by-line cross-reference and comparison.

III

Text

THE REIGN OF KING EDWARD THE THIRD

[Act I Scene i]

Enter King Edward, Derby, Prince Edward, Audley,
[Warwick] and Artois

KING:
> Robert of Artois, banished though thou be
> from France thy native country, yet with us   5
> thou shalt retain as great a seigniory
> for we create thee Earl of Richmond here
> and now go forwards with our pedigree.
> Who next succeeded Philip le Beau?

ARTOIS:
> Three sons of his which all successfully   10
> did sit upon their father's regal throne
> yet died and left no issue of their loins.

KING:
> But was my mother sister unto those?

ARTOIS:
> She was, my lord, and only Isabel
> was all the daughters that this Philip had   15
> whom afterward your father took to wife
> and from the fragrant garden of her womb
> your gracious self, the flower of Europe's hope,
> derivéd is inheritor to France
> but note the rancour of rebellious minds   20
> when thus the lineage of Beau was out
> the French obscured your mother's privilege
> and though she were the next of blood proclaimed
> John of the house of Valois, now their king.
> The reason was they say the realm of France   25
> replete with princes of great parentage
> ought not admit a governor to rule
> except he be descended of the male
> and that's the special ground of their contempt

wherewith they study to exclude your grace   30
but they shall find that forgéd ground of theirs
to be but dusty heaps of brittle sand.
Perhaps it will be thought a heinous thing
that I a Frenchman should discover this
but heaven I call to record of my vows   35
it is not hate nor any private wrong
but love unto my country and the right
provokes my tongue thus lavish in report.
You are the lineal watchman of our peace
and John of Valois indirectly climbs.   40
What then should subjects but embrace their king?
Ah, wherein may our duty more be seen
than striving to rebate a tyrant's pride
and place the true shepherd of our commonwealth?

KING: This counsel, Artois, like to fruitful showers   45
hath added growth unto my dignity
and by the fiery vigour of thy words
hot courage is engendered in my breast
which heretofore was racked in ignorance
but now doth mount with golden wings of fame   50
and will approve fair Isabel's descent
able to yoke their stubborn necks with steel
that spurn against my sovereignty in France.

Sound a horn

A messenger! Lord Audley, know from whence.

Enter a messenger, Lorraine   55

AUDLEY: The Duke of Lorraine having crossed the seas
entreats he may have conference with your highness.

KING: Admit him lords that we may hear the news.
Say Duke of Lorraine wherefore art thou come?

LORRAINE: The most renownéd prince King John of France   60
doth greet thee Edward and by me commands
that for so much as by his liberal gift
the Guyenne dukedom is entailed to thee
thou do him lowly homage for the same
and for that purpose here I summon thee   65
repair to France within these forty days
that there according as the custom is

thou mayst be sworn true liegeman to our king
or else thy title in that province dies
and he himself will repossess the place.   70

KING: See how occasion laughs me in the face!
No sooner minded to prepare for France
but straight I am invited, nay with threats
upon a penalty enjoined to come.
Twere but a childish part to say him nay.   75
Lorraine, return this answer to thy lord –
I mean to visit him as he requests.
But how? Not servilely disposed to bend
but like a conqueror to make him bow.
His lame unpolished shifts are come to light   80
and truth hath pulled the vizard from his face
that set a gloss upon his arrogance.
Dare he command a fealty in me?
Tell him the crown that he usurps is mine
and where he sets his foot he ought to kneel.   85
Tis not a petty dukedom that I claim
but all the whole dominions of the realm
which if with grudging he refuse to yield
I'll take away those borrowed plumes of his
and send him naked to the wilderness.   90

LORRAINE: Then Edward here in spite of all thy lords
I do pronounce defiance to thy face.

PRINCE: Defiance, Frenchman? We rebound it back
even to the bottom of thy master's throat
and be it spoke with reverence of the king   95
my gracious father and these other lords
I hold thy message but as scurrilous
and him that sent thee like the lazy drone
crept up by stealth unto the eagle's nest
from whence we'll shake him with so rough a storm   100
as others shall be warnèd by his harm.

WARWICK: Bid him leave off the lion's case he wears
lest meeting with the lion in the field
he chance to tear him piecemeal for his pride.

ARTOIS: The soundest counsel I can give his grace   105
is to surrender ere he be constrained.
A voluntary mischief hath less scorn
than when reproach with violence is borne.

LORRAINE: Regenerate traitor, viper to the place
where thou wast fostered in thine infancy   110
bear'st thou a part in this conspiracy?

He [King] draws his sword

KING:	Lorraine, behold the sharpness of this steel!
	Fervent desire that sits against my heart
	is far more thorny-pricking than this blade 115
	that with the nightingale I shall be scarred
	as oft as I dispose myself to rest
	until my colours be displayed in France.
	This is thy final answer, so be gone.
LORRAINE:	It is not that nor any English brave 120
	afflicts me so as doth his poisoned view
	that is most false should most of all be true.

[Exit Lorraine]

KING:　　　　Now lords our fleeting bark is under sail
　　　　　　our gage is thrown and war is soon begun
　　　　　　but not so quickly brought unto an end.　　125

Enter Montague

　　　　　　But wherefore comes Sir William Montague?
　　　　　　How stands the league between the Scot and us?
MONTAGUE:　Cracked and dissevered, my renownéd lord.
　　　　　　The treacherous king no sooner was informed　130
　　　　　　of your withdrawing of your army back
　　　　　　but straight forgetting of his former oath
　　　　　　he made invasion on the bordering towns.
　　　　　　Berwick is won, Newcastle spoiled and lost
　　　　　　and now the tyrant hath begirt with siege　135
　　　　　　the castle of Roxborough where enclosed
　　　　　　the Countess Salisbury is like to perish.
KING:　　　That is thy daughter, Warwick, is it not
　　　　　　whose husband hath in Brittaine served so long
　　　　　　about the planting of Lord Mountford there?　140
WARWICK:　It is, my lord.
KING:　　　Ignoble David hast thou none to grieve
　　　　　　but silly ladies with thy threatening arms?
　　　　　　But I will make you shrink your snaily horns.
　　　　　　First therefore Audley this shall be thy charge　145
　　　　　　go levy footmen for our wars in France
　　　　　　and Ned take muster of our men at arms
　　　　　　in every shire elect a several band
　　　　　　let them be soldiers of a lusty spirit
　　　　　　such as dread nothing but dishonour's blot.　150

Be wary therefore since we do commence
a famous war and with so mighty a nation.
Derby, be thou ambassador for us
unto our father-in-law the Earl of Hainault
make him acquainted with our enterprise   155
and likewise will him with our own allies
that are in Flanders to solicit to
the Emperor of Almaine in our name.
Myself, whilst you are jointly thus employed
will with these forces that I have at hand   160
march and once more repulse the traitorous Scot.
But sirs be resolute, we shall have wars
on every side and Ned thou must begin
now to forget thy study and thy books
and ure thy shoulders to an armour's weight.   165

PRINCE: As cheerful-sounding to my youthful spleen
this tumult is of war's increasing broils
as at the coronation of a king
the joyful clamours of the people are
when '*Ave, Caesar!*' they pronounce aloud.   170
Within this school of honour I shall learn
either to sacrifice my foes to death
or in a rightful quarrel spend my breath.
Then cheerfully forward, each a several way!
In great affairs tis naught to use delay.   175

Exeunt

[Act I Scene ii]

Enter the Countess

COUNTESS: Alas, how much in vain my poor eyes gaze
for succour that my sovereign should send.
Ah cousin Montague I fear thou wants   180
the lively spirit sharply to solicit
with vehement suit the king in my behalf.
Thou dost not tell him what a grief it is
to be the scornful captive to a Scot
either to be wooed with broad untunéd oaths   185
or forced by rough insulting barbarism.
Thou dost not tell him if he here prevail
how much they will deride us in the north
and in their vild uncivil skipping jigs

bray forth their conquest and our overthrow 190
even in the barren bleak and fruitless air.

Enter David and Douglas, Lorraine

I must withdraw, the everlasting foe
comes to the wall. I'll closely step aside
and list their babble blunt and full of pride. 195

KING DAVID: My lord of Lorraine, to our brother of France
commend us as the man in Christendom
that we must reverence and entirely love.
Touching your embassage, return and say
that we with England will not enter parley 200
nor never make fair weather or take truce
but burn their neighbour towns and so persist
with eager roads beyond their city York
and never shall our bonny riders rest
nor rust in canker have the time to eat 205
their light-borne snaffles nor their nimble spurs
nor lay aside their jacks of gimmaled mail
nor hang their staves of grainéd Scottish ash
in peaceful wise upon their city walls
nor from their buttoned tawny leathern belts 210
dismiss their biting whinyards till your king
cry out 'enough, spare England now for pity'.
Farewell, and tell him that you leave us here
before this castle, say you came from us
even when we had that yielded to our hands. 215

LORRAINE: I take my leave, and fairly will return
your acceptable greeting to my king.

Exit Lorraine

KING DAVID: Now Douglas to our former task again
for the division of this certain spoil.

DOUGLAS: My liege I crave the lady and no more. 220

KING DAVID: Nay soft ye sir, first I must make my choice
and first I do bespeak her for myself.

DOUGLAS: Why then my liege let me enjoy her jewels.

KING DAVID: Those are her own, still liable to her
and who inherits her hath those with all. 225

Enter a Scot in haste

MESSENGER: My liege, as we were pricking on the hills
to fetch in booty, marching hitherward

we might descry a mighty host of men.
The sun reflecting on the armour showed   230
a field of plate, a wood of pikes advanced.
Bethink your highness speedily herein.
An easy march within four hours will bring
the hindmost rank unto this place, my liege.

KING DAVID: Dislodge, dislodge, it is the King of England!   235
DOUGLAS: Jemmy my man, saddle my bonny black.
KING DAVID: Meanst thou to fight, Douglas we are too weak.
DOUGLAS: I know it well my liege and therefore fly.
COUNTESS: My lords of Scotland, will ye stay and drink?
KING DAVID: She mocks at us Douglas, I cannot endure it.   240
COUNTESS: Say good my lord which is he must have the lady
and which her jewels? I am sure my lords
ye will not hence till you have shared the spoils.
KING DAVID: She heard the messenger and heard our talk
and now that comfort makes her scorn at us.   245

Another messenger

MESSENGER II: Arm, my good lord! Oh we are all surprised!
COUNTESS: After the French ambassador my liege
and tell him that you dare not ride to York.
Excuse it that your bonny horse is lame.   250
KING DAVID: She heard that too. Intolerable grief!
Woman, farewell. Although I do not stay –

Exeunt Scots

COUNTESS: Tis not for fear, and yet you run away.
O happy comfort, welcome to our house.
The confident and boisterous-boasting Scot   255
that swore before my walls they would not back
for all the arméd power of this land
with faceless fear that ever turns his back
turned hence against the blasting north-east wind
upon the bare report and name of arms.   260

Enter Montague

O summer's day! see where my cousin comes!
MONTAGUE: How fares my aunt? We are not Scots
why do you shut your gates against your friends?
COUNTESS: Well may I give a welcome, cousin, to thee   265
for thou com'st well to chase my foes from hence.

MONTAGUE:	The king himself is come in person hither.
	Dear aunt, descend and gratulate his highness.
COUNTESS:	How may I entertain his majesty
	to show my duty and his dignity? 270

[Exeunt]
Enter King Edward, Warwick, Artois, with others

KING EDWARD:	What, are the stealing foxes fled and gone
	before we could uncouple at their heels?
WARWICK:	They are my liege, but with a cheerful cry
	hot hounds and hardy chase them at the heels. 275

Enter Countess

KING EDWARD:	This is the Countess, Warwick, is it not?
WARWICK:	Even she, my liege, whose beauty tyrant's fear
	as a May blossom with pernicious winds
	hath sullied, withered, overcast and done. 280
KING EDWARD:	Hath she been fairer, Warwick, than she is?
WARWICK:	My gracious king, fair is she not at all
	if that herself were by to stain herself
	as I have seen her when she was herself.
KING EDWARD:	What strange enchantment lurked in those her eyes 285
	when they excelled this excellence they have
	that now her dim decline hath power to draw
	my subject eyes from piercing majesty
	to gaze on her with doting admiration.
COUNTESS:	In duty lower than the ground I kneel 290
	and for my dull knees bow my feeling heart
	to witness my obedience to your highness
	with many millions of a subject's thanks
	for this your royal presence whose approach
	hath driven war and danger from my gate. 295
KING EDWARD:	Lady, stand up. I come to bring thee peace
	however thereby I have purchased war.
COUNTESS:	No war to you my liege, the Scots are gone
	and gallop home toward Scotland with their hate.
KING EDWARD:	Lest yielding here I pine in shameful love, 300
	come, we'll pursue the Scots. Artois, away!
COUNTESS:	A little while my gracious sovereign stay
	and let the power of a mighty king
	honour our roof. My husband in the wars
	when he shall hear it will triumph for joy. 305
	Then dear my liege, now niggard not thy state

	being at the wall, enter our homely gate.	
KING EDWARD:	Pardon me Countess I will come no near.	
	I dreamed tonight of treason and I fear.	
COUNTESS:	Far from this place let ugly treason lie.	310
KING EDWARD:	No farther off than her conspiring eye	
	which shoots infected poison in my heart	
	beyond repulse of wit or cure of art.	
	Now in the sun alone it doth not lie	
	with light to take light from a mortal eye	315
	for here two day-stars that mine eyes would see	
	more than the sun steals mine own light from me.	
	Contemplative desire, desire to be	
	in contemplation that may master thee.	
	Warwick, Artois, to horse and let's away.	320
COUNTESS:	What might I speak to make my sovereign stay?	
KING EDWARD:	What needs a tongue to such a speaking eye	
	that more persuades than winning oratory?	
COUNTESS:	Let not thy presence like the April sun	
	flatter our earth and suddenly be done.	325
	More happy do not make our outward wall	
	than thou wilt grace our inner house withal.	
	Our house my liege is like a country swain	
	whose habit rude and manners blunt and plain	
	presageth naught yet inly beautified	330
	with bounties, riches and fair hidden pride	
	for where the golden ore doth buried lie	
	the ground undecked with nature's tapestry	
	seems barren, sere, unfertile, fruitless, dry	
	and where the upper turf of earth doth boast	335
	his pride, perfumes and parti-coloured cost	
	delve there and find this issue and their pride	
	to spring from ordure and corruption's side.	
	But to make up my all too long compare	
	these ragged walls no testimony are	340
	what is within but like a cloak doth hide	
	from weather's waste the under-garnished pride.	
	More gracious than my terms can let thee be	
	entreat thyself to stay a while with me.	
KING EDWARD:	As wise as fair! What fond fit can be heard	345
	when wisdom keeps the gate as beauty's guard?	
	Countess, albeit my business urgeth me	
	it shall attend while I attend on thee.	
	Come on my lords, here will I host tonight.	

Exeunt

[Act II Scene i]

[Enter Lodowick]

LODOWICK:	I might perceive his eye in her eye lost	350

LODOWICK: I might perceive his eye in her eye lost   350
his ear to drink her sweet tongue's utterance
and changing passion like inconstant clouds
that rack upon the carriage of the winds
increase and die in his disturbéd cheeks.
Lo when she blushed even then did he look pale   355
as if her cheeks by some enchanted power
attracted had the cherry blood from his.
Anon with reverent fear when she grew pale
his cheeks put on their scarlet ornaments
but no more like her oriental red   360
than brick to coral or live things to dead.
Why did he then thus counterfeit her looks?
If she did blush twas tender modest shame
being in the sacred presence of a king.
If he did blush twas red immodest shame   365
to vail his eyes amiss, being a king.
If she looked pale twas silly woman's fear
to bear herself in presence of a king.
If he looked pale, it was with guilty fear
to dote amiss, being a mighty king.   370
Then Scottish wars farewell, I fear twill prove
a lingering English siege of peevish love.
Here comes his highness walking all alone.

Enter King Edward

KING EDWARD: She is grown more fairer far since I came thither   375
her voice more silver every word than other
her wit more fluent. What a strange discourse
unfolded she of David and his Scots.
'Even thus' quoth she 'he spake' and then spoke broad
with epithets and accents of the Scot   380
but somewhat better than the Scot could speak
'And thus' quoth she, and answered then herself
for who could speak like her but she herself?
Breathes from the wall an angel's note from heaven
of sweet defiance to her barbarous foes.   385
When she would talk of peace methinks her tongue
commanded war to prison, when of war
it wakened Caesar from his Roman grave

to hear war beautified by her discourse.
Wisdom is foolishness but in her tongue 390
beauty a slander but in her fair face
there is no summer but in her cheerful looks
nor frosty winter but in her disdain.
I cannot blame the Scots that did besiege her
for she is all the treasure of our land 395
but call them cowards that they ran away
having so rich and fair a cause to stay.
Art thou there, Lod'wick? Give me ink and paper.

LODOWICK: I will my liege.
KING EDWARD: And bid the lords hold on their play at chess 400
for we will walk and meditate alone.
LODOWICK: I will my sovereign.

[Exit Lodowick]

KING EDWARD: This fellow is well read in poetry
and hath a lusty and persuasive spirit.
I will acquaint him with my passion 405
which he shall shadow with a veil of lawn
through which the queen of beauty's queen shall see
herself the ground of my infirmity.

Enter Lodowick

KING EDWARD: Hast thou pen ink and paper ready Lodowick? 410
LODOWICK: Ready my liege.
KING EDWARD: Then in the summer arbour sit by me
make it our council house or cabinet
since green our thoughts green be the conventicle
where we will ease us by disburdening them. 415
Now Lod'wick invocate some golden Muse
to bring thee hither an enchanted pen
that may for sighs set down true sighs indeed
talking of grief to make thee ready groan
and when thou writest of tears encouch the word 420
before and after with such sweet laments
that it may raise drops in a Tartar's eye
and make a flint-heart Scythian pitiful
for so much moving hath a poet's pen.
Then if thou be a poet move thou so 425
and be enrichéd by thy sovereign's love
for if the touch of sweet concordant strings
could force attendance in the ears of hell

how much more shall the strains of poet's wit
beguile and ravish soft and human minds? 430

LODOWICK: To whom my lord shall I direct my style?

KING EDWARD: To one that shames the fair and sots the wise
whose body is an abstract or a brief
contains each general virtue in the world.
'Better than beautiful' thou must begin 435
devise for fair a fairer word than fair
and every ornament that thou wouldest praise
fly it a pitch above the soar of praise.
For flattery fear thou not to be convicted
for were thy admiration ten times more 440
ten times ten thousand more the worth exceeds
of that thou art to praise, thy praise's worth.
Begin! I will to contemplate the while.
Forget not to set down how passionate
how heart-sick and how full of languishment 445
her beauty makes me.

LODOWICK: Write I to a woman?

KING EDWARD: What beauty else could triumph on me
or who but women do our love-lays greet?
What, thinkest thou I did bid thee praise a horse? 450

LODOWICK: Of what condition or estate she is
twere requisite that I should know, my lord.

KING EDWARD: Of such estate that hers is as a throne
and my estate the footstool where she treads.
Then mayst thou judge what her condition is 455
by the proportion of her mightiness.
Write on while I peruse her in my thoughts.
Her voice, to music or the nightingale?
To music every summer-leaping swain
compares his sunburnt lover when she speaks 460
and why should I speak of the nightingale?
The nightingale sings of adulterate wrong
and that compared is too satirical
for sin though sin would not be so esteemed
but rather virtue sin, sin virtue deemed. 465
Her hair far softer than the silkworm's twist
like to a flattering glass doth make more fair
the yellow amber – 'like a flattering glass'
comes in too soon, for writing of her eyes
I'll say that like a glass they catch the sun 470
and thence the hot reflection doth rebound
against my breast and burns my heart within.

Ah what a world of descant makes my soul
upon this voluntary ground of love!
Come Lod'wick, hast thou turned thy ink to gold?   475
If not, write but in letters capital
my mistress' name and it will gild thy paper.
Read, lord, read!   477a
Fill thou the empty hollows of mine ears
with the sweet hearing of thy poetry.

LODOWICK: I have not to a period brought her praise.   480
KING EDWARD: Her praise is as my love, both infinite
which apprehend such violent extremes
that they disdain an ending period.
Her beauty hath no match but my affection.
Hers more than most, mine most and more than more 485
hers more to praise than tell the sea by drops
nay more than drop the massy earth by sands
and sand by sand print them in memory
then wherefore talkest thou of a period
to that which craves unended admiration?   490
Read, let us hear.

LODOWICK: 'More fair and chaste than is the queen of shades'
KING EDWARD: That line hath two faults gross and palpable.
Comparest thou her to the pale queen of night
who being set in dark seems therefore light?   495
What is she, when the sun lifts up his head
but like a fading taper dim and dead?
My love shall brave the eye of heaven at noon
and being unmasked outshine the golden sun.

LODOWICK: What is the other fault my sovereign lord?   500
KING EDWARD: Read o'er the line again.
LODOWICK: 'More fair and chaste'
KING EDWARD: I did not bid thee talk of chastity
to ransack so the treasure of her mind
for I had rather have her chased than chaste.   505
Out with the moon line, I will none of it
and let me have her likened to the sun
say she hath thrice more splendour than the sun
that her perfections emulates the sun
that she breeds sweets as plenteous as the sun   510
that she doth thaw cold winter like the sun
that she doth cheer fresh summer like the sun
that she doth dazzle gazers like the sun
and in this application to the sun
bid her be free and general as the sun   515

	who smiles upon the basest weed that grows	
	as lovingly as on the fragrant rose.	
	Let's see what follows that same moonlight line.	
LODOWICK:	'More fair and chaste than is the queen of shades,	
	more bold in constancy' –	520
KING EDWARD:	In constancy than who?	
LODOWICK:	'than Judith was'.	
KING EDWARD:	O monstrous line! put in the next a sword	
	and I shall woo her to cut off my head.	
	Blot, blot, good Lod'wick, let us hear the next.	525
LODOWICK:	There's all that yet is done.	
KING EDWARD:	I thank thee then, thou hast done little ill	
	but what is done is passing passing ill.	
	No, let the captain talk of boist'rous war	
	the prisoner of immuréd dark constraint	530
	the sick man best sets down the pangs of death	
	the man that starves the sweetness of a feast	
	the frozen soul the benefit of fire	
	and every grief his happy opposite.	
	Love cannot sound well but in lovers' tongues	535
	give me the pen and paper, I will write –	

Enter Countess

	But soft, here comes the treasurer of my spirit.	
	Lod'wick, thou knowst not how to draw a battle	
	these wings these flankers and these squadrons	540
	argue in thee defective discipline	
	thou shouldest have placed this here, this other here.	
COUNTESS:	Pardon my boldness, my thrice-gracious lords	
	let my intrusion here be called my duty	
	that comes to see my sovereign how he fares.	545
KING EDWARD:	Go draw the same I tell thee in what form.	
LODOWICK:	I go.	

[Exit]

COUNTESS:	Sorry I am to see my liege so sad.	
	What may thy subject do to drive from thee	
	thy gloomy consort, sullen melancholy?	550
KING EDWARD:	Ah lady I am blunt and cannot straw	
	the flowers of solace in a ground of shame.	
	Since I came hither Countess I am wronged.	
COUNTESS:	Now God forbid that any in my house	
	should think my sovereign wrong! thrice-gentle king	555
	acquaint me with thy cause of discontent.	

KING EDWARD:	How near then shall I be to remedy?
COUNTESS:	As near, my liege, as all my woman's power
	can pawn itself to buy thy remedy.
KING EDWARD:	If thou speakst true then have I my redress 560
	engage thy power to redeem my joys
	and I am joyful Countess, else I die.
COUNTESS:	I will, my liege.
KING EDWARD:	Swear Countess that thou wilt.
COUNTESS:	By heaven I will. 565
KING EDWARD:	Then take thyself a little way aside
	and tell thyself a king doth dote on thee
	say that within thy power [it] doth lie
	to make him happy and that thou hast sworn
	to give him all the joy within thy power 570
	do this and tell me when I shall be happy.
COUNTESS:	All this is done, my thrice-dread sovereign.
	That power of love that I have power to give
	thou hast with all devout obedience
	employ me how thou wilt in proof thereof. 575
KING EDWARD:	Thou hearst me say that I do dote on thee.
COUNTESS:	If on my beauty take it if thou canst
	though little I do prize it ten times less
	if on my virtue take it if thou canst
	for virtue's store by giving doth augment 580
	be it on what it will that I can give
	and thou canst take away, inherit it.
KING EDWARD:	It is thy beauty that I would enjoy.
COUNTESS:	O were it painted I would wipe it off
	and dispossess myself to give it thee 585
	but sovereign it is soldered to my life.
	Take one and both for like an humble shadow
	it haunts the sunshine of my summer's life.
KING EDWARD:	But thou mayst leave it me to sport withal.
COUNTESS:	As easy may my intellectual soul 590
	be lent away and yet my body live
	as lend my body, palace to my soul,
	away from her and yet retain my soul.
	My body is her bower her court her abbey
	and she an angel pure divine unspotted 595
	if I should leave her house my lord to thee
	I kill my poor soul and my poor soul me.
KING EDWARD:	Didst thou not swear to give me what I would?
COUNTESS:	I did my liege, so what you would I could.
KING EDWARD:	I wish no more of thee than thou mayst give 600
	nor beg I do not but I rather buy

that is thy love and for that love of thine
in rich exchange I tender to thee mine.

COUNTESS:　　　But that your lips were sacred my lord
you would profane the holy name of love.　　　　605
That love you offer me you cannot give
for Caesar owes that tribute to his queen.
That love you beg of me I cannot give
for Sara owes that duty to her lord.
He that doth clip or counterfeit your stamp　　　610
shall die my lord and will your sacred self
commit high treason against the King of heaven
to stamp his image in forbidden metal
forgetting your allegiance and your oath?
In violating marriage sacred law　　　　　　615
you break a greater honour than yourself
to be a king is of a younger house
than to be married. Your progenitor
sole-reigning Adam on the universe
by God was honoured for a married man　　　620
but not by him anointed for a king.
It is a penalty to break your statutes
though not enacted with your highness' hand
how much more to infringe the holy act
made by the mouth of God, sealed with his hand?　625
I know my sovereign in my husband's love
who now doth loyal service in his wars
doth but to try the wife of Salisbury
whether she will hear a wanton's tale or no
lest being therein guilty by my stay　　　　630
from that not from my liege I turn away.

Exit

KING EDWARD:　　Whether is her beauty by her words divine
or are her words sweet chaplains to her beauty
like as the wind doth beautify a sail
and as a sail becomes the unseen wind　　　635
so do her words her beauties, beauty words.
O that I were a honey-gathering bee
to bear the comb of virtue from his flower
and not a poison-sucking envious spider
to turn the juice I take to deadly venom.　　640
Religion is austere and beauty gentle
too strict a guardian for so fair a weed
oh that she were as is the air to me

why so she is for when I would embrace her
this do I and catch nothing but myself.   645
I must enjoy her for I cannot beat
with reason and reproof fond love away.

Enter Warwick

Here comes her father, I will work with him
to bear my colours in this field of love.   650

WARWICK: How is it that my sovereign is so sad?
May I with pardon know your highness' grief?
An that my old endeavour will remove it
it shall not cumber long your majesty.

KING EDWARD: A kind and voluntary gift thou profferest   655
that I was forward to have begged of thee
but O thou world great nurse of flattery
why dost thou tip men's tongues with golden words
and peise their deeds with weight of heavy lead
that fair performance cannot follow promise?   660
O that a man might hold the heart's close book
and choke the lavish tongue when it doth utter
the breath of falsehood not charactered there.

WARWICK: Far be it from the honour of my age
that I should owe bright gold and render lead.   665
Age is a cynic not a flatterer
I say again that if I knew your grief
and that by me it may be lessenéd
my proper harm should buy your highness' good.

KING EDWARD: These are the vulgar tenders of false men   670
that never pay the duty of their words
thou wilt not stick to swear what thou hast said
but when thou knowest my grief's condition
this rash-disgorgéd vomit of thy word
thou wilt eat up again and leave me helpless.   675

WARWICK: By heaven I will not though your majesty
did bid me run upon your sword and die.

KING EDWARD: Say that my grief is no way medicinable
but by the loss and bruising of thine honour?

WARWICK: If nothing but that loss may vantage you   680
I would account that loss my vantage too.

KING EDWARD: Thinkst that thou canst unswear thy oath again?

WARWICK: I cannot nor I would not if I could.

KING EDWARD: But if thou dost what shall I say to thee?

WARWICK: What may be said to any perjured villain   685
that breaks the sacred warrant of an oath.

KING EDWARD: What wilt thou say to one that breaks an oath?
WARWICK: That he hath broke his faith with God and man
                 and from them both stands excommunicate.
KING EDWARD: What office were it to suggest a man   690
                 to break a lawful and religious vow?
WARWICK: An office for the devil not for man.
KING EDWARD: That devil's office must thou do for me
                 or break thy oath or cancel all the bonds
                 of love and duty twixt thyself and me   695
                 and therefore Warwick if thou art thyself
                 the lord and master of thy word and oath
                 go to thy daughter and in my behalf
                 command her, woo her, win her anyways
                 to be my mistress and my secret love   700
                 I will not stand to hear thee make reply
                 thy oath break hers or let thy sovereign die.

                            Exit King

WARWICK: O doting king or detestable office
                 well may I tempt myself to wrong myself
                 when he hath sworn me by the name of God   705
                 to break a vow made by the name of God.
                 What if I swear by this right hand of mine
                 to cut this right hand off? The better way
                 were to profane the idol than confound it
                 but neither will I do. I'll keep mine oath   710
                 and to my daughter make a recantation
                 of all the virtue I have preached to her
                 I'll say she must forget her husband Salisbury
                 if she remember to embrace the King
                 I'll say an oath may easily be broken   715
                 but not so easily pardoned being broken
                 I'll say it is true charity to love
                 but not true love to be so charitable
                 I'll say his greatness may bear out the shame
                 but not his kingdom can buy out the sin   720
                 I'll say it is my duty to persuade
                 but not her honesty to give consent.

                            Enter Countess

                 See where she comes. Was never father had
                 against his child an embassage so bad.   725
COUNTESS: My lord and father, I have sought for you
                 my mother and the peers importune you

	to keep in promise of his majesty	
	and do your best to make his highness merry.	
WARWICK:	How shall I enter in this graceless arrant?	730
	I must not call her 'child', for where's the father	
	that will in such a suit seduce his child?	
	Then 'wife of Salisbury' – shall I so begin?	
	No, he's my friend, and where is found the friend	
	that will do friendship such endamagement?	735
	Neither my daughter nor my dear friend's wife.	
	I am not Warwick as thou thinkst I am	
	but an attorney from the court of hell	
	that thus have housed my spirit in his form	
	to do a message to thee from the king	740
	the mighty king of England dotes on thee	
	he that hath power to take away thy life	
	hath power to take thy honour, then consent	
	to pawn thine honour rather than thy life	
	honour is often lost and got again	745
	but life once gone hath no recovery	
	the sun that withers hay doth nourish grass	
	the king that would distain thee will advance thee	
	the poets write that great Achilles' spear	
	could heal the wound it made, the moral is	750
	what mighty men misdo they can amend	
	the lion doth become his bloody jaws	
	and grace his foragement by being mild	
	when vassal fear lies trembling at his feet	
	the king will in his glory hide thy shame	755
	and those that gaze on him to find out thee	
	will lose their eyesight looking in the sun	
	what can one drop of poison harm the sea	
	whose hugey vastures can digest the ill	
	and make it lose his operation	760
	the king's great name will temper thy misdeeds	
	and give the bitter portion of reproach	
	a sugared sweet and most delicious taste	
	besides it is no harm to do the thing	
	which without shame could not be left undone	765
	thus have I in his majesty's behalf	
	apparelled sin in virtuous sentences	
	and dwell upon thy answer in his suit.	
COUNTESS:	Unnatural besiege, woe me unhappy	
	to have escaped the danger of my foes	770
	and to be ten times worse envired by friends.	
	Hath he no means to stain my honest blood	
	but to corrupt the author of my blood	

to be his scandalous and vile solicitor?
No marvel though the branches be then infected   775
when poison hath encompasséd the root
no marvel though the leprous infant die
when the stern dame envenometh the dug
why then give sin a passport to offend
and youth the dangerous reign of liberty   780
blot out the strict forbidding of the law
and cancel every canon that prescribes
a shame for shame or penance for offence
no let me die if his too boisterous will
will have it so, before I will consent   785
to be an actor in his graceless lust.

WARWICK: Why now thou speakst as I would have thee speak
and mark how I unsay my words again
an honourable grave is more esteemed
than the polluted closet of a king   790
the greater man the greater is the thing
be it good or bad that he shall undertake
an unreputed mote flying in the sun
presents a greater substance than it is
the freshest summer's day doth soonest taint   795
the loathéd carrion that it seems to kiss
deep are the blows made with a mighty axe
that sin doth ten times aggravate itself
that is committed in a holy place
an evil deed done by authority   800
is sin and subornation. Deck an ape
in tissue and the beauty of the robe
adds but the greater scorn unto the beast.
A spacious field of reasons could I urge
between his glory, daughter, and thy shame   805
that poison shows worst in a golden cup
dark night seems darker by the lightning flash
lilies that fester smell far worse than weeds
and every glory that inclines to sin
the shame is treble by the opposite.   810
So leave I with my blessing in thy bosom
which then convert to a most heavy curse
when thou convertest from honour's golden name
to the black faction of bed-blotting shame.

COUNTESS: I'll follow thee and when my mind turns so   815
my body sink my soul in endless woe.

Exeunt

[Act II Scene ii]

Enter at one door Derby from France
at another door Audley with a drum

DERBY:	Thrice-noble Audley, well encountered here	
	how is it with our sovereign and his peers?	820
AUDLEY:	Tis full a fortnight since I saw his highness	
	what time he sent me forth to muster men	
	which I accordingly have done and bring them hither	
	in fair array before his majesty.	
	What news my lord of Derby from the emperor?	825
DERBY:	As good as we desire, the emperor	
	hath yielded to his highness friendly aid	
	and makes our king lieutenant-general	
	in all his lands and large dominions	
	then *via* for the spacious bounds of France.	830
AUDLEY:	What, doth his highness leap to hear these news?	
DERBY:	I have not yet found time to open them	
	the king is in his closet malcontent	
	for what I know not, but he gave in charge	
	till after dinner none should interrupt him.	835
	The Countess Salisbury and her father Warwick,	
	Artois and all look underneath the brows.	
AUDLEY:	Undoubtedly then something is amiss.	

Enter the King

DERBY:	The trumpets sound, the king is now abroad.	840
AUDLEY:	Here comes his highness.	
DERBY:	Befall my sovereign all my sovereign's wish!	
KING EDWARD:	Ah that thou wert a witch to make it so.	
DERBY:	The emperor greeteth you.	
KING EDWARD:	Would it were the Countess.	845
DERBY:	And hath accorded to your highness' suit.	
KING EDWARD:	Thou liest, she hath not but I would she had.	
AUDLEY:	All love and duty to my lord the king.	
KING EDWARD:	Well all but one is none, what news with you?	
AUDLEY:	I have my liege levied those horse and foot	850
	according as your charge and brought them hither.	
KING EDWARD:	Then let those foot trudge hence upon those horse	
	according to our discharge and be gone.	
	Derby, I'll look upon the Countess' mind anon.	
DERBY:	The Countess' mind, my liege?	855

KING EDWARD: I mean the emperor, leave me alone.
AUDLEY: What is his mind?
DERBY: Let's leave him to his humour.

Exeunt

KING EDWARD: Thus from the heart's abundance speaks the tongue
Countess for emperor and indeed why not?   860
She is as imperator over me and I to her
am as a kneeling vassal that observes
the pleasure or displeasure of her eye.

Enter Lodowick

What says the more than Cleopatra's match   865
to Caesar now?
LODOWICK: that yet my liege ere night
she will resolve your majesty.
KING EDWARD: What drum is this that thunders forth this march
to start the tender Cupid in my bosom?   870
Poor sheepskin, how it brawls with him that beateth it!
Go break the thundering parchment bottom out
and I will teach it to conduct sweet lines
unto the bosom of a heavenly nymph
for I will use it as my writing-paper   875
and so reduce him from a scolding drum
to be the herald and dear counsel-bearer
betwixt a goddess and a mighty king.
Go bid the drummer learn to touch the lute
or hang him in the braces of his drum   880
for now we think it an uncivil thing
to trouble heaven with such harsh resounds. Away!

Exit [Lodowick]

The quarrel that I have requires no arms
but these of mine and these shall meet my foe
in a deep march of penetrable groans.   885
My eyes shall be my arrows, and my sighs
shall serve me as the vantage of the wind
to whirl away my sweetest artillery.
Ah, but alas she wins the sun of me
for that is she herself and thence it comes   890
that poets term the wanton warrior blind
but love hath eyes as judgment to his steps

till too much lovéd glory dazzles them.
How now?

Enter Lodowick   895

LODOWICK: My liege the drum that struck the lusty march
                   stands with Prince Edward your thrice-valiant son.

Enter Prince Edward

KING EDWARD: I see the boy, oh how his mother's face
                   modelled in his, corrects my strayed desire   900
                   and rates my heart and chides my thievish eye
                   who being rich enough in seeing her
                   yet seeks elsewhere, and basest theft is that
                   which cannot cloak itself on poverty.
                   Now boy, what news?   905
PRINCE EDWARD: I have assembled, my dear lord and father
                   the choicest buds of all our English blood
                   for our affairs to France and here we come
                   to take direction from your majesty.
KING EDWARD: Still do I see in him delineate   910
                   his mother's visage, those his eyes are hers
                   who looking wistly on me make me blush
                   for faults against themselves give evidence.
                   Lust is a fire and men like lanthorns show
                   light lust within themselves, even through themselves. 915
                   Away, loose silks of wavering vanity!
                   Shall the large limit of fair Brittany
                   by me be overthrown, and shall I not
                   master this little mansion of my self?
                   Give me an armour of eternal steel   920
                   I go to conquer kings and shall I not then
                   subdue myself and be my enemy's friend?
                   It must not be. Come boy, forward, advance!
                   Let's with our colours sweet the air of France.

Enter Lodowick   925

LODOWICK: My liege, the Countess with a smiling cheer
                   desires access unto your majesty.
KING EDWARD: Why there it goes, that very smile of hers
                   hath ransomed captive France and set the King
                   the Dolphin and the peers at liberty.   930
                   Go leave me Ned and revel with thy friends.

Exit Prince

Thy mother is but black and thou like her
dost put it in my mind how foul she is.
Go fetch the Countess hither in thy hand

Exit Lodowick

and let her chase away these winter clouds   935
for she gives beauty to both heaven and earth.
The sin is more to hack and hew poor men
than to embrace in an unlawful bed
the register of all rarieties
since leathern Adam till this youngest hour.   940

Enter Countess [and Lodowick]

Go, Lod'wick, put thy hand into thy purse
play, spend, give, riot, waste, do what thou wilt
so thou wilt hence awhile and leave me here.

[Exit Lodowick]

Now my soul's playfellow art thou come   945
to speak the more than heavenly word of yea
to my objection in thy beauteous love?
COUNTESS: My father on his blessing hath commanded –
KING EDWARD: – that thou shalt yield to me?
COUNTESS: Ay, dear my liege, your due.   950
KING EDWARD: And that my dearest love can be no less
than right for right and render love for love.
COUNTESS: Than wrong for wrong and endless hate for hate
but sith I see your majesty so bent
that my unwillingness, my husband's love   955
your high estate nor no respect respected
can be my help but that your mightiness
will overbear and awe these dear regards
I bind my discontent to my content
and what I would not I'll compel I will   960
provided that yourself remove those lets
that stand between your highness' love and mine.
KING EDWARD: Name them fair Countess and by heaven I will.
COUNTESS: It is their lives that stand between our love
that I would have choked up, my sovereign.   965
KING EDWARD: Whose lives, my lady?

COUNTESS:	My thrice-loving liege
	your queen and Salisbury my wedded husband
	who living have that title in our love
	that we cannot bestow but by their death. 970
KING EDWARD:	Thy opposition is beyond our law.
COUNTESS:	So is your desire. If the law
	can hinder you to execute the one
	let it forbid you to attempt the other.
	I cannot think you love me as you say 975
	unless you do make good what you have sworn.
[KING EDWARD]:	No more, thy husband and the queen shall die.
	Fairer thou art by far than Hero was,
	beardless Leander not so strong as I.
	He swum an easy current for his love 980
	but I will throng a Hellespont of blood
	to arrive at Sestos where my Hero lies.
COUNTESS:	Nay you'll do more, you'll make the river too
	with their heart-bloods that keep our love asunder
	of which my husband and your wife are twain. 985
KING EDWARD:	Thy beauty makes them guilty of their death
	and gives in evidence that they shall die
	upon which verdict I their judge condemn them.
COUNTESS:	O perjured beauty, more corrupted judge!
	When to the great Star-Chamber o'er our heads 990
	the universal sessions calls to count
	this packing evil, we both shall tremble for it.
KING EDWARD:	What says my fair love, is she resolute?
COUNTESS:	Resolute to be dissolved and therefore this –
	keep but thy word great king and I am thine. 995
	Stand where thou dost, I'll part a little from thee
	and see how I will yield me to thy hands.
	Here by my side doth hang my wedding-knives.
	Take thou the one and with it kill thy queen
	and learn by me to find her where she lies 1000
	and with this other I'll dispatch my love
	which now lies fast asleep within my heart.
	When they are gone then I'll consent to love.
	Stir not lascivious king to hinder me
	my resolution is more nimbler far 1005
	than thy prevention can be in my rescue
	and if thou stir I strike, therefore stand still
	and hear the choice that I will put thee to.
	Either swear to leave thy most unholy suit
	and never henceforth to solicit me 1010
	or else by heaven this sharp-pointed knife

shall stain thy earth with that which thou would stain,
my poor chaste blood. Swear, Edward, swear
or I will strike and die before thee here.

KING EDWARD: Even by that power I swear that gives me now   1015
the power to be ashaméd of myself
I never mean to part my lips again
in any words that tends to such a suit.
Arise, true English lady, whom our isle
may better boast of than ever Roman might   1020
of her whose ransacked treasury hath tasked
the vain endeavour of so many pens.
Arise, and be my fault thy honour's fame
which after-ages shall enrich thee with.
I am awakéd from this idle dream.   1025
Warwick, my son, Derby, Artois and Audley,
brave warriors all, where are you all this while?

                          Enter all

Warwick, I make thee warden of the north
thou, Prince of Wales, and Audley, straight to sea   1030
scour to Newhaven, some there stay for me.
Myself, Artois and Derby will through Flanders
to greet our friends there and to crave their aid.
This night will scarce suffice me to discover
my folly's siege against a faithful lover   1035
for ere the sun shall gild the eastern sky
we'll wake him with our martial harmony.

                          Exeunt

[Act III Scene i]

Enter King John of France, his two sons, Charles of Normandy and Philip,
and the Duke of Lorraine

KING JOHN:	Here till our navy of a thousand sail	
	have made a breakfast to our foe by sea	
	let us encamp to wait their happy speed.	1045
	Lorraine, what readiness is Edward in?	
	How hast thou heard that he provided is	
	of martial furniture for this exploit?	
LORRAINE:	To lay aside unnecessary soothing	
	and not to spend the time in circumstance	1050
	tis bruited for a certainty my lord	
	that he's exceeding strongly fortified	
	his subjects flock as willingly to war	
	as if unto a triumph they were led.	
CHARLES:	England was wont to harbour malcontents	1055
	bloodthirsty and seditious Catilines	
	spendthrifts and such as gape for nothing else	
	but changing and alteration of the state	
	and is it possible	
	that they are now so loyal in themselves?	1060
LORRAINE:	All but the Scot, who solemnly protests	
	as heretofore I have informed his grace	
	never to sheathe his sword or take a truce.	
KING JOHN:	Ah, that's the anchorage of some better hope	
	but on the other side to think what friends	1065
	King Edward hath retained in Netherland	
	among those ever-bibbing epicures	
	those frothy Dutchmen puffed with double beer	
	that drink and swill in every place they come	
	doth not a little aggravate mine ire	1070
	besides we hear the emperor conjoins	
	and stalls him in his own authority	
	but all the mightier that their number is	
	the greater glory reaps the victory.	
	Some friends have we beside domestic power	1075
	the stern Polonian and the warlike Dane	
	the king of Bohemia and of Sicily	
	are all become confederates with us	
	and as I think are marching hither apace.	
	But soft I hear the music of their drums	1080
	by which I guess that their approach is near.	

*Enter the King of Bohemia with Danes, and a Polonian
captain with other soldiers another way*

KING OF BOHEMIA:	King John of France, as league and neighbourhood
	requires when friends are any way distressed
	I come to aid thee with my country's force.
POLONIAN CAPTAIN:	And from great Moscow, fearful to the Turk,
	and lofty Poland, nurse of hardy men 1090
	I bring these servitors to fight for thee
	who willingly will venture in thy cause.
KING JOHN:	Welcome Bohemian king and welcome all
	this your great kindness I will not forget
	besides your plentiful rewards in crowns 1095
	that from our treasury ye shall receive.
	There comes a hare-brained nation decked in pride
	the spoil of whom will be a treble gain
	and now my hope is full, my joy complete
	at sea we are as puissant as the force 1100
	of Agamemnon in the haven of Troy
	by land with Xerxes we compare of strength
	whose soldiers drank up rivers in their thirst
	then Bayard-like, blind overweening Ned
	to reach at our imperial diadem 1105
	is either to be swallowed of the waves
	or hacked apieces when thou comest ashore.

Enter [a mariner]

MARINER:	Near to the coast I have described my lord
	as I was busy in my watchful charge 1110
	the proud Armado of King Edward's ships
	which at the first far off when I did ken
	seemed as it were a grove of withered pines
	but drawing near their glorious bright aspect
	their streaming ensigns wrought of coloured silk 1115
	like to a meadow full of sundry flowers
	adorns the naked bosom of the earth
	majestical the order of their course
	figuring the hornéd circle of the moon
	and on the top-gallant of the admiral 1120
	and likewise all the handmaids of his train
	the arms of England and of France unite
	are quartered equally by herald's art
	thus tightly carried with a merry gale
	they plough the ocean hitherward amain. 1125

KING JOHN:	Dare he already crop the fleur de luce?
	I hope the honey being gathered thence
	he with the spider afterward approached
	shall suck forth deadly venom from the leaves
	but where's our navy, how are they prepared 1130
	to wing themselves against this flight of ravens?
MARINER:	They having knowledge brought them by the scouts
	did break from anchor straight and, puffed with rage
	no otherwise than were their sails with wind
	made forth as when the empty eagle flies 1135
	to satisfy his hungry griping maw.
KING JOHN:	These for thy news, return unto thy bark
	and if thou scape the bloody stroke of war
	and do survive the conflict, come again
	and let us hear the manner of the fight. 1140

Exit [mariner]

	Meanspace my lords tis best we be dispersed
	to several places lest they chance to land.
	First you my lord with your Bohemian troops
	shall pitch your battles on the lower hand
	my eldest son the Duke of Normandy 1145
	together with this aid of Muscovites
	shall climb the higher ground another way
	here in the middle coast betwixt you both
	Philip my youngest boy and I will lodge
	so lords begone and look unto your charge 1150
	you stand for France, an empire fair and large.

Exeunt

	Now tell me Philip what is thy concept
	touching the challenge that the English make?
PHILIP:	I say my lord claim Edward what he can
	and bring he ne'er so plain a pedigree 1155
	tis you are in possession of the crown
	and that's the surest point of all the law
	but were it not, yet ere he should prevail
	I'll make a conduit of my dearest blood
	or chase those straggling upstarts home again. 1160
KING JOHN:	Well said young Philip, call for bread and wine
	that we may cheer our stomachs with repast
	to look our foes more sternly in the face.

The battle heard afar off

Now is begun the heavy day at sea.
Fight, Frenchmen, fight! Be like the field of bears   1165
when they defend their younglings in their caves.
Stir, angry Nemesis, the happy helm
that with the sulphur battles of your rage
the English fleet may be dispersed and sunk.

Shot

PHILIP: O father how this echoing cannon-shot   1170
               like sweet harmony disgests my cates.
KING JOHN: Now boy thou hearest what thund'ring terror tis
               to buckle for a kingdom's sovereignty.
               The earth with giddy trembling when it shakes
               or when the exhalations of the air   1175
               breaks in extremity of lightning flash
               affrights not more than kings when they dispose
               to shew the rancour of their high-swoll'n hearts.

Retreat

Retreat is sounded, one side hath the worse.
O if it be the French, sweet Fortune turn   1180
and in thy turning change the forward winds
that with advantage of a favouring sky
our men may vanquish and th'other fly.

Enter mariner

My heart misgives, say mirror of pale death   1185
to whom belongs the honour of this day?
Relate I pray thee if thy breath will serve
the sad discourse of this discomfiture.
MARINER: I will my lord
               my gracious sovereign France hath ta'en the foil   1190
               and boasting Edward triumphs with success.
               These iron-hearted navies
               when last I was reporter to your grace
               both full of angry spleen of hope and fear
               hasting to meet each other in the face   1195
               at last conjoined and by their admiral

our admiral encountered many shot
by this the other that beheld these twain
give earnest penny of a further wrack
like fiery dragons took their haughty flight   1200
and likewise meeting, from their smoky wombs
sent many grim ambassadors of death.
Then gan the day to turn to gloomy night
and darkness did as well enclose the quick
as those that were but newly reft of life   1205
no leisure served for friends to bid farewell
and if it had, the hideous noise was such
as each to other seeméd deaf and dumb
purple the sea whose channel filled as fast
with streaming gore that from the maiméd fell   1210
as did her gushing moisture break into
the cranny cleftures of the through-shot planks.
Here flew a head dissevered from the trunk
there mangled arms and legs were tossed aloft
as when a whirlwind takes the summer dust   1215
and scatters it in middle of the air
then might ye see the reeling vessels split
and tottering sink into the ruthless flood
until their lofty tops were seen no more.
All shifts were tried both for defence and hurt   1220
and now the effect of valour and of force
of resolution and of cowardice
we lively pictured, how the one for fame
the other by compulsion, laid about.
Much did the *Nonpareil,* that brave ship   1225
so did the *Black Snake of Bullen,* than which
a bonnier vessel never yet spread sail
but all in vain, both sun the wind and tide
revolted all unto our foemen's side
that we perforce were fain to give them way   1230
and they are landed, thus my tale is done
we have untimely lost and they have won.

KING JOHN: Then rests there nothing but with present speed
to join our several forces all in one
and bid them battle ere they range too far.   1235
Come gentle Philip let us hence depart
this soldier's words have pierced thy father's heart.

*Exeunt. Enter two Frenchmen, a woman and two little children
meet them and other citizens*

[Act III Scene ii]

ONE:	Well met my masters, how now, what's the news	1240
	and wherefore are ye laden thus with stuff?	
	What, is it quarter-day that you remove	
	and carry bag and baggage too?	
TWO:	Quarter-day, aye, and quartering-day, I fear.	
	Have ye not heard the news that flies abroad?	1245
ONE:	What news?	
THREE:	How the French navy is destroyed at sea	
	and that the English army is arrived.	
ONE:	What then?	
TWO:	What then? quoth you, why, is't not time to fly	1250
	when envy and destruction is so nigh?	
ONE:	Content thee man, they are far enough from hence	
	and will be met I warrant ye to their cost	
	before they break so far into the realm.	
TWO:	Aye, so the grasshopper doth spend the time	1255
	in mirthful jollity till winter come	
	and then too late he would redeem his time	
	when frozen cold hath nipped his careless head.	
	He that no sooner will provide a cloak	
	than when he sees it doth begin to rain	1260
	may peradventure for his negligence	
	be throughly washed when he suspects it not.	
	We that have charge and such a train as this	
	must look in time to look for them and us	
	lest when we would we cannot be relieved.	1265
ONE:	Belike you then despair of ill success	
	and think your country will be subjugate.	
THREE:	We cannot tell, tis good to fear the worst.	
ONE:	Yet rather fight than like unnatural sons	
	forsake your loving parents in distress.	1270
TWO:	Tush, they that have already taken arms	
	are many fearful millions in respect	
	of that small handful of our enemies	
	but tis a rightful quarrel must prevail	
	Edward is son unto our late king's sister	1275
	where John Valois is three degrees removed.	
WOMAN:	Besides, there goes a prophecy abroad	
	published by one that was a friar once	
	whose oracles have many times proved true	
	and now he says the time will shortly come	1280
	whenas a lion rouséd in the west	
	shall carry hence the fleur de luce of France	

these I can tell ye and such-like surmises
strike many Frenchmen cold unto the heart.

Enter a Frenchman 1285

FRENCHMAN: Fly, countrymen and citizens of France!
Sweet-flowering peace, the root of happy life
is quite abandoned and expulsed the land
instead of whom ransacked constraining war
sits like to ravens upon your houses' tops 1290
slaughter and mischief walk within your streets
and unrestrained make havoc as they pass
the form whereof even now myself beheld
upon this fair mountain whence I came
for so far off as I directed mine eyes 1295
I might perceive five cities all on fire
cornfields and vineyards burning like an oven
and as the leaking vapour in the wind
turned but aside I likewise might discern
the poor inhabitants escaped the flame 1300
fall numberless upon the soldiers' pikes.
Three ways these dreadful ministers of wrath
do tread the measures of their tragic march
upon the right hand comes the conquering king
upon the left his hot unbridled son 1305
and in the midst our nation's glittering host
all which though distant yet conspire in one
to leave a desolation where they come
fly therefore citizens if you be wise
seek out some habitation further off 1310
here if you stay your wives will be abused
your treasure shared before your weeping eyes
shelter you yourselves for now the storm doth rise.
Away, away, methinks I hear their drums
ah wretched France I greatly fear thy fall 1315
thy glory shaketh like a tottering wall.

[Exeunt]

[Act III Scene iii]

Enter King Edward and the Earl of Derby with soldiers
and Gobin de Grey

KING EDWARD: Where's the Frenchman by whose cunning guide
we found the shallow of this river Somme 1320
and had direction how to pass the sea?

GOBIN:	Here my good lord.
KING EDWARD:	How art thou called? tell me thy name.
GOBIN:	Gobin de Grey, if please your excellence.
KING EDWARD:	Then Gobin for the service thou hast done 1325
	we here enlarge and give thee liberty
	and for recompence beside this good
	thou shalt receive five hundred marks in gold
	I know not how we should have met our son
	whom now in heart I wish I might behold. 1330

Enter Artois

ARTOIS:	Good news my lord the prince is hard at hand
	and with him comes Lord Audley and the rest
	whom since our landing we could never meet.

Enter Prince Edward, Lord Audley and soldiers   1335

KING EDWARD:	Welcome, fair prince, how hast thou sped, my son
	since thy arrival on the coast of France?
PRINCE EDWARD:	Successfully, I thank the gracious heavens
	some of their strongest cities we have won
	as Harfleur, Lie, Crotay and Carentigne 1340
	and others wasted, leaving at our heels
	a wide apparent field and beaten path
	for solitariness to progress in
	yet those that would submit we kindly pardoned
	for who in scorn refused our proffered peace 1345
	endured the penalty of sharp revenge.
KING EDWARD:	Ah France why shouldest thou be this obstinate
	against the kind embracement of thy friends?
	how gently had we thought to touch thy breast
	and set our foot upon thy tender mould 1350
	but that in froward and disdainful pride
	thou like a skittish and untaméd colt
	dost start aside and strike us with thy heels.
	But tell me Ned in all thy warlike course
	hast thou not seen the usurping king of France? 1355
PRINCE EDWARD:	Yes my good lord and not two hours ago
	with full a hundred thousand fighting men
	upon the one side with the river's bank
	and on the other both his multitudes
	I feared he would have cropped our smaller power 1360
	but happily perceiving your approach
	he hath withdrawn himself to Crécy plains

	where as it seemeth by his good array	
	he means to bid us battle presently.	
KING EDWARD:	He shall be welcome, that's the thing we crave.	1365

Enter King John, Dukes of Normandy and Lorraine,
King of Boheme, young Philip and soldiers

KING JOHN: Edward, know that John the true king of France
musing thou shouldst encroach upon his land
and in thy tyrannous proceeding slay   1370
his faithful subjects and subvert his towns
spits in thy face and in this manner following
obraids thee with thine arrogant intrusion.
First I condemn thee for a fugitive
a thievish pirate and a needy mate   1375
one that hath either no abiding place
or else inhabiting some barren soil
where neither herb or fruitful grain is had
dost altogether live by pilfering
next insomuch thou hast infringed thy faith   1380
broke league and solemn covenant made with me
I hold thee for a false pernicious wretch
and last of all although I scorn to cope
with one so much inferior to myself
yet in respect thy thirst is all for gold   1385
thy labour rather to be feared than loved
to satisfy thy lust in either part
here am I come and with me have I brought
exceeding store of treasure, pearl and coin
leave therefore now to persecute the weak   1390
and arméd entering conflict with the armed
let it be seen mongst other petty thefts
how thou canst win this pillage manfully.

KING EDWARD: If gall or wormwood have a pleasant taste
then is thy salutation honey-sweet   1395
but as the one hath no such property
so is the other most satirical
yet wot how I regard thy worthless taunts
if thou have uttered them to soil my fame
or dim the reputation of my birth   1400
know that thy wolvish barking cannot hurt
if slily to insinuate with the world
and with a strumpet's artificial line
to paint thy vicious and deforméd cause
be well assured the counterfeit will fade   1405

and in the end thy foul defects be seen
but if thou didst it to provoke me on
as who should say I were but timorous
or coldly negligent did need a spur
bethink thyself how slack I was at sea.   1410
Now since my landing I have won no towns
entered no further but upon the coast
and there have ever since securely slept
but if I have been otherwise employed
imagine, Valois, whether I intend   1415
to skirmish not for pillage but for the crown
which thou dost wear and that I vow to have
or one of us shall fall into his grave.

PRINCE EDWARD: Look not for cross invectives at our hands
or railing execrations of despite   1420
let creeping serpents hid in hollow banks
sting with their tongues, we have remorseless swords
and they shall plead for us and our affairs
yet thus much briefly by my father's leave
as all the immodest poison of thy throat   1425
is scandalous and most notorious lies
and our pretended quarrel is truly just
so end the battle when we meet today
may either of us prosper and prevail
or luckless cursed receive eternal shame.   1430

KING EDWARD: That needs no further question and I know
his conscience witnesseth it is my right
therefore, Valois, say, wilt thou yet resign
before the sickle's thrust into the corn
or that enkindled fury turn to flame?   1435

KING JOHN: Edward, I know what right thou hast in France
and ere I basely will resign my crown
this champion field shall be a pool of blood
and all our prospect as a slaughter-house.

PRINCE EDWARD: Aye, that approves thee, tyrant, what thou art   1440
no father, king or shepherd of thy realm
but one that tears her entrails with thy hands
and like a thirsty tiger suckst her blood.

AUDLEY: You peers of France, why do you follow him
that is so prodigal to spend your lives?   1445

CHARLES: Whom should they follow, agéd impotent,
but he that is their true-born sovereign?

KING EDWARD: Obraidst thou him because within his face
time hath engraved deep characters of age?
Know that these grave scholars of experience   1450

	like stiff-grown oaks will stand immovable	
	when whirlwind quickly turns up younger trees.	
DERBY:	Was ever any of thy father's house	
	king but thyself before this present time?	

DERBY:
like stiff-grown oaks will stand immovable
when whirlwind quickly turns up younger trees.
Was ever any of thy father's house
king but thyself before this present time?
Edward's great lineage by the mother's side   1455
five hundred years hath held the sceptre up
judge then, conspirators, by this descent
which is the true-born sovereign, this or that.

PHILIP:
Father, range your battles, prate no more
these English fain would spend the time in words   1460
that, night approaching, they might escape unfought.

KING JOHN:
Lords and my loving subjects, now's the time
that your intended force must bide the touch
therefore my friends consider this in brief
he that you fight for is your natural king   1465
he against whom you fight a foreigner
he that you fight for rules in clemency
and reins you with a mild and gentle bit
he against whom you fight if he prevail
will straight enthrone himself in tyranny   1470
make slaves of you and with a heavy hand
curtail and curb your sweetest liberty
then to protect your country and your king
let but the haughty courage of your hearts
answer the number of your able hands   1475
and we shall quickly chase these fugitives
for what's this Edward but a belly-god
a tender and lascivious wantonness
that th'other day was almost dead for love?
and what I pray you is his goodly guard   1480
such as but scant them of their chines of beef
and take away their downy featherbeds
and presently they are as resty-stiff
as twere a many over-ridden jades
then Frenchmen scorn that such should be your lords 1485
and rather bind ye them in captive bands.

ALL FRENCHMEN:
Vive le roi! God save King John of France!

KING JOHN:
Now on this plain of Crécy spread yourselves
and Edward when thou darest, begin the fight.

KING EDWARD:
We presently will meet thee, John of France   1490
and, English lords, let us resolve the day
either to clear us of that scandalous crime
or be entombéd in our innocence
and Ned because this battle is the first
that ever yet thou foughtest in pitchéd field   1495

as ancient custom is of martialists
to dub thee with the type of chivalry
in solemn manner we will give thee arms
come therefore heralds, orderly bring forth
a strong attirement for the prince my son.   1500

Enter four heralds bringing in a coat armour,
a helmet a lance and a shield

Edward Plantagenet in the name of God
as with this armour I impall thy breast
so be thy noble unrelenting heart   1505
walled in with flint of matchless fortitude
that never base affections enter there.
Fight and be valiant, conquer where thou comst!
Now follow, lords, and do him honour too.

DERBY: Edward Plantagenet Prince of Wales   1510
as I do set this helmet on thy head
wherewith the chamber of this brain is fenced
so may thy temples with Bellona's hand
be still adorned with laurel victory.
Fight and be valiant, conquer where thou comst!   1515

AUDLEY: Edward Plantagenet Prince of Wales
receive this lance into thy manly hand
use it in fashion of a brazen pen
to draw forth bloody stratagems in France
and print thy valiant deeds in honour's book.   1520
Fight and be valiant, vanquish where thou comst!

ARTOIS: Edward Plantagenet, Prince of Wales
hold, take this target, wear it on thy arm
and may the view thereof like Perseus' shield
astonish and transform thy gazing foes   1525
to senseless images of meagre death.
Fight and be valiant, conquer where thou comst!

KING EDWARD: Now wants there naught but knighthood which deferred
we leave till thou hast won it in the field.

PRINCE EDWARD: My gracious father and ye forward peers   1530
this honour you have done me animates
and cheers my green yet scarce-appearing strength
with comfortable good-presaging signs
no otherwise than did old Jacob's words
whenas he breathed his blessing on his sons.   1535
These hallowed gifts of yours when I profane
or use them not to glory of my God
to patronage the fatherless and poor

or for the benefit of England's peace
be numb my joints, wax feeble both mine arms 1540
wither my heart that like a sapless tree
I may remain the map of infamy.

KING EDWARD: Then thus our steeléd battles shall be ranged
the leading of the vaward Ned is thine
to dignify whose lusty spirit the more 1545
we temper it with Audley's gravity
that courage and experience joined in one
your manage may be second unto none.
For the main battles I will guide myself
and Derby in the rearward march behind. 1550
That orderly disposed and set in ray
let us to horse and God grant us the day.

Exeunt

[Act III Scene iv]

*Alarum. Enter a many Frenchmen flying. After them Prince
Edward running. Then enter King John and Duke of Lorraine* 1555

KING JOHN: Oh Lorraine say what mean our men to fly?
Our number is far greater than our foe's.

LORRAINE: The garrison of Genoese my lord
that came from Paris weary with their march
grudging to be suddenly employed 1560
no sooner in the forefront took their place
but straight retiring so dismayed the rest
as likewise they betook themselves to flight
in which for haste to make a safe escape
more in the clustering throng are pressed to death 1565
than by the enemy a thousandfold.

KING JOHN: O hapless fortune, let us yet assay
if we can counsel some of them to stay.

[Exeunt]

[Act III Scene v]

Enter King Edward and Audley

KING EDWARD: Lord Audley, whiles our son is in the chase 1570
withdraw our powers unto this little hill
and here a season let us breathe ourselves.

AUDLEY: I will my lord.

Exit, sound retreat

KING EDWARD: Just-dooming heaven, whose secret providence
                 to our gross judgement is inscrutable   1575
                 how are we bound to praise thy wondrous works
                 that hast this day given way unto the right
                 and made the wicked stumble at themselves.

Enter Artois

ARTOIS: Rescue, King Edward, rescue for thy son!   1580
KING EDWARD: Rescue, Artois? what, is he prisoner
                 or by violence fell beside his horse?
ARTOIS: Neither my lord but narrowly beset
                 with turning Frenchmen whom he did pursue
                 as tis impossible that he should scape   1585
                 except your highness presently descend.
KING EDWARD: Tut, let him fight, we gave him arms today
                 and he is labouring for a knighthood, man.

Enter Derby

DERBY: The prince, my lord, the prince, oh succour him   1590
                 he's close encompassed with a world of odds.
KING EDWARD: Then will he win a world of honour too
                 if he by valour can redeem him thence
                 if not, what remedy, we have more sons
                 than one, to comfort our declining age.   1595

Enter Audley

AUDLEY: Renownéd Edward, give me leave I pray
                 to lead my soldiers where I may relieve
                 your grace's son, in danger to be slain.
                 The snares of French like emmets on a bank   1600
                 muster about him whilst he lion-like
                 entangled in the net of their assaults
                 franticly rends and bites the woven toil
                 but all in vain, he cannot free himself.
KING EDWARD: Audley, content. I will not have a man   1605
                 on pain of death sent forth to succour him.
                 This is the day ordained by destiny
                 to season his courage with those grievous thoughts

	that if he breaketh out, Nestor's years on earth	
	will make him savour still of this exploit.	1610
DERBY:	Ah, but he shall not live to see those days.	
KING EDWARD:	Why then his epitaph is lasting praise.	
AUDLEY:	Yet good my lord tis too much wilfulness	
	to let his blood be spilt that may be saved.	
KING EDWARD:	Exclaim no more for none of you can tell	1615
	whether a borrowed aid will serve or no.	
	Perhaps he is already slain or ta'en	
	and dare a falcon when she's in her flight	
	and ever after she'll be haggard-like.	
	Let Edward be delivered by our hands	1620
	and still in danger he'll expect the like	
	but if himself himself redeem from thence	
	he will have vanquished cheerful death and fear	
	and ever after dread their force no more	
	than if they were but babes or captive slaves.	1625
AUDLEY:	O cruel father, farewell Edward then.	
DERBY:	Farewell, sweet prince, the hope of chivalry.	
ARTOIS:	O would my life might ransom him from death.	
KING EDWARD:	But soft methinks I hear	
	the dismal charge of trumpets' loud retreat.	1630
	All are not slain I hope that went with him	
	some will return with tidings good or bad.	

Enter Prince Edward in triumph, bearing in his hand
his shivered lance, and the King of Boheme borne before
wrapped in the colours. They run and embrace him.   1635

AUDLEY:	O joyful sight, victorious Edward lives!	
DERBY:	Welcome brave prince.	
KING EDWARD:	Welcome Plantagenet.	

kneel and kiss his father's hand

PRINCE EDWARD:	First, having done my duty as beseemed	
	lords I regreet you all with hearty thanks	1640
	and now behold after my winter's toil	
	my painful voyage on the boisterous sea	
	of war's devouring gulfs and steely rocks	
	I bring my fraught unto the wishéd port	
	my summer's hope, my travel's sweet reward	1645
	and here with humble duty I present	
	this sacrifice, this first fruit of my sword	
	cropped and cut down even at the gate of death	
	the King of Boheme, father, whom I slew	

whose thousands had entrenched me round about   1650
and lay as thick upon my battered crest
as on an anvil with their ponderous glaives
yet marble courage still did underprop
and when my weary arms with often blows
like the continual labouring woodman's axe   1655
that is enjoined to fell a load of oaks
began to falter, straight I would recover
my gifts you gave me and my zealous vow
and then new courage made me fresh again
that in despite I carved my passage forth   1660
and put the multitude to speedy flight.
Lo thus hath Edward's hand filled your request
and done I hope the duty of a knight.

his sword borne by a soldier

KING EDWARD: Aye, well hast thou deserved a knighthood, Ned,
                      and therefore with thy sword yet reeking warm   1665
                      with blood of those that fought to be thy bane
                      arise Prince Edward trusty knight at arms
                      this day thou hast confounded me with joy
                      and proved thyself fit heir unto a king.
PRINCE EDWARD: Here is a note my gracious lord of those   1670
                      that in this conflict of our foes were slain
                      eleven princes of esteem, fourscore barons
                      a hundred and twenty knights and thirty thousand
                      common soldiers and of our men a thousand.
KING EDWARD: Our God be praised. Now, John of France, I hope 1675
                      thou knowest King Edward for no wantonness
                      no love-sick cockney nor his soldiers jades
                      but which way is the fearful king escaped?
PRINCE EDWARD: Towards Poitiers, noble father, and his sons.
KING EDWARD: Ned, thou and Audley shall pursue them still.   1680
                      Myself and Derby will to Calais straight
                      and there begirt that haven-town with siege.
                      Now lies it on an upshot, therefore strike
                      and wistly follow whiles the game's on foot.
                      What picture's this?   1685
PRINCE EDWARD: A pelican my lord
                      wounding her bosom with her crookéd beak
                      that so her nest of young ones might be fed
                      with drops of blood that issue from her heart.
                      The motto *sic et vos* – 'and so should you'.   1690

Exeunt

[Act IV Scene i]

Enter Lord Mountford with a coronet in his hand
with him the Earl of Salisbury

MOUNTFORD: My lord of Salisbury since by our aid
mine enemy Sir Charles of Blois is slain
and I again am quietly possessed   1695
in Brittaine's dukedom, know that I resolve
for this kind furtherance of your king and you
to swear allegiance to his majesty
in sign whereof receive this coronet
bear it unto him and withal mine oath   1700
never to be but Edward's faithful friend.

SALISBURY: I take it Mountford, thus I hope ere long
the whole dominions of the realm of France
will be surrendered to his conquering hand.

Exit [Mountford]

Now if I knew but safely how to pass   1705
I would to Calais gladly meet his grace
whither I am by letters certified
that he intends to have his host removed.
It shall be so, this policy will serve.
Ho, who's within? Bring Villiers to me.   1710

Enter Villiers

Villiers, thou knowest thou art my prisoner
and that I might for ransom if I would
require of thee a hundred thousand francs
or else retain and keep thee captive still   1715
but so it is that for a smaller charge
thou mayst be quit and if thou wilt thyself
and this it is, procure me but a passport
of Charles the Duke of Normandy, that I
without restraint may have recourse to Calais   1720
through all the countries where he hath to do
which thou mayst easily obtain I think
by reason I have often heard thee say
he and thou were students once together
and then thou shalt be set at liberty   1725
how sayst thou, wilt thou undertake to do it?

VILLIERS:	I will my lord but I must speak with him.
SALISBURY:	Why so thou shalt, take horse and post from hence
	only before thou goest, swear by thy faith
	that if thou canst not compass my desire 1730
	thou wilt return my prisoner back again
	and that shall be sufficient warrant for me.
VILLIERS:	To that condition I agree, my lord
	and will unfeignedly perform the same.

Exit

SALISBURY:	Farewell Villiers.	1735
	Thus once I mean to try a Frenchman's faith.	

Exit

[Act IV Scene ii]

Enter King Edward and Derby with soldiers

KING EDWARD:	Since they refuse our proffered league my lord	
	and will not ope their gates and let us in	
	we will entrench ourselves on every side	1740
	that neither victuals nor supply of men	
	may come to succour this accursèd town	
	famine shall combat where our swords are stopped.	

Enter six poor Frenchmen

DERBY:	The promised aid that made them stand aloof	1745
	is now retired and gone another way	
	it will repent them of their stubborn will	
	but what are these poor ragged slaves my lord?	
KING EDWARD:	Ask what they are, it seems they come from Calais.	1750
DERBY:	You wretched patterns of despair and woe	
	what are you, living men or gliding ghosts	
	crept from your graves to walk upon the earth?	
A POOR FRENCHMAN:	No ghosts my lord but men that breathe a life	
	far worse than is the quiet sleep of death.	1755
	We are distressèd poor inhabitants	
	that long have been diseasèd sick and lame	
	and now because we are not fit to serve	
	the captain of the town hath thrust us forth	

	that so expense of victuals may be saved.	1760
KING EDWARD:	A charitable deed no doubt and worthy praise	
	but how do you imagine then to speed?	

KING EDWARD: A charitable deed no doubt and worthy praise
but how do you imagine then to speed?
we are your enemies in such a case
we can no less but put ye to the sword
since when we proffered truce it was refused. 1765

POOR FRENCHMEN: And if your grace no otherwise vouchsafe
as welcome death is unto us as life.

KING EDWARD: Poor silly men much wronged and more distressed
go, Derby, go and see they be relieved
command that victuals be appointed them 1770
and give to every one five crowns apiece.

[Exeunt Derby and Frenchmen]

The lion scorns to touch the yielding prey
and Edward's sword must fresh itself in such
as wilful stubbornness hath made perverse.

Enter Lord Percy 1775

Lord Percy, welcome. What's the news in England?

PERCY: The Queen, my lord, comes here to your grace
and from her highness and the lord vicegerent
I bring this happy tidings of success:
David of Scotland, lately up in arms 1780
thinking belike he soonest should prevail
your highness being absent from the realm
is by the fruitful service of your peers
and painful travail of the Queen herself
that big with child was every day in arms 1785
vanquished subdued and taken prisoner.

KING EDWARD: Thanks Percy for thy news with all my heart.
What was he took him prisoner in the field?

PERCY: An esquire my lord, John Copeland is his name
who since entreated by her majesty 1790
denies to make surrender of his prize
to any but unto your grace alone
whereat the Queen is grievously displeased.

KING EDWARD: Well then we'll have a pursuivant despatched
to summon Copeland hither out of hand 1795
and with him he shall bring his prisoner king.

PERCY: The Queen my lord herself by this at sea
and purposeth as soon as wind will serve

	to land at Calais and to visit you.	
KING EDWARD:	She shall be welcome, and to wait her coming	1800
	I'll pitch my tent near to the sandy shore.	

Enter a captain

CAPTAIN:	The burgesses of Calais, mighty king	
	have by a council willingly decreed	
	to yield the town and castle to your hands	1805
	upon condition it will please your grace	
	to grant them benefit of life and goods.	
KING EDWARD:	They will so? Then belike they may command	
	dispose elect and govern as they list.	
	No sirrah, tell them since they did refuse	1810
	our princely clemency at first proclaimed	
	they shall not have it now although they would.	
	I will accept of naught but fire and sword	
	except within these two days six of them	
	that are the wealthiest merchants in the town	1815
	come naked all but for their linen shirts	
	with each a halter hanged about his neck	
	and prostrate yield themselves upon their knees	
	to be afflicted, hanged or what I please	
	and so you may inform their masterships.	1820

Exeunt [King Edward and Percy]

CAPTAIN:	Why, this it is to trust a broken staff.	
	Had we not been persuaded John our king	
	would with his army have relieved the town	
	we had not stood upon defiance so	
	but now tis past that no man can recall	1825
	and better some do go to wrack than all.	

Exit

[Act IV Scene iii]

Enter Charles of Normandy and Villiers

CHARLES:	I wonder Villiers thou shouldest importune me	
	for one that is our deadly enemy.	
VILLIERS:	Not for his sake my gracious lord so much	1830
	am I become an earnest advocate	

as that thereby my ransom will be quit.

CHARLES: Thy ransom, man? why needest thou talk of that?
art thou not free? and are not all occasions
that happen for advantage of our foes   1835
to be accepted of and stood upon?

VILLIERS: No, good my lord, except the same be just
for profit must with honour be commixed
or else our actions are but scandalous
but letting pass these intricate objections   1840
wilt please your highness to subscribe or no?

CHARLES: Villiers, I will not nor I cannot do it.
Salisbury shall not have his will so much
to claim a passport how it pleaseth himself.

VILLIERS: Why then I know the extremity my lord   1845
I must return to prison whence I came.

CHARLES: Return? I hope thou wilt not.
What bird that hath escaped the fowler's gin
will not beware how she's ensnared again?
or what is he so senseless and secure   1850
that having hardly passed a dangerous gulf
will put himself in peril there again?

VILLIERS: Ah but it is mine oath my gracious lord
which I in conscience may not violate
or else a kingdom should not draw me hence.   1855

CHARLES: Thine oath? why that doth bind thee to abide
hast thou not sworn obedience to thy prince?

VILLIERS: In all things that uprightly he commands
but either to persuade or threaten me
not to perform the covenant of my word   1860
is lawless and I need not to obey.

CHARLES: Why is it lawful for a man to kill
and not to break a promise with his foe?

VILLIERS: To kill, my lord, when war is once proclaimed
so that our quarrel be for wrongs received   1865
no doubt is lawfully permitted us
but in an oath we must be well advised
how do we swear, and when we once have sworn
not to infringe it though we die therefor.
Therefore, my lord, as willing I return   1870
as if I were to fly to paradise.

CHARLES: Stay my Villiers, thine honourable mind
deserves to be eternally admired
thy suit shall be no longer thus deferred.
Give me the paper, I'll subscribe to it   1875
and wheretofore I loved thee as Villiers

hereafter I'll embrace thee as myself.
Stay and be still in favour with thy lord.

VILLIERS: I humbly thank your grace, I must dispatch
and send this passport first unto the earl   1880
and then I will attend your highness' pleasure.

CHARLES: Do so, Villiers, and Charles when he hath need
be such his soldiers howsoever he speed.

                    Exit Villiers. Enter King John

KING JOHN: Come Charles and arm thee, Edward is entrapped   1885
the Prince of Wales is falln into our hands
and we have compassed him, he cannot scape.

CHARLES: But will your highness fight today?

KING JOHN: What else, my son? he's scarce eight thousand strong
and we are threescore thousand at the least.   1890

CHARLES: I have a prophecy, my gracious lord
wherein is written what success is like
to happen us in this outrageous war
it was delivered me at Crécy's field
by one that is an agéd hermit there   1895
'when feathered fowl shall make thine army tremble
and flintstones rise and break the battle ray
then think on him that doth not now dissemble
for that shall be the hapless dreadful day
yet in the end thy foot shalt thou advance   1900
as far in England as thy foe in France'.

KING JOHN: By this it seems we shall be fortunate
for as it is impossible that stones
should ever rise and break the battle ray
or airy fowl make men in arms to quake   1905
so is it like we shall not be subdued
or say this might be true yet in the end
since he doth promise we shall drive him hence
and forage their country as they have done ours
by this revenge, that loss will seem the less   1910
but all are frivolous fancies toys and dreams
once we are sure we have ensnared the son
catch we the father after how we can.

                            Exeunt

[Act IV Scene iv]

Enter Prince Edward, Audley and others

PRINCE EDWARD: Audley, the arms of death embrace us round   1915
and comfort have we none save that to die
we pay sour earnest for a sweeter life.
At Crécy field our clouds of warlike smoke
choked up those French mouths and dissevered them
but now their multitudes of millions hide   1920
masking as twere the beauteous burning sun
leaving no hope to us but sullen dark
and eyeless terror of all-ending night.

AUDLEY: This sudden mighty and expedient head
that they have made, fair prince, is wonderful.   1925
Before us in the valley lies the king
vantaged with all that heaven and earth can yield
his party stronger-battled than our whole
his son the braving duke of Normandy
hath trimmed the mountain on our right hand up   1930
in shining plate that now the aspiring hill
shows like a silver quarry or an orb
aloft the which the banners, bannerets
and new-replenished pendants cuff the air
and beat the winds that for their gaudiness   1935
struggles to kiss them. On our left hand lies
Philip the younger issue of the king
coating the other hill in such array
that all his gilded upright pikes do seem
straight trees of gold, the pendants leaves,   1940
and their device of antique heraldry
quartered in colours seeming sundry fruits
makes it the orchard of the Hesperides.
Behind us two the hill doth bear his height
for like a half-moon opening but one way   1945
it rounds us in, there at our backs are lodged
the fatal crossbows and the battle there
is governed by the rough Chatillion.
Then thus it stands, the valley for our flight
the king binds in, the hills on either hand   1950
are proudly royaliséd by his sons
and on the hill behind stands certain death
in pay and service with Chatillion.

PRINCE EDWARD: Death's name is much more mighty than his deeds
                 thy parcelling this power hath made it more   1955
                 than all the world, and call it but a power.
                 As many sands as these my hands can hold
                 are but my handful of so many sands
                 easily ta'en up and quickly thrown away
                 but if I stand to count them sand by sand   1960
                 the number would confound my memory
                 and make a thousand millions of a task
                 which briefly is no more indeed than one.
                 These quarters, squadrons and these regiments
                 before, behind us and on either hand   1965
                 are but a power. When we name a man
                 his hand his foot his head hath several strengths
                 and being all but one self instant strength
                 why all this many, Audley, is but one
                 and we can call it all but one man's strength.   1970
                 He that hath far to go tells it by miles
                 if he should tell the steps it kills his heart.
                 The drops are infinite that make a flood
                 and yet thou knowest we call it but a rain.
                 There is but one France, one king of France   1975
                 that France hath no more kings, and that same king
                 hath but the puissant legion of one king
                 and we have one. Then apprehend no odds
                 for one to one is fair equality.

                              Enter a herald from King John   1980

                 What tidings, messenger? be plain and brief.
HERALD: The King of France my sovereign lord and master
                 greets by me his foe the Prince of Wales.
                 If thou call forth a hundred men of name
                 of lords, knights, esquires and English gentlemen   1985
                 and with thyself and those kneel at his feet
                 he straight will fold his bloody colours up
                 and ransom shall redeem lives forfeited.
                 If not, this day shall drink more English blood
                 than e'er was buried in our British earth.   1990
                 What is the answer to his proffered mercy?
PRINCE EDWARD: This heaven that covers France contains the mercy
                 that draws from me submissive orisons.
                 That such base breath should vanish from my lips
                 to urge the plea of mercy to a man   1995
                 the Lord forbid. Return and tell the King

my tongue is made of steel and it shall beg
my mercy on his coward burgonet
tell him my colours are as red as his
my men as bold, our English arms as strong   2000
return him my defiance in his face.

HERALD: I go.

[Exit] Enter another

PRINCE EDWARD: What news with thee?

HERALD: The Duke of Normandy my lord and master   2005
pitying thy youth is so engirt with peril
by me hath sent a nimble-jointed jennet
as swift as ever yet thou didst bestride
and therewithal he counsels thee to fly
else death himself hath sworn that thou shalt die.   2010

PRINCE EDWARD: Back with the beast unto the beast that sent him
tell him I cannot sit a coward's horse
bid him today bestride the jade himself
for I will stain my horse quite o'er with blood
and double-gild my spurs but I will catch him   2015
so tell the capering boy and get thee gone.

[Exit] Enter another

HERALD: Edward of Wales, Philip the second son
to the most mighty Christian king of France
seeing thy body's living date expired   2020
all full of charity and Christian love
commends this book full fraught with prayers
to thy fair hand and for thy hour of life
entreats thee that thou meditate therein
and arm thy soul for her long journey towards.   2025
Thus have I done his bidding and return.

PRINCE EDWARD: Herald of Philip greet thy lord from me
all good that he can send I can receive
but thinkst thou not the unadviséd boy
hath wronged himself in this far tendering me?   2030
Happily he cannot pray without the book
I think him no divine extemporal
then render back this commonplace of prayer
to do himself good in adversity.
Besides, he knows not my sin's quality   2035
and therefore knows no prayers for my avail.
Ere night his prayer may be to pray to God
to put it in my heart to hear his prayer

so tell the courtly wanton and be gone.

HERALD: I go.   2040

[Exit]

PRINCE EDWARD: How confident their strength and number makes them.
Now Audley sound those silver wings of thine
and let those milk-white messengers of time
show thy time's learning in this dangerous time
thyself art busy and bit with many broils   2045
and stratagems forepast with iron pens
are texted in thine honourable face
thou art a married man in this distress
but danger woos me as a blushing maid
teach me an answer to this perilous time.   2050

AUDLEY: To die is all as common as to live
the one in choice the other holds in chase
for from the instant we begin to live
we do pursue and hunt the time to die.
First bud we, then we blow and after seed   2055.
then presently we fall, and as a shade
follows the body so we follow death
if then we hunt for death why do we fear it?
if we fear it why do we follow it?
if we do follow it how can we shun it?   2060
If we do fear, with fear we do but aid
the thing we fear to seize on us the sooner
if we fear not then no resolvéd proffer
can overthrow the limit of our fate
for whether ripe or rotten, drop we shall   2065
as we do draw the lottery of our doom.

PRINCE EDWARD: Ah good old man, a thousand thousand armours
these words of thine have buckled on my back
ah what an idiot hast thou made of life
to seek the thing it fears, and how disgraced   2070
the imperial victory of murdering death
since all the lives his conquering arrows strike
seek him and he not them, to shame his glory.
I will not give a penny for a life
nor half a halfpenny to shun grim death   2075
since for to live is but to seek to die
and dying but beginning of new life
let come the hour when he that rules it will
to live or die I hold indifferent.

Exeunt

[Act IV Scene v]

KING JOHN: A sudden darkness hath defaced the sky
the winds are crept into their caves for fear
the leaves move not, the world is hushed and still
the birds cease singing and the wandering brooks
murmur no wonted greeting to their shores   2085
silence attends some wonder and expecteth
that heaven should pronounce some prophecy.
Where or from whom proceeds this silence, Charles?

CHARLES: Our men with open mouths and staring eyes
look on each other as they did attend   2090
each other's words and yet no creature speaks.
A tongue-tied fear hath made a midnight hour
and speeches sleep through all the waking regions.

KING JOHN: But now the pompous sun in all his pride
looked through his golden coach upon the world   2095
and on a sudden hath he hid himself
that now the under earth is as a grave
dark, deadly, silent and uncomfortable.

A clamour of ravens

Hark, what a deadly outcry do I hear?

CHARLES: Here comes my brother Philip.   2100

KING JOHN: All dismayed.
What fearful words are those thy looks presage?

PHILIP: A flight, a flight!

KING JOHN: Coward, what flight? thou liest, there needs no flight.

PHILIP: A flight!   2105

KING JOHN: Awake thy craven powers and tell on
the substance of that very fear indeed
which is so ghastly printed in thy face.
What is the matter?

PHILIP: A flight of ugly ravens   2110
do croak and hover o'er our soldiers' heads
and keep in triangles and cornered squares
right as our forces are embattléd.
With their approach there came this sudden fog
which now hath hid the airy flower of heaven   2115
and made at noon a night unnatural
upon the quaking and dismayéd world.

	In brief our soldiers have let fall their arms	
	and stand like metamorphosed images	
	bloodless and pale, one gazing on another.	2120
KING JOHN:	Aye, now I call to mind the prophecy	
	but I must give no entrance to a fear.	
	Return and hearten up these yielding souls	
	tell them the ravens seeing them in arms	
	so many fair against a famished few	2125
	come but to dine upon their handiwork	
	and prey upon the carrion that they kill	
	for when we see a horse laid down to die	
	although not dead, the ravenous birds	
	sit watching the departure of his life	2130
	even so these ravens for the carcasses	
	of those poor English that are marked to die	
	hover about and if they cry to us	
	tis but for meat that we must kill for them.	
	Away and comfort up my soldiers	2135
	and sound the trumpets and at once dispatch	
	this little business of a silly fraud.	

Exit Prince. Another noise. Salisbury
brought in by a French captain

CAPTAIN:	Behold my liege this knight and forty mo	2140
	of whom the better part are slain and fled	
	with all endeavour sought to break our ranks	
	and make their way to the encompassed prince.	
	Dispose of him as please your majesty.	
KING JOHN:	Go, and the next bough, soldier, that thou seest	2145
	disgrace it with his body presently	
	for I do hold a tree in France too good	
	to be the gallows of an English thief.	
SALISBURY:	My lord of Normandy, I have your pass	
	and warrant for my safety through this land.	2150
CHARLES:	Villiers procured it for thee did he not?	
SALISBURY:	He did.	
CHARLES:	And it is current, thou shalt freely pass.	
KING JOHN:	Ay, freely to the gallows to be hanged	
	without denial or impediment.	2155
	Away with him!	
CHARLES:	I hope your highness will not so disgrace me	
	and dash the virtue of my seal at arms.	
	He hath my never-broken name to show	
	charactered with this princely hand of mine	2160

and rather let me leave to be a prince
than break the stable verdict of a prince.
I do beseech you let him pass in quiet.

KING JOHN:
Thou and thy word lie both in my command
what canst thou promise that I cannot break?   2165
which of these twain is greater infamy
to disobey thy father or thyself?
Thy word nor no man's may exceed his power
nor that same man doth never break his word
that keeps it to the utmost of his power.   2170
The breach of faith dwells in the soul's consent
which if thyself without consent do break
thou art not chargéd with the breach of faith.
Go hang him for thy licence lies in me
and my constraint stands the excuse for thee.   2175

CHARLES:
What, am I not a soldier in my word?
Then arms adieu and let them fight that list.
Shall I not give my girdle from my waist
but with a guardian I shall be controlled
to say I may not give my things away?   2180
Upon my soul, had Edward Prince of Wales
engaged his word, writ down his noble hand
for all your knights to pass his father's land
the royal king to grace his warlike son
would not alone safe conduct give to them   2185
but with all bounty feasted them and theirs.

KING JOHN:
Dwellst thou on precedents? then be it so.
Say, Englishman, of what degree thou art.

SALISBURY:
An earl in England though a prisoner here
and those that know me call me Salisbury.   2190

KING JOHN:
Then, Salisbury, say whither thou art bound.

SALISBURY:
To Calais where my liege King Edward is.

KING JOHN:
To Calais, Salisbury, then to Calais pack
and bid the king prepare a noble grave
to put his princely son black Edward in   2195
and as thou travelst westward from this place
some two leagues hence there is a lofty hill
whose top seems topless, for the embracing sky
doth hide his high head in her azure bosom
upon whose tall top when thy foot attains   2200
look back upon the humble vale beneath
humble of late but now made proud with arms
and thence behold the wretched Prince of Wales
hooped with a bond of iron round about
after which sight to Calais spur amain   2205

and say the prince was smothered and not slain
and tell the king this is not all his ill
for I will greet him ere he thinks I will.
Away, be gone, the smoke but of our shot
will choke our foes though bullets hit them not.   2210

Exeunt

[Act IV Scene vi]

Alarum. Enter Prince Edward and Artois

ARTOIS: How fares your grace? are you not shot my lord?
PRINCE EDWARD: No, dear Artois, but choked with dust and smoke
                    and stepped aside for breath and fresher air.
ARTOIS: Breathe then and to it again, the amazéd French   2215
                    are quite distract with gazing on the crows
                    and were our quivers full of shafts again
                    your grace should see a glorious day of this.
                    O for more arrows, lord, that's our want.
PRINCE EDWARD: Courage, Artois, a fig for feathered shafts   2220
                    when feathered fowls do bandy on our side.
                    What need we fight and sweat and keep a coil
                    when railing crows outscold our adversaries?
                    Up, up Artois, the ground itself is armed
                    with fire-containing flint, command our bows   2225
                    to hurl away their pretty-coloured yew
                    and to it with stones. Away, Artois, away
                    my soul doth prophesy we win the day.

Exeunt

[Act IV Scene vii]

Alarum. Enter King John

KING JOHN: Our multitudes are in themselves confounded   2230
                    dismayéd and distraught. Swift-starting fear
                    hath buzzed a cold dismay through all our army
                    and every petty disadvantage prompts
                    the fear-possesséd abject soul to fly.
                    Myself, whose spirit is steel to their dull lead   2235
                    what with recalling of the prophecy

and that our native stones from English arms
rebel against us, find myself attainted
with strong surprise of weak and yielding fear.

                  Enter Charles   2240

CHARLES: Fly, father, fly! The French do kill the French.
Some that would stand let drive at some that fly.
Our drums strike nothing but discouragement
our trumpets sound dishonour and retire
the spirit of fear that feareth nought but death   2245
cowardly works confusion on itself.

                  Enter Philip

PHILIP: Pluck out your eyes and see not this day's shame
an arm hath beat an army, one poor David
hath with a stone foiled twenty stout Goliahs.   2250
Some twenty naked starvelings with small flints
hath driven back a puissant host of men
arrayed and fenced in all accomplements.
KING JOHN: *Mortdieu*! they quait at us and kill us up.
No less than forty thousand wicked elders   2255
have forty lean slaves this day stoned to death.
CHARLES: O that I were some other countryman.
This day hath set derision on the French
and all the world will blurt and scorn at us.
KING JOHN: What, is there no hope left?   2260
CHARLES: No hope but death to bury up our shame.
KING JOHN: Make up once more with me, the twentieth part
of those that live are men enow to quail
the feeble handful on the adverse part.
CHARLES: Then charge again, if heaven be not opposed   2265
we cannot lose the day.
KING JOHN: On, away!

                  Exeunt

[Act IV Scene viii]

Enter Audley wounded and rescued by two squires

ESQUIRE: How fares my lord?
AUDLEY: Even as a man may do   2270
that dines at such a bloody feast as this.

ESQUIRE: I hope, my lord, that is no mortal scar.
AUDLEY: No matter if it be, the count is cast
                 and in the worst ends but a mortal man.
                 Good friends, convey me to the princely Edward   2275
                 that in the crimson bravery of my blood
                 I may become him with saluting him.
                 I'll smile and tell him that this open scar
                 doth end the harvest of his Audley's war.

                            Exeunt

[Act IV Scene ix]

*Enter Prince Edward, King John, Charles and all with
ensigns spread. Retreat sounded*

PRINCE EDWARD: Now John in France and lately John of France
                 thy bloody ensigns are my captive colours
                 and you high-vaunting Charles of Normandy   2285
                 that once today sent me a horse to fly
                 are now the subjects of my clemency.
                 Fie, lords, is it not a shame that English boys
                 whose early days are not yet worth a beard
                 should in the bosom of your kingdom thus   2290
                 one against twenty beat you up together?
KING JOHN: Thy fortune not thy force hath conquered us.
PRINCE EDWARD: An argument that heaven aids the right.

                      [Enter Artois and Philip]

                 See, see, Artois doth bring with him along
                 the late good counsel-giver to my soul.   2295
                 Welcome Artois and welcome Philip too.
                 Who now of you or I have need to pray?
                 Now is the proverb verified in you
                 'too bright a morning breeds a lowring day'.

                      Sound trumpets, enter Audley   2300

                 But say, what grim discouragement comes here?
                 Alas, what thousand arméd men of France
                 have writ that note of death in Audley's face?
                 Speak thou that wooest death with thy careless smile

	and lookst so merrily upon thy grave	2305
	as if thou wert enamoured on thine end	
	what hungry sword hath so bereaved thy face	
	and lopped a true friend from my loving soul?	
AUDLEY:	O prince thy sweet bemoaning speech to me	
	is as a mournful knell to one dead-sick.	2310
PRINCE EDWARD:	Dear Audley, if my tongue ring out thy end	
	my arms shall be the grave. What may I do	
	to win thy life or to revenge thy death?	
	If thou wilt drink the blood of captive kings	
	or that it were restorative, command	2315
	a health of king's blood and I'll drink to thee.	
	If honour may dispense for thee with death	
	the never-dying honour of this day	
	share wholly Audley to thyself and live.	
AUDLEY:	Victorious prince, that thou art so, behold	2320
	a Caesar's fame in kings' captivity.	
	If I could hold dim death but at a bay	
	till I did see my liege thy loyal father	
	my soul should yield this castle of my flesh	
	this mangled tribute with all willingness	2325
	to darkness, consummation, dust and worms.	
PRINCE EDWARD:	Cheerly, bold man, thy soul is all too proud	
	to yield her city for one little breach	
	should be divorcéd from her earthly spouse	
	by the soft temper of a Frenchman's sword.	2330
	Lo, to repair thy life I give to thee	
	three thousand marks a year in English land.	
AUDLEY:	I take thy gift to pay the debts I owe.	
	These two poor esquires redeemed me from the French	
	with lusty and dear hazard of their lives.	2335
	What thou hast given me I give to them	
	and as thou lovest me, prince, lay thy consent	
	to this bequeath in my last testament.	
PRINCE EDWARD:	Renownéd Audley, live and have from me	
	this gift twice doubled to these esquires and thee.	2340
	But live or die, what thou hast given away	
	to these and theirs shall lasting freedom stay.	
	Come, gentlemen, I will see my friend bestowed	
	within an easy litter, then we'll march	
	proudly towards Calais with triumphant pace	2345
	unto my royal father and there bring	
	the tribute of my wars, fair France his king.	

Exeunt

[Act V Scene i]

Enter six citizens in their shirts, barefoot, with
halters about their necks. Enter King Edward,
Queen Philippa, Derby, soldiers   2350

KING EDWARD:	No more, Queen Philip, pacify yourself.
	Copeland, except he can excuse his fault
	shall find displeasure written in our looks
	and now unto this proud resisting town
	soldiers assault, I will no longer stay 2355
	to be deluded by their false delays.
	Put all to sword and make the spoil your own.
CITIZENS:	Mercy, King Edward, mercy, gracious lord.
KING EDWARD:	Contemptuous villains, call ye now for truce?
	mine ears are stopped against your bootless cries 2360
	sound drums' alarum, draw threatening swords!
[CITIZEN ONE]:	Ah, noble prince, take pity on this town
	and hear us mighty king
	we claim the promise that your highness made
	the two days' respite is not yet expired 2365
	and we are come with willingness to bear
	what torturing death or punishment you please
	so that the trembling multitude be saved.
KING EDWARD:	My promise, well I do confess as much
	but I require the chiefest citizens 2370
	and men of most account that should submit.
	You peradventure are but servile grooms
	or some felonious robbers on the sea
	whom apprehended, law would execute
	albeit severity lay dead in us. 2375
	No, no, ye cannot overreach us thus.
[CITIZEN] TWO:	The sun, dread lord, that in the western fall
	beholds us now low-brought through misery
	did in the orient purple of the morn
	salute our coming forth when we were known 2380
	or may our portion be with damnéd fiends.
KING EDWARD:	If it be so then let our covenant stand.
	We take possession of the town in peace
	but for yourselves look you for no remorse
	but as imperial justice hath decreed 2385
	your bodies shall be dragged about these walls
	and after feel the stroke of quartering steel.
	This is your doom, go, soldiers, see it done.

QUEEN PHILIPPA:	Ah, be more mild unto these yielding men.
	It is a glorious thing to stablish peace 2390
	and kings approach the nearest unto God
	by giving life and safety unto men.
	As thou intendest to be king of France
	so let her people live to call thee king
	for what the sword cuts down or fire hath spoiled 2395
	is held in reputation none of ours.
KING EDWARD:	Although experience teach us this is true
	that peaceful quietness brings most delight
	when most of all abuses are controlled
	yet insomuch it shall be known that we 2400
	as well can master our affections
	as conquer other by the dint of sword
	Philip prevail, we yield to thy request
	these men shall live to boast of clemency
	and tyranny strike terror to thyself. 2405
[CITIZEN] TWO:	Long live your highness, happy be your reign.
KING EDWARD:	Go get you hence, return unto the town
	and if this kindness hath deserved your love
	learn then to reverence Edward as your king.

Exeunt [citizens]   2410

Now might we hear of our affairs abroad
we would till gloomy winter were o'erspent
dispose our men in garrison a while
but who comes here?

Enter Copeland and King David

DERBY:	Copeland, my lord, and David King of Scots. 2415
KING EDWARD:	Is this the proud presumptuous esquire of the north
	that would not yield his prisoner to my queen?
COPELAND:	I am, my liege, a northern esquire indeed
	but neither proud nor insolent, I trust. 2420
KING EDWARD:	What moved thee to be so obstinate
	to contradict our royal queen's desire?
COPELAND:	Not wilful disobedience, mighty lord,
	but my desert and public law at arms.
	I took the king myself in single fight 2425
	and like a soldier would be loth to lose
	the least pre-eminence that I had won
	and Copeland straight upon your highness' charge
	is come to France and with a lowly mind

doth vail the bonnet of his victory.   2430
Receive, dread lord, the custom of my fraught
the wealthy tribute of my labouring hands
which should long since have been surrendered up.
had but your gracious self been there in place.

QUEEN PHILIPPA: But, Copeland, thou didst scorn the king's command 2435
neglecting our commission in his name.

COPELAND: His name I reverence but his person more.
His name shall keep me in allegiance still
but to his person I will bend my knee.

KING EDWARD: I pray thee, Philip, let displeasure pass.   2440
This man doth please me and I like his words
for what is he that will attempt great deeds
and lose the glory that ensues the same?
All rivers have recourse unto the sea
and Copeland's faith relation to his king.   2445
Kneel therefore down, now rise King Edward's knight
and to maintain thy state I freely give
five hundred marks a year to thee and thine.

Enter Salisbury

Welcome, Lord Salisbury, what news from Brittaine? 2450

SALISBURY: This, mighty king, the country we have won
and Charles de Mountford regent of that place
presents your highness with this coronet
protesting true allegiance to your grace.

KING EDWARD: We thank thee for thy service valiant earl   2455
challenge our favour for we owe it thee.

SALISBURY: But now my lord as this is joyful news
so must my voice be tragical again
and I must sing of doleful accidents.

KING EDWARD: What, have our men the overthrow at Poitiers   2460
or is our son beset with too much odds?

SALISBURY: He was, my lord, and as my worthless self
with forty other serviceable knights
under safe conduct of the Dolphin's seal
did travel that way, finding him distressed   2465
a troop of lances met us on the way
surprised and brought us prisoners to the king
who proud of this and eager of revenge
commanded straight to cut off all our heads
and surely we had died but that the duke   2470
more full of honour than his angry sire
procured our quick deliverance from thence.

But ere we went, 'salute your king' quoth he
'bid him provide a funeral for his son
today our sword shall cut his thread of life   2475
and sooner than he thinks we'll be with him
to quittance those displeasures he hath done',
This said, we passed, not daring to reply
our hearts were dead, our looks diffused and wan
wandering at last we climbed unto a hill   2480
from whence, although our grief were much before
yet now to see the occasion with our eyes
did thrice so much increase our heaviness
for there my lord oh there we did descry
down in a valley how both armies lay.   2485
The French had cast their trenches like a ring
and every barricado's open front
was thick embossed with brazen ordinance.
Here stood a battle of ten thousand horse
there twice as many pikes in quadrant wise   2490
here crossbows and deadly-wounding darts
and in the midst like to a slender point
within the compass of the horizon
as twere a rising bubble in the sea
a hazel wand amidst a wood of pines   2495
or as a bear fast-chained unto a stake
stood famous Edward still expecting when
those dogs of France would fasten on his flesh.
Anon the death-procuring knell begins
off go the cannons that with trembling noise   2500
did shake the very mountain where they stood.
Then sound the trumpets' clangour in the air
the battles join and when we could no more
discern the difference twixt the friend and foe
so intricate the dark confusion was   2505
away we turned our watery eyes with sighs
as black as powder fuming into smoke
and thus I fear unhappy have I told
the most untimely tale of Edward's fall.

QUEEN PHILIPPA: Ah me, is this my welcome into France?   2510
Is this the comfort that I looked to have
when I should meet with my belovéd son?
Sweet Ned, I would thy mother in the sea
had been prevented of this mortal grief.

KING EDWARD: Content thee, Philip, tis not tears will serve   2515
to call him back if he be taken hence.
Comfort thyself as I do gentle queen

with hope of sharp unheard-of dire revenge.
He bids me to provide his funeral
and so I will, but all the peers in France   2520
shall mourners be and weep out bloody tears
until their empty veins be dry and sere.
The pillars of his hearse shall be their bones
the mould that covers him, their city ashes
his knell that groaning cries of dying men   2525
and in the stead of tapers on his tomb
an hundred fifty towers shall burning blaze
while we bewail our valiant son's decease.

After a flourish sounded within, enter a herald

HERALD: Rejoice my lord, ascend the imperial throne!   2530
The mighty and redoubted Prince of Wales
great servitor to bloody Mars in arms
the Frenchman's terror and his country's fame
triumphant rideth like a Roman peer
and lowly at his stirrup comes afoot   2535
King John of France together with his son
in captive bonds, whose diadem he brings
to crown thee with and to proclaim thee king.

KING EDWARD: Away with mourning, Philip, wipe thine eyes.
Sound trumpets, welcome in Plantagenet!   2540

Enter Prince Edward, King John, Philip, Audley, Artois

As things long lost when they are found again
so doth my son rejoice his father's heart
for whom even now my soul was much perplexed.   2545

QUEEN PHILIPPA: Be this a token to express my joy

Kiss him

for inward passions will not let me speak.

PRINCE EDWARD: My gracious father here receive the gift
this wreath of conquest and reward of war
got with as mickle peril of our lives   2550
as ere was thing of price before this day.
Install your highness in your proper right
and herewithal I render to your hands
these prisoners, chief occasion of our strife.

KING EDWARD: So, John of France, I see you keep your word.   2555
You promised to be sooner with ourself
than we did think for, and tis so indeed.

But had you done at first as now you do
how many civil towns had stood untouched
that now are turned to ragged heaps of stones?   2560
how many people's lives mightst thou have saved
that are untimely sunk into their graves?

KING JOHN: Edward, recount not things irrevocable.
              Tell me what ransom thou requirest to have?

KING EDWARD: Thy ransom John hereafter shall be known   2565
              but first to England thou must cross the seas
              to see what entertainment it affords.
              Howe'er it falls it cannot be so bad
              as ours hath been since we arrived in France.

KING JOHN: Accursèd man, of this I was foretold   2570
              but did misconster what the prophet told.

PRINCE EDWARD: Now, father, this petition Edward makes
              to thee whose grace hath been his strongest shield
              that as thy pleasure chose me for the man
              to be the instrument to show thy power   2575
              so thou wilt grant that many princes more
              bred and brought up within that little isle
              may still be famous for like victories.
              And for my part the bloody scars I bear
              the weary nights that I have watched in field   2580
              the dangerous conflicts I have often had
              the fearful menaces were proffered me
              the heat and cold and what else might displease
              I wish were now redoubled twentyfold
              so that hereafter ages when they read   2585
              the painful traffic of my tender youth
              might thereby be inflamed with such resolve
              as not the territories of France alone
              but likewise Spain, Turkey and what countries else
              that justly would provoke fair England's ire   2590
              might at their presence tremble and retire.

KING EDWARD: Here, English lords, we do proclaim a rest
              an intercession of our painful arms.
              Sheathe up your swords, refresh your weary limbs
              peruse your spoils and after we have breathed   2595
              a day or two within this haven town
              God willing then for England we'll be shipped
              where in a happy hour I trust we shall
              arrive three kings two princes and a queen.

                        FINIS   2600

IV

Notes

The following abbreviations are used for the canonical and other works (the former cited from the Riverside Edition 1974, as in Spevack 1973); the dates given are those of the first publication of each significantly different version.

Ado	*Much Ado about Nothing*, 1600
Ant	*Antony and Cleopatra*, 1623
AWEW	*All's Well that Ends Well*, 1623
AYLI	*As You Like It*, 1623
Cont	*The First Part of the Contention*, 1594
Cor	*Coriolanus*, 1623
Cym	*Cymbeline*, 1623
E3	*The Reign of King Edward III*, 1596
EI	*Edmund Ironside*, 1926
Err	*The Comedy of Errors*, 1623
FV	*The Famous Victories of Henry V*, 1598
Ham	*Hamlet*, 1603, 1604–5, 1623
1H4	*Henry IV, Part 1*, 1598
2H4	*Henry IV, Part 2*, 1600
H5	*Henry V*, 1600, 1623
1H6	*1 Henry VI*, 1623
2H6	*2 Henry VI*, 1623 (but 1594 for lines also found in *The First Part of the Contention*)
3H6	*3 Henry VI*, 1623 (but 1595 for lines also found in *The True Tragedy of Richard, Duke of York*)
H8	*Henry VIII*, 1623
JC	*Julius Caesar*, 1623
JN	*King John*, 1623
LC	*A Lover's Complaint*, 1609
Leir	*The True Chronicle History of King Leir*, 1605
LLL	*Love's Labour's Lost*, 1598
Lr	*King Lear*, 1608, 1623
Luc	*The Rape of Lucrece*, 1594
Mac	*Macbeth*, 1623
MM	*Measure for Measure*, 1623
MND	*A Midsummer Night's Dream*, 1600
MV	*The Merchant of Venice*, 1600
MWW	*The Merry Wives of Windsor*, 1602, 1623
Oth	*Othello*, 1622
Per	*Pericles*, 1609
PP	*The Passionate Pilgrim*, 1599

PT	*The Phoenix and the Turtle*, 1601
R2	*Richard II*, 1597
R3	*Richard III*, 1597, 1623
Rom	*Romeo and Juliet*, 1597, 1599
Shr	*The Taming of the Shrew*, 1623
Sonn	*The Sonnets*, 1609
TGV	*The Two Gentlemen of Verona*, 1623
Tim	*Timon of Athens*, 1623
Titus	*Titus Andronicus*, 1594, 1623
Tmp	*The Tempest*, 1623
TN	*Twelfth Night*, 1623
1TR	*The Troublesome Reign of King John, Part 1*
2TR	*The Troublesome Reign of King John, Part 2*
Tro	*Troilus and Cressida*, 1609
TT	*The True Tragedy of Richard, Duke of York*, 1595
Ven	*Venus and Adonis*, 1593
WT	*The Winter's Tale*, 1623
F	*First Folio*, 1623
Q1	*First Quarto*
Q2	*Second Quarto*

4   **Robert of Artois** see Froissart XXV, XXVI, XXVIII.

6   **seigniory** lordship, rank, status.

7   **we create thee . . . here** cf. *1H6*, III.iv.26 'we here create you . . .', *2H6*, I.i.64 'we here create thee . . .'. The attendant ceremonial lends an effective touch of solemnity to state occasions and battle-fields, as in lines 1503ff. and 1528 below.

7   **Earl of Richmond** this historical detail derives from Holinshed, not Froissart.

8   **now go forwards** cf. *H5*, I.ii.9 'we pray you to proceed', also a deliberate preamble to a long speech about the Edward III geneal-ogy and succession; cf. also *2H6*, II.ii.7 'Sweet York, begin' to introduce the same genealogy in support of 'my . . . title to the English crown'.

9   **Philip le Beau** (Phillip of Bew, Q1) king of France, who had died in 1314; his daughter Isabel was the wife of Edward II of England and mother of Edward III.

9–10   **succeeded . . . successfully** cf. *R3* 1597, III.i.71, 73 'succeeding . . . successfully'. *R3* editors silently prefer the Folio reading 'succes-sively', as if the Quarto adverb was a mere mistake. But this loses Shakespeare's deliberate early word-play on both senses; he is the earliest recorded authority (*OED*) for most modern meanings of 'successful' (*Titus*, I.i.66, 172) and 'successfully' (ibid., 194, *AYLI*, I.ii.153).

10   **Three sons** – Louis X, Philip V and Charles IV.

10   **successfully**; this usage (*OED* 2 = successively) antedates the given 1651 citation.

11   **sit . . . regal throne** cf. *3H6*, IV.iii.64 'seated . . . regal throne' and V.vii.1 'sit . . . royal throne'; also *R2*, IV.i.113 'regal throne'.

12   **issue of their loins** not a biblical phrase; this may be its first published use. It occurs in various forms in *R3*, I.iii.231, *Cym*, V.v.330 and *Leir*, 26. Such emphasis on physical generation is a feature of the canonical genealogies; cf. also 'womb' in line 17 here and *1TR*, 6, and see 17–18 below.

13   **But was . . . ?** the rather stilted enquiry suggests dramatic inexperience.

17   **fragrant garden** cf. *Titus*, II.ii.2 'the fields are fragrant', and II.iv.54 'the fragrant meads'.

17–18   **garden . . . womb . . . flower** typical imagery of the Edward III family tree, as in *R2*, I.ii.18, 22 'branch . . . root . . . womb'.

18   **your gracious self** cf. *R3*, III.vii.131, also about the last lineal descendant.

18   **the flower of Europe's hope** cf. *R2*, III.iii.97 'the flower of England's face'.

19   **derivéd** the first recorded use (*OED* ppl.a.) is *MND*, I.i.99.

21   **out** at an end (*OED* 23).

22   **obscured** a strong usage not clearly defined in the *OED*. The meaning here is 'deliberately misrepresented', as in *1H6*, V.iv.22 'obscure my noble birth'.

22   **privilege** right, prerogative.

23   **the next of blood** cf. *2H6*, I.i.151 and I.ii.63 'the next of blood'.

23   **proclaimed** elliptical for 'proclaimed . . . king', as in *3H6*, IV.vii.69, which far antedates *OED* v. 2d.

24   **John . . . now their king** John II; in fact Philip of Valois was king at this time.

25   **the realm of France** a favourite phrase in *1H6* (six times), *2H6* (twice) and *H5* (twice); in *1H6*, I.vi.15 France is also 'replete with', as here.

26   **parentage** lineage, ancestry, as in *2H6*, IV.ii.144 'birth and parentage', the first recorded literary use (*OED* 3).

27   **ought not admit** 'to' omitted as in line 419 below and *JC*, I.i.3 'ought not walk'.

28   **except . . . descended of the male** as in the *H5*, I.ii.35f. account of this French subterfuge, which closely follows Holinshed.

29–32   **ground . . . ground . . . dusty . . . sand** deliberate word-play, with biblical overtones of building on sand, Matthew 7:26–7.

29   **contempt** in the strong legal sense (*OED* 4) of disobedience to the lawful sovereign; this antedates the first recorded use (1621).

30   **study to** find some pretext to, as in *LLL*, I.i.66.

31–3   'Since Q1 prefixes *Artois* to line 33 it seems likely that 31–2 were originally intended to be a passionate interjection by the king', as Armstrong (1965) points out; Edward's character is thus deftly delineated.

34   **discover** disclose.

35   **call to record** a legal expression; call to witness.

36   **not . . . nor . . . private wrong** cf. *R2*, II.i.165–6 'not . . . nor . . . nor . . . nor . . . private wrongs', also in a context of Edward III

genealogy and his war with France, and the same contrast with patriotism and rectitude.

36–7   **hate . . . wrong . . . love . . . right** deliberate intertwined antithesis.

38   **my tongue . . . lavish** cf. *1H6*, II.v.47 'his lavish tongue'; and see line 662 below.

39   **lineal** the first recorded use of this epithet applied to a person (*OED* A2c) is *H5*, I.ii.82; there too it denotes the direct descent of Edward III from the rightful heirs to the throne of France.

39   (special, 29) **the . . . watchman of our peace** cf. *1H6*, III.i.66 'the special watchmen of our . . . weal'.

40   **indirectly** as distinct from lineal; cf. *H5*, II.iv.94 'your crown and kingdom indirectly held', said of a later French king for the same reason, namely that the direct descent belongs to Edward III and his line.

40   **climbs** attains sovereignty; cf. *3H6*, IV.vii.62 'fearless minds climb soonest unto crowns'.

41   **embrace their king** joyfully accept his authority, a sense not clearly defined in the *OED*; but cf. *1H6*, V.iii.171–2 'embrace . . . King Henry', also said by a French nobleman about the king of England.

43–4   **tyrant . . . shepherd** the antithesis recurs in lines 1440–41.

45–6   **fruitful showers . . . growth** for the idea that rain promotes growth, cf. *Sonn*, 75.1–2 'as food to life . . . showers to the ground' and *H8*, III.i.6–8 'plants and flowers/ever sprung, as sun and showers/there had made a lasting spring'.

48   **hot courage** cf. *Ven*, 276 'hot courage'.

48   **courage . . . engendered in my breast** cf. *1H6*, III.iii.87 'beget new courage in our breasts'.

49–50   **ignorance . . . doth mount with . . . wings** for the same antithesis and imagery cf. *2H6*, IV.vii.73–4 'ignorance is the curse of God, knowledge the wing whereon we fly to heaven' and *Sonn*, 78.6 'heavy ignorance aloft to fly'.

50   **golden** i.e. in the sunshine.

51   **approve** demonstrate.

52   **yoke . . . stubborn necks** cf. *EI*, 114–15 'yoke . . . stubborn necks', *1H6*, II.iii.64 'yoketh . . . rebellious necks'.

53   **spurn against** kick out at; cf. *EI*, 1684, *JN*, III.i.141–2.

54   **know** find out.

56   The Duke of Lorraine unhistorically created ambassador by the playwright.

56   **crossed the seas** this grandiose locution also describes the Channel crossing in *1H6*, III.i.179, V.v.90 and *3H6*, III.iii.235.

57   **entreats** earnestly requests, as in *EI*, 1486; both far antedate the first recorded use (*OED* v. II 8), *Tmp*, V.i.118.

60f.   It was Philip, not John, who summoned Edward to do homage for the dukedom; and Edward obeyed, in 1329. The playwright is adapting Froissart XXIV.

60   **renowned prince** as in *MV*, II.i.20 and *3H6*, III.iii.214.

63   **entailed** a legal technicality: transferred to a stipulated succession, as in *3H6*, I.i.194 'entail the crown to thee and to thine heirs'.

65–6 **I summon thee repair** I command you to come.

67 **as the custom is** cf. *Rom*, IV.v.80 'as the custom is'.

68 **sworn true liegeman to our king** cf. *1H4*, II.ii.337–8 'swore . . . true liegeman', *1H6*, V.iv. 128 'true liegeman to his crown'; the terminology of feudal law.

69 **title in** a legal term; right to possession of property.

70 **repossess** found only four times in the canon, all in *3H6*; again a legal term.

71 **occasion laughs** Fortune is personified, as in *Ham*, I.iii.54 'occasion smiles', also said before a voyage to France.

72–3 **No sooner . . . but straight** as in *Sonn*, 129.5; see also lines 130–38 and 1561–2 below.

73 **nay** in the Shakespearean sense exemplified by Onions (*Glossary*) of correcting and amplifying what precedes.

75 **Twere** the first recorded use (*OED*) is *Mac*, I.vii.1; also in lines 452, 1484, 1921 and 2494.

76 **return this answer** the first recorded use (*OED* return v. 19) is *1H6*, II.v.20 'answer was return'd'; the second is *TN*, I.i.24 'return this answer'; see line 2001 below.

78–9 **servilely . . . conqueror** the same antithesis between the proud palfrey 'servilely' tied to a tree but imperious when released occurs in *Ven*, 260–65, 392.

80 **unpolished** in the supposed sense 'left rude or imperfect' (*OED* ppl.a.3), this is the first recorded use; but it surely exemplifies the Shakespearean coinage *OED* 4, 'not refined, unmannerly' as in *2H6*, III.ii.271, *LLL*, IV.ii.17, *Shr*, IV.i.125.

81 **(truth) . . . vizard** mask; cf. 'unmask . . . truth' *Luc*, 940.

82 **set a gloss upon his arrogance** cf. *1H6*, IV.i.103 'set a gloss upon his bold intent'.

83 **command a fealty in me** cf. *2H6*, V.i.49–50 'command . . . fealty'.

84–5 **crown . . . usurps . . . mine . . . foot** cf. *EI*, 1807, 1816–17, 1822 'feet . . . mine . . . mine . . . usurpation . . . crown', also in a dispute between kings about realms.

89 **take away those borrowed plumes of his** cf. *1H6*, III.iii.7 'we'll pull his plumes and take away his train', *2H6*, III.i.75 'his feathers are but borrowed', *EI*, 283 'make thy peacock plumes fall down'; all four references equate feathers with social status instead of the more usual analogue of plagiarism.

90 **naked to the wilderness** with biblical overtones; Joseph was 'stript . . . out of his coat' and 'cast in the pit that is in the wilderness', Genesis 37: 22–4; a pit in a wilderness also occurs in *Titus* II.iii.

92–4 **defiance . . . face, defiance . . . throat** cf. *EI*, 719 'defiance . . . face', *JN*, I.i.21, *1H4*, III.ii.116, 'defiance . . . mouth', *2H4*, III.i.64–5 'defiance . . . eyes', *JC*, V.i.64–5 'defiance . . . teeth', *Rom*, I.i.110 'defiance . . . ears'; and see line 2001 below.

93–4 **rebound . . . throat** cf. *R2*, I.i.56–7 'returned doubled down his throat'.

95 **with reverence** an apology for impending outspokenness.

98	**lazy drone** cf. *H5*, I.ii.204 'lazy . . . drone'.
98–9	**drone . . . crept up by stealth . . . eagle's nest** cf. *H5*, I.ii.169f. 'eagle . . . nest . . . weasel . . . sneaking', *2H6*, IV.i.109 'drones . . . eagles'.
100–1	**storm/harm** the assonance serves as a cue to Warwick.
102	**lion's case** lion-skin mantle, a garment apparently introduced by the playwright for the sake of the quip that follows. Similar jesting allusions are found in *JN*, II.i.141f., III.i.128f. and *1TR*, 574; and cf. *H5*, IV.iii.93f.
104	**for his pride** perhaps with word-play on 'a pride of lions'.
107	**A voluntary mischief** etc. better confess a mistake than suffer rebuke and punishment. The latent thought is that submission attracts clemency, cf. lines 752–4.
107–8	**scorn/borne** the first of many rhymes introduced more for stylistic effect than as cues; here they indicate an epigram.
109	**Regenerate** *sic*; duly included in the *OED* (ppl.a.3) as the first recorded use (= 'degenerate'), but it seems just as likely to be one of the many Quarto misprints.
109–10	**[d]egenerate traitor, viper** cf. *EI*, 166–7 'degenerate . . . viper, traitor' and *Cor*, III.i.285 'viperous traitor'.
109–10	**viper to the place where thou wast fostered in thine infancy** A typical early Shakespeare image of treachery to one's native land is the fabled viper that bites the maternal bosom or womb. This passage is cited as the first recorded reference to the former (*OED* viper 3a); but the latter may well be the intended meaning here, as in *1H6*, III.i.72–3 'a viperous worm/that gnaws the bowels of the commonwealth'; cf. also *EI*, 167 where a traitor is called a 'mother-killing viper'.
115	**thorny-pricking** the first of many inventive compounds, duly acknowledged (*OED* thorny 5) as the first recorded use.
116	**nightingale** fabled to wound its breast against a thorn while singing.
116	**scarred** here as in the canon (e.g. *H5*, V.i.88) the concept of scars or scarring includes recently inflicted as well as healed wounds; see also lines 2272, 2278, 2579 below and *EI*, 1712, 1714.
120	**brave** threat.
121	**poisoned view** the traitor Artois, viper in line 109, is now a basilisk, the serpent whose glance was fabled to be fatally venomous. The traitor Edricus is also both viper and basilisk (*EI*, 167, 1651–2); the treachery of Suffolk is basilisk-like in the same sense (*2H6*, III.ii.52–3).
122	**false . . . true** cf. among many other such examples *R2*, IV.i.64.
123	**fleeting** afloat, launched.
124–5	**begun . . . end** for war and its uncertainty as the unifying theme of the antithesis, cf. *Cor*, III.i.326–7 'the end of it unknown to the beginning'.
126	**Montague** for his journey south in search of aid see Froissart LXXVI.
128–9	**the league between . . . us? Cracked** cf. *H8*, II.ii.24–5 'cracked the league between us'.

129	**Cracked and dissevered** a mannered combination of near-synonyms from different roots, e.g. Anglo-Saxon and Latin, as in *Titus*, V.ii.78 and *1H6*, II.i.76 'scatter(ed) and disperse(d)'.
130–33	**no sooner . . . but straight** see lines 72–3 and 1561–2.
134	**spoiled** sacked.
134f.	**Berwick** etc., the details are drawn from Froissart LV, LXIII–LXVI.
135–6	**the [Scot] hath begirt with siege/the castle** cf. *H5*, I.ii.152 'girding with . . . siege castles' and *Luc*, 221 'siege . . . engirt'.
136f	**Roxborough** this spelling suggests that Holinshed was also consulted; Froissart LXXIII has 'Rousburge'. The dramatist has transferred the Countess here from Wark Castle in Northumberland and made her Warwick's daughter instead of the King's own ward, thus already following the Painter source (*Palace of Pleasure*) used in more detail for the following love scenes.
136	**enclosed** hemmed in by an army; this antedates the first recorded use (*OED* v. 6) in *JC*, V.iii.28 'enclosed round about with horsemen'.
140	**the planting** cf. *1H6*, II.v.80 'plant the rightful heir', *EI*, 135 'plant you in your former quiet states'.
140	**Lord Mountford** Froissart LXXVIII describes the contention between Mountford and Charles de Blois over the dukedom of Brittany.
142	**ignoble** dishonourable. This may antedate the first recorded use (*OED* 2, Nashe 1592); the second is *R3*, III.v.22.
142	**David II** of Scotland.
143	**silly [ladies]** defenceless; cf. *TGV*, IV.i.69–70 'and do no outrages on silly women', and see also line 367 below.
144	**shrink . . . snaily horns** when hit, as in *Ven*, 1033–4 'snail . . . horns . . . hit . . . shrinks'.
144	**snaily** this is the first recorded use (*OED* 1).
148	**elect** choose, select.
148	**a several band** separate bands, one for each shire; cf. *LC*, 206 'a several fair', i.e. individual women, and line 174 below.
150	**dishonour's blot** cf. *2H6*, IV.i.39–40 'dishonour . . . blot', *EI*, 748 'dishonourable blot'.
151–2	**wary . . . war** no doubt deliberate word-play.
154	**the Earl of Hainault** father of Edward's wife Philippa; this allegiance and the others mentioned derive from Froissart XXXIIf.
158	**Almaine** Germany.
164	**thy study and thy books** cf. *1H6*, II.iv.56 'my study and my books'.
165	**ure** accustom.
165	**armour** a suit of armour, as in *Ado*, II.iii.16.
166	**cheerful-sounding** no doubt a new-coined compound, though not so listed in the *OED*. Cf. also *R3*, V.iii.269 'sound . . . cheerfully', i.e. drums and trumpets for battle, as here.
166	**youthful spleen** cf. *EI*, 1798, 1801 'youthful blood . . . spleen'.
166	**spleen** high spirit, courage; the first recorded use (*OED* sb. 5a) is *Rom*, III.i.157. Senses 3, 4a, 4b, 5b and 6 are also recorded as Shakespeare coinages.
167	**increasing** the first recorded use (*OED* ppl.a.) is *2H4*, I.ii.182.

169–70   **clamours . . . people . . . Ave** the notion of a crowd crying '*Ave*' recurs in *MM*, I.i.67, 70 'people . . . loud applause . . . aves', which is the first recorded use of that plural noun in the sense (*OED* B la) 'shouts of welcome', as here.

170   **'Ave, Caesar!'** presumably Julius, who is much in the playwright's mind; see also line 388 etc. and the Plutarch *Life*: 'the people welcomed Caesar with loud applause', as in the *MM* lines cited above.

173   **quarrel** violent contention (as in lines 1274, 1427 and 1865): the first recorded literary use (*OED* sb. 4) is *MV*, V.i.238 and the second *Shr*, I.ii.27.

174   **a several** see line 148 above.

175   **In great affairs** cf. *2H6*, III.i.224 'in great affairs'.

175   **tis naught to use delay** rhymed end-scene tag, as in *EI*, 276 'delay of time is vain' and *1H4*, III.ii.180 'let's away , . . [do not] delay'.

175   **naught** worse than useless, hurtful; this is the first recorded use (*OED* B adj. 3).

178   **poor eyes** no mere cliché; the eyes invite compassion because they have visibly been weeping, as in *JN*, II.i.169, *R3*, I.ii.13.

179, 181   the deliberate alliteration avouches that the style has been heightened in order to portray the Countess as a poetic heroine.

180   **thou wants** *sic*. Some editors amend to 'wantest', which obscures the singularity of this grammatical form, also often found in the First Folio; see Abbott 1869, 242.

182   **vehement suit** cf. *JN*, I.i.254 'vehement suit'.

182   **in my behalf** the playwright demotes Montague into a mere messenger and gives him an ineffectual character.

183, 187   **Thou dost not tell him** the repetition presents both the Countess and her creator as self-conscious stylists.

183   **what a grief it is** cf. *EI*, 234 'what a grief it is'.

184   **scornful** despised, as in *Luc*, 520.

185   **broad** as in Lowland Scots vernacular; cf. also line 379 below.

185   **untunéd** a technical term: off-key. The first recorded use of this figurative sense (*OED* ppl.a. la transf.) is *Err* V.i.311, and of the literal sense *R2*, I.iii.134 'boisterous untuned drums'. For 'boisterous' also applied to the Scots speech see line 255 below.

186   **insulting** the first recorded use (*OED* ppl.a.) is *1H6*, I.ii.138.

186   **barbarism** uncivilised behaviour, a usage overlooked by the *OED* (2b, 3); this should have been the first recorded use.

187   **him . . . he** King Edward, King David.

189   **vild** the already old-fashioned form of 'vile' also preferred in *EI* and *Sonn*.

189   **uncivil** rough, rude, of actions (*OED* 3a); the first recorded use is *TGV*, V.iv.60. Cf. also *2H6*, III.i.310 'uncivil kerns' (i.e. Irish irregulars).

189   **skipping** this is the first recorded use (*OED* ppl.a.2); cf. also *Mac*, I.ii.30 'skipping kerns' (i.e. Scottish irregulars).

189   **jigs** i.e. their musical accompaniment; the first recorded use (*OED* sb. 2) is *LLL*, IV.iii.166.

190   **bray forth** a contemptuous phrase for the dance music of the

despised soldiery, presumably played on trumpets and drums; cf. *Ham*, I.iv.ii 'the kettle-drum and trumpet thus bray out', with similar allusions in *R2*, I.iii.135, *JN*, III.i.303, *Tim*, II.ii.161. These are the only canonical mentions of braying; all four have the same associations as here.

190   **their conquest . . . our overthrow** for the same one-line antithesis cf. *LLL*, V.ii.574 'overthrown . . . conqueror'.

191   **barren bleak and fruitless air** the Countess continues to display her rhetorical skills. 'Bleak' here means 'cold or chilly, of wind or weather' (*OED* a. 3); its first recorded use is *JN*, V.vii.40 'bleak winds'. 'Barren' and 'fruitless' also connote a cold climate; cf. *2H6*, II.iv.3 'barren winter' and *MND*, I.i.72–3 'barren . . . cold fruitless'. For the association with Scotland cf. *Err*, III.ii.119–20 'Where Scotland? I found it by the barrenness'. See also line 334 below.

192   **Lorraine** Froissart XXXIII says only that the French king had sent messengers to Scotland; the dramatist economically employs the ambassador Lorraine. That actual duke is also mentioned in the Edward genealogy of *H5*, I.ii.70, 83.

193   **the everlasting foe** i.e. the Scots.

194   **closely** secretly, as in *LLL*, IV.iii.135.

194–5   **aside/pride** the rhyme is King David's cue.

195   **babble** meaning 'prattle, inarticulate or imperfect speech', to clinch the Countess's contempt for the broad Scots accent (lines 185, 379–80). This anticipates the first recorded use (*OED* sb. 1) by nearly a century.

195   **blunt** coarse.

196ff.   Note the structure of King David's speech; plain bread-and-butter messages sandwich a rich filling of Scottish-sounding rhetoric.

196–7   **our brother . . . the man** both are King John.

196   **brother of France** fellow-monarch, a courtesy title as in *JN*, II.i.547, III.i.161 'brother of England', and cf. *H5*, V.ii.2 'brother France'; the usage is frequent in *FV*, scene xx.

198   **entirely love** 'entirely' appears only nine times in the canon, four times in immediate association with 'love' (*Lr*, I.ii.96, *Ado*, III.i.37, *AWEW*, I.iii.100, *Oth*, III.iv.60) and thrice in close association (*LLL*, IV.iii.321, 324, *Oth*, III.iv.112–14, *Ant*, IV.xiv.24–5).

199   **Touching your embassage** as regards your ambassadorial function.

201   **make fair weather** make peace, a usage unrecorded in the *OED*, but cf. *JN*, V.i.20–21 'hush . . . this storm of war/and make fair weather', *2H6*, V.i.30–31 'make fair weather . . . till Henry be more weak'.

201ff.   **nor** used five times, to begin the line, as e.g. thrice in *2H6*, I.i.244–6.

201   **take truce** as in *Rom*, III.i.157 and *Ven*, 82.

202   **neighbour** nearest.

203   **eager** fierce.

203   **roads** (Q1 *rods*) inroads, forays; the word is found in Holinshed.

204   **bonny** introduced as a Scotticism, here and in lines 236 (q.v.) and 250. The whole speech is deliberately bombastic.

204–8	**riders . . . rust . . . eat . . . gimmaled . . . staves** cf. *H5*, IV.ii.44–50 'rusty . . . horsemen . . . staves . . . gimmaled . . . chawed'.
205	**rust in canker . . . eat** for these associations cf. *Ven*, 767 'cankering rust', 656 'canker . . . eats', *2H4*, I.ii.219 'eaten . . . with a rust', *TGV*, I.i.43 'eating canker', *1H6*, II.iv.71 'canker eats', *Sonn*, 99.13 'canker eat'.
206	**light-borne** unknown to the *OED*, but surely a coinage.
206	**snaffles** another Scotticism; the first recorded use, dated 1533, is 'a Scottish snaffle', i.e. a plain bridle-bit.
206	**nimble** frequently applied, an inventive usage not specifically noted in the *OED*.
207	**jacks** tunics.
207	**gimmaled** jointed. This is the first recorded use (*OED* ppl.a.), and the next is *H5*, IV.ii.49 (originally spelt 'gymould' and jymold', respectively); there are no other examples.
208	**grainéd . . . ash** cf. *Cor*, IV.v.108 'my grainéd ash' which must surely mean 'staff' as here, not 'lance' or 'spear'.
210	**buttoned** not just ornamented but fastened with buttons (*OED* 2, first recorded from 1826).
211	**dismiss** in the sense 'give egress to' (*OED* v. 2b), the first recorded use is *JC*, I.iii.97. Here it serves as a high-flown term for drawing a sword, as in the comic usage *TN*, III.iv.224 'dismount thy tuck'.
211	**biting** painfully sharp, as in *Lr*, V.iii.277 'biting falchion'.
211	**whinyards** short swords; another Scotticism (cf. the *OED* 1856 example 'this Scots whinyard').
216	**fairly** courteously and suitably, *OED* 2 and 4, respectively; the first recorded use of the former is *Err*, V.i.233 and of the latter *MV*, I.i.128.
217	**acceptable** gratifying.
219	**this certain spoil** these prizes which are sure to fall into our hands; the coming comic anticlimax is carefully prepared. This episode is invented, not derived from Froissart.
221	**soft ye** this locution (*OED* adv.8a(c)) antedates the first recorded use (1599); the second is *Ham*, III.i.87 'soft you now'.
224	**liable to her** rightfully in her possession, a technical legal term also found in *JN*, II.i.490 'liable to our crown'.
227	**we were pricking on the hills** riding; the audience might have recognised an ironic allusion to 'A gentle knight was pricking on the plain', the first line of Spenser's *The Faerie Queene*, Cantos I–III of which had been published in 1590 after circulating in manuscript from *c.* 1587.
228–9	**marching hitherward . . . a mighty host** cf. *2H6*, IV.ix.25, 27 'a mighty power . . . marching hitherward' and *EI*, 916, 'coming hitherward', 1748 'a mighty power', 1765 'a mighty host'.
230	**sun reflecting** shining, casting light upon; the first recorded use (*OED* v.II 8b) is *Titus*, I.ii.226–7 'reflect . . . as Titan's rays'.
231	**a field of plate** the sunlit armour glittered like polished silver and gold utensils, as in *H5*, IV.ii.1 'the sun doth gild our armour' and *R2*, I.iii.28 'plated in habiliments of war'; see also the next note.

231   **a wood of pikes** cf. *3H6*, V.iv.67 'the thorny wood', i.e. a hostile
          army, which in *EI*, 1339–41 carries 'bristle-pointed spears . . . like
          a new-shred grove of ashes tall/or else a wood of pines and cedars'.
          In lines 1939–40 below (q.v.) such images of gold plate and trees
          combine; see also line 1113.

235   **dislodge** strike camp; cf. *Cor*, V.iv.41, the only canonical example.

236   **bonny black** [horse]; cf. *2H6*, V.ii.12 'bonny beast', also a favourite
          horse.

237–8   **fight . . . fly** antithesis as in *1H6*, IV.v.37, *3H6*, I.iv.40, *EI*,
          182.

240   **She mocks at us** as Armstrong (1965) suggests, this episode may
          have have been adapted from Holinshed's account of the Countess
          of March at the siege of Dunbar castle 1337–8; 'she used many
          pleasant words in jesting and taunting at the enemy's doings'. There
          the enemy was the English army under the Earl of Salisbury, hus-
          band of the Countess here, which may well have been the associa-
          tive link.

248   **After** ride after; the first recorded use with the verb of motion
          omitted, as here (*OED* B prep.I 1a) is *2H6* V.iii.27 'shall we after
          them?'

251   **She heard that too** i.e. the proposed cross-border forays.

253   **Tis not for fear** the increasingly confident Countess not only inter-
          rupts King David but mockingly anticipates and rejects his self-
          justification.

255   **confident** over-bold, presumptuous (*OED* A I4); the first recorded
          use is *2H4*, II.i.111. See also line 2041 below.

255   **boisterous-boasting** a coinage unrecorded in the *OED*, though the
          quasi-adverbial use of the former component is first recorded (*OED*
          10) from *JN*, IV.i.75.

256–9   **back . . . turns . . . back . . . turned** apparently inadvertent repeti-
          tion, as often in e.g. *Titus* Act I.

258   **faceless fear that ever turns his back** this bold personification
          incorporates the first recorded use of 'faceless' in modern English
          (*OED* a.).

259   **against the blasting north-east wind** cf. *R2*, I.iv.6–7 'north-east
          wind . . . blew bitterly against our faces'.

259   **blasting . . . wind** this may antedate the first recorded use (*OED*
          ppl.a., in a 1591 dictionary); the next is *MM*, V.i.122 'blasting
          . . . breath'.

262   **O summer's day!** no mere cliché, but a picture of joy and bliss; cf.
          Sonn, 18.1 'Shall I compare thee to a summer's day?'

262–3   **cousin . . . aunt** Montague is her husband's nephew; see Froissart
          II.

265–6   **welcome . . . thou com'st well** serious word-play, with deliberate
          chiasmus.

268   **descend** the Countess stands on an upper stage.

268   **gratulate** greet, salute, as in *R3*, IV.i.10, *Titus*, I.i.221.

271   **Enter King Edward** the source for his arrival as the Scots decamp
          and his infatuation with the Countess is Froissart LXXVII; details

	of the latter episode are drawn from Painter, *Palace of Pleasure* XLVI.
272	**stealing** combines 'moving stealthily' and 'thieving'.
272	**foxes** symbols of treachery to the realm, as in *1–3 H6* and *EI*.
273	**uncouple** set the hounds free for pursuit, as in *Titus*, II.ii.3 and *MND*, IV.i.107.
273–5	**uncouple . . . cheerful cry . . . hounds . . . chase** cf. *MND*, IV.i. 107–25 'uncouple . . . hounds . . . cry . . . hounds . . . pursuit . . . cry . . .cheered'.
275	**hot hounds** cf. *Ven*, 692 'hot . . . hounds'.
278	**tyrant's fear** the terror inspired by King David.
279–80	**May blossom . . . winds . . . overcast** cf. *Sonn*, 18.3 'winds . . . shake . . . buds of May'.
280	**sullied** this usage (*OED* v. 1b) is first recorded from *1H6*, IV.iv.6; the other senses are first recorded from *WT*, I.ii.326 and *1H4*, II.iv.75.
280	**sullied, withered, overcast and done** the deliberately rich diction here is more poetic exuberance than characterisation.
282ff.	Her normal beauty would eclipse her present appearance, if it were possible to compare both together.
283–4	**herself . . . stain herself . . . herself** cf. *Ven*, 1129 'herself herself beheld', *Luc*, 1566 'herself herself detest', *Rom*, I.ii.95 'herself poised with herself', and similarly *Ven*, 161 'himself himself forsook', *Luc*, 157 'himself himself . . . forsake', 160 'himself himself confounds', 998 'himself himself seek . . . to kill', all with the same schizoid connotations; see also lines 566–7, 704–5 and 1622 below.
284	**herself** her true self. A comparable usage of 'himself' (*OED* 3b) is first recorded from *TGV*, II.iii.22.
285	**enchantment** alluring charm (*OED* 2 fig.), far antedating the first recorded use.
286	**excelled this excellence** surpassed this beauty; again, serious word-play.
287	**dim decline** the latent thought is that although the King's glory is steadfastly dazzling, like the noonday sun, and the Countess's beauty is in decline, like the setting sun, her gaze is nevertheless the more compelling, as if she were the monarch and he the subject.
288	**eyes . . . piercing majesty** cf. *3H6*, V.ii.16–17 'eyes . . . piercing as the midday sun', as Warwick says when comparing himself to a king.
288, 293	**subject . . . subject's** the repetition is no doubt deliberately rhetorical.
291	**dull** unfeeling, in contrast to the heart.
293, 304	**a subject's thanks . . . honour our roof** cf. *EI*, 93–4 'honour my castle . . . a subject's welcome', in the same context of soliciting a royal visit.
294	**this your royal presence** cf. *WT*, I.ii.38 'your royal presence', *R2*, IV.i.115, *R3*, II.i.79, *Per*, II.iii.49 'this royal presence'.
296–7	**peace . . . war** an antithesis which the Countess fails to (or feigns not to) understand; see also lines 386–7.

300 **pine** consume with longing or desire; the first recorded use (*OED* 6) is *Rom*, V.iii.236.

304 **roof** the first recorded use (*OED* Ic, denoting a house) is *1H6*, II.iii.56 and the second is *AYLI*, II.iii.17.

305 **triumph** apparently scanned as an iamb not a trochee, cf. *1H4*, V.iii.14.

306 **niggard not** be not ungenerous with; the first recorded uses of any such verbal form are (*OED* trans.) *JC*, IV.iii.228 and (intrans.) *Sonn*, 1.12.

308 **near** nearer: cf. Abbott 1869, 367, citing *R2*, III.ii.64, V.i.88; *Mac* II.iii.140.

310 **ugly treason** cf. *1H6*, V.iii.189 'ugly treasons', also in association with fabulous beasts (there 'Minotaurs') and the beauty of an illicitly loved woman; see also *MV*, III.ii.28 'ugly treason'.

311–12 **eye . . . shoots infected poison** cf. *R3*, I.ii.147–50 'poison . . . poison . . . poison . . . sight . . . infect . . . eyes . . . eyes . . . infected . . . basilisks' with the same serious pun, here unspoken save in the word 'shoots' (basilisk = cannon). In both contexts these incongruously unflattering comparisons occur to a wooing monarch.

312 **shoots** discharges, like a cannon; this far antedates the first recorded use (*OED* III 21e) of the metaphor.

314–17 **sun . . . light . . . take light . . . eye . . . day-stars . . . eyes . . . sun . . . steals light** in allusion to the theory that the eye creates the light it sees by, which is in turn outshone and blinded by brighter sources such as (the poet feigns) a woman's eyes; cf. *LLL*, I.i.77–89 'light . . . blind . . . eyesight . . . light . . . [six times] . . . losing of your eyes . . . a fairer eye . . . sun . . . star' etc., with the same theory and the same thought.

316 **day-stars** suns, i.e. the eyes of the Countess; this completes the chiasmus begun in line 314, 'sun . . . light . . . light . . . [sun]'.

316–17 **day-stars steals** noun-verb discord.

318–19 **Contemplative desire . . . desire . . . contemplation** a further chiasmus, with personification and word-play in continuation of the previous conceit: 'let my lust, brought on by looking, look into itself, reflect on its own nature and thus subside'.

322 **speaking eye** cf. *Lr*, IV.v.25 'speaking looks', *Sonn*, 23.10 'speaking breast', *Tro*, IV.v.55 'language in her eye'.

323 **winning** alluring; this is the first recorded use (*OED* 3).

323 **oratory** rhetoric, eloquence; the former sense (*OED* 1) is first recorded from *Luc*, 815, the latter (*OED* 2) from *Titus*, V.iii. 90.

324–5 **[king's] presence . . . April sun . . . flatter . . . suddenly be done** for these associations of king, sun, flatter and transience cf. *Sonn*, 33, 2, 9, 11 'flatter . . . sovereign . . . sun . . . but one hour'.

330 **presageth** foretells, leads one to expect; this is the second recorded use in this non-supernatural sense (*OED* 1b); the first is *1H6*, IV.i.191. See also lines 1533 and 2102 below.

331–6 **riches . . . pride . . . buried . . . cost** cf. *Sonn*, 64.2 'rich proud cost . . . buried'.

331, 336, 337, 342	**pride** these repetitions are perhaps inadvertent, as in *Titus* Act I.
333	**undecked** this is the first recorded literary use (*OED* ppl.a.1); the parent verb 'undeck' is first recorded from *R2*, IV.i.250.
333	**nature's tapestry** plants and flowers.
334	**barren, sere, unfertile, fruitless, dry** for the idea of barrenness yielding a rich crop of synonyms cf. *Ven*, 136 'barren, lean and lacking juice', *R2*, I.iii.168 'dull unfeeling barren', *Err*, IV.ii.19 'deformed, crooked, old and sere'. See also line 191 above.
334	**unfertile** this is the first recorded use (*OED* 1).
335	**turf of earth** cf. *LLL*, IV.ii.88 'turf of earth'.
336	**parti-coloured cost** variegated treasure; the natural riches of growth above ground are compared to the mineral wealth below.
338–41	**spring ... ordure ... what is within ... like a cloak ... hide** cf. *H5*, II.iv.37–40 'outside ... covering with a coat ...ordure ... spring'.
339	**all too long** perhaps a compound epithet, like *Sonn*, 86.2 'all-too-precious'.
339, 343	**my ... compare ... my terms** rhetorical devices; the orator disclaims any special skills.
340–2	**ragged walls ... pride** cf. *R2*, V.v.21–2 'ragged ... walls ... pride'.
342	**waste** damage, devastation.
342	**under-garnished** the first and only recorded use of this coinage (*OED* ppl.a.), with the same meaning as 'inly beautified' at line 330.
344	**entreat thyself** i.e. to visit the Countess's humble castle; cf. *1H6*, II.ii.40–41 'the Countess ... entreats [you], great lord, to visit her poor castle'.
345	**As wise as fair** high praise; cf. *TGV*, IV.ii.41–2 'fair and wise is she, the heaven such grace did lend her' and similar encomia in *Rom*, *Ham*, *Oth*, etc.
345	**fond fit** foolish mood.
348	**attend ... attend on** the second component is intended to be startling in its self-abasing role reversal that makes the monarch the servant of his subject. The first recorded use of 'attend [up]on' in this sense (*OED* 8b) is *TGV*, II.iv.121.
349	**host** be a guest, lodge, as in *Err*, I.ii.9, which is the first recorded use so spelt (*OED* v. 2. intr.).
350–73	the entire speech is carefully constructed from the colour contrasts of 'red' and 'pale' in facial expressions connoting desire as in *Ven*, 346f. or fear as in *Luc*, 1353f., with the same litany of 'he ... she ... his ... her' as in those contexts; cf. also the same red and white confrontation in *1H6*, II.iv.30f., again with 'thy ... my', etc., and see also line 354 below.
350	**might** could, as often in Shakespeare; see Abbott 1869, 221–2.
351	**ear ... drink ... her ... tongue's utterance** cf. *Rom*, II.ii.58–9 'ears ... drunk ... thy tongue's uttering'.
352–3	**inconstant clouds ... winds** cf. *Rom*, I.iv.100 'inconstant ... wind'.

352–4	**clouds ... rack ... cheeks** cf. *Sonn*, 33.5–6 'clouds ... rack ... face', *3H6*, II.i.27 'racking clouds'.
353	**rack upon the carriage of** are driven apart by.
354–8	**die ... cheeks ... pale ... cheeks ... blood ... pale** cf. *R2*, III.ii. 75–9 'pale ... blood ... face ... blood ... pale ... dead'.
354	**disturbéd** agitated; the first recorded use (*OED* ppl.a.) is *Ven*, 340, where it describes the blushing Adonis.
354–63	**cheeks ... look pale ... cheeks ... blood ... fear ... pale ... red ... counterfeit ... looks ... blush ... shame** cf. *1H6*, II.iv. 61–6 'white ... bloody red ... cheeks ... counterfeit ... pale they look with fear ... fear ... cheeks blush ... shame ... counterfeit'. See also line 362 below.
359.	**their scarlet ornaments** cf. *Sonn*, 142.6 'their scarlet ornaments'. See also line 437 below.
360	**oriental red** like the rising sun.
360–61	**[sun] red ... coral** cf. *Sonn*, 130.1–2 'sun ... coral ... red'.
361	**brick ... coral ... live ... dead** antithesis combines with chiasmus.
362	**counterfeit ... looks** cf. *MND*, III.ii.237 'counterfeit ... looks'.
363, 365, 367	**twas** the first recorded use (*OED*) is *Oth*, III.iii.158.
364	**sacred presence of a king** cf. *JN*, III.i.148, *R2*, III.iii.9 'sacred king', *1H6*, III.i.180 'the presence of a king', etc.
364, 366, 368, 370	**king** rhetorically repeated as in *EI*, 106–8.
366	**vail ... eyes amiss** to lower, as in *Ham*, I.ii.70 'vailéd lids', and look away, as in *Err*, II.ii.184 'eyes amiss'.
367	**silly woman** the epithet connotes innocence and defencelessness, as in *3H6*, I.i.243 'silly woman'; cf. line 143 above.
369	**with guilty fear** cf. *R3*, V.iii.142 'with guilty fear'.
370	**dote amiss** characteristic compression of thought: 'fall in love in the wrong direction; become a slave to a mere subject'.
372	**a lingering English siege of peevish love** a line notable for its humour and euphony. 'Lingering' shares the canonical connotations of protracted suffering, as in its first recorded use in that sense (*OED* 2b), *2H6*, III.ii.247 'grievous lingering death'.
375	**more fairer far** intensive comparative, as in *3H6*, II.ii.146 'fairer far' and *LLL*, IV.i.62 'more fairer than fair'; see Abbott 1869, 22.
375ff.	The heightened poetic style continues to be notable for its repetitions, both deliberate ('herself', 382–3) and perhaps inadvertent ('discourse', 377 and 389).
375–7	**more fairer ... her voice ... her wit** cf. *3H6*, III.ii.84–5 'her looks ... her words ... her wit' in the parallel wooing scene between Lady Grey and King Edward IV.
376	**her voice more silver** cf. *Rom*, II.ii.165–6 'silver-sweet ... lovers' tongues ... music', IV.v.128 'music ... silver sound'.
376	**every word than other** cf. *JC*, I.ii.230 'every time gentler than other'.
378	**unfolded** the *OED* does not clearly distinguish this special sense of 'tell a story', which antedates *Ham*, I.v.15 'a tale unfold'.

379	**broad** as in line 185.
380	**epithets** expressions, phrases, terms: the first recorded use (sb. *OED* 3) is *Ado*, V.ii.66 (overlooking *LLL*, IV.ii.8, V.i.15 or V.ii.171) and the second is *Oth*, I.i.14. According to Onions (*Glossary*) this loose usage is Shakespearean.
380	**accents** modes of utterance, such as the 'broad oaths' of line 185. The first recorded use (*OED* 3) is *AYLI*, III.ii.341, also a Shakespearean usage (Onions, *Glossary*); the sense 'speech, language, including both the tones and their meaning' (*OED* 5) is cited first from *JN*, V.vi.14 and next from *JC*, III.i.113.
382–3	**herself . . . herself** see lines 704 and 1622.
384	**Breathes** utters softly; the first recorded use (*OED* 12) is *JN*, IV.ii.36. The notion that breezes breathe sweetly (*OED* 8) is also first recorded from Shakespeare, *Tmp*, II.i.47, though this overlooks *LC*, 103. The idea may derive from the soft playing of a wind instrument. Cf. also *EI*, 1174–5 'Muses breathe . . . melodious'. Several other senses of the verb (*OED* 4b, 7, 9, 10c, 11) are first recorded from Shakespeare.
384	**from the wall . . . angel's note** cf. Painter, *Palace of Pleasure* XLVI, 338, 340 'upon one of the ramparts . . . angel's voice'.
384	**note** song, as in *MND*, III.i.137–8 'sing . . . thy note'.
384–9	**note . . . talk . . . of war . . . discourse** cf. *H5*, I.i.43–4 'discourse of war . . . music'.
385	**defiance** rejection, contempt; the first recorded use (*OED* 5) is *MM*, III.i.142, and cf. also *EI*, 719.
387	**commanded . . . to prison** cf. *TGV*, III.i.237 'to prison . . . commanded'.
388	**wakened . . . grave** cf. *Tmp*, V.i.48 'graves . . . waked'.
388–9	**Caesar . . . war** Caesar was an authority on war in *De Bello Gallico*, which is quoted in *2H6*, IV.vii.60–61 and mentioned in *R3*, III.i.84–6. The dramatist seems also to have been familiar with Plutarch's *Life*, which again describes Caesar the seasoned campaigner.
391	**beauty a slander** in a context of antitheses, cf. *Sonn*, 127.4 'beauty slandered'.
392	**cheerful looks** cf. *1H4*, II.iv.423 'cheerful look'.
393	**frosty . . . disdain** cf. *Luc*, 691 'cold disdain'.
394	**besiege** connotes the metaphorical sense first recorded (*OED* v, 1b) from *Sonn*, 2.1 and next from *AWEW*, II.i.10.
398, 411	**Give me ink and paper . . . [exit, enter] . . . Hast thou pen/ink and paper ready?/Ready, my liege** cf. *Luc*, 1289 'go get me hither paper, ink and pen', *R3*, V.iii.49 'give me some ink and paper', 75 'is ink and paper ready? It is, my lord', and *EI*, 1137f., which not only allows the same short interval with the same stage business but describes a letter in similar terms (see lines 416–30); cf. also *TN*, *Ant*, etc.
400	**chess** mentioned once in the canon, in a stage direction before *Tmp*, V.i.172.
401	**meditate** 'exercise the mental faculties in contemplation' (*OED* 4); the first recorded use is *R3*, III.vii.75.

403   **well read in poetry** cf. *Shr*, I.ii.169 'well-read in poetry', the first recorded use of that compound epithet (*OED* 1) or that phrase.

405   **passion** amorous feeling; the first recorded use (*OED* 8a) is *Titus*, II.i.36.

406   **shadow** obscure, conceal, as in *Ven*, 533 'clouds that shadow heaven's light'.

406   **veil of lawn** fine white cambric; cf. *Ven*, 589–91 'pale . . . lawn . . . spread . . . blushing rose . . . her cheek' and *Luc*, 258–9 'red . . . lawn . . . white', with the same colour contrasts as in lines 355–69 above.

407   **the queen of beauty's queen** the Countess surpasses even Venus.

407–8   **beauty . . . infirmity** contrast her excellence with his frailty; cf. *Ven*, 735 'mingle beauties with infirmities'.

413   **council house** presumably a private chamber, as in *R3*, III.v.38–9 'plotted, in the council-house, to murder me'; in this sense (not noted in the *OED*) these would be the first usages.

413   **cabinet** summer-house (*OED* 2) and private room (*OED* 3); the former is a Spenserian usage, in both *The Shepherd's Calendar* (December, 17: 'green cabinet') and *The Faerie Queene* (II.xii.83).

414   **green our thoughts** amorous, for a reason known to Shakespeare but not to the *OED*, namely that 'green indeed is the colour of lovers' (*LLL*, I.ii.86).

414   **green . . . green** with added word-play; the former means 'strong, vital', as in line 1532 below.

414   **conventicle** secret meeting-place; this is the first recorded use (*OED* II6). Cf. also *2H6*, III.i.166, the sole canonical occurrence.

415   **ease . . . disburdening** with covert antithesis; the latter verb appears only once in the canon, *R2*, II.i.229, in the same context of easing the feelings.

416–30   See p. 414 for the ideas and vocabulary shared with the otherwise quite different letter-writing scene in *EI*, 1171ff.

416   **invocate . . . Muse** cf. *Sonn*, 38.10 'Muse . . . invocate'.

418, 424   **for sighs/set down true sighs . . . poet's pen** cf. *LLL*, IV.iii.343–4 'poet . . . pen . . . ink tempered with love's sighs', and see lines 422–3 below.

419   **ready** inclined, disposed, with 'to' omitted as in line 27.

420   **encouch** this is duly recorded as a first citation (*OED* en- prefix 1) but without definition; its sense of 'surround', with connotations of 'express in terms', is matched in *2H6*, III.i.179 'clerkly couched'.

421   **laments** the first recorded use (*OED* 1) is *1H6*, I.i.103.

422–3   **[the word may] raise drops in a Tartar's eye/and make a flint-heart Scythian pitiful** cf. *LLL*, IV.iii.345–6, where the poet's 'lines would ravish savage ears and plant in tyrants mild humility'; see also lines 418 and 424 above.

423   **flint-heart Scythian** perhaps a topical allusion to Marlowe's cruel tyrant the Scythian Tamburlaine, famous on the London stage since 1587; for the epithet, cf. *Titus*, V.iii.88 'heart . . . flint', *Ven*, 95 'flint-hearted'.

423–4	**pitiful . . . moving** cf. *EI*, 1115–16 'pitiful . . . moving', also in the context of letter-writing.
427–8	**touch of . . . strings could** i.e. Orpheus. Cf. *TGV*, III.ii.77–8 'Orpheus' lute, whose . . . touch could'.
427–8	**touch . . . ears of hell** an allusion to the story of Orpheus in the underworld, as told in Book X of Ovid's *Metamorphoses*.
427–8	**sweet concordant strings . . . ears** cf. *Sonn*, 8.5–7, 9 'concord . . . ear , , . sweetly . . . string . . . sweet'.
428	**attendance** attention.
430	**beguile** charm, amuse: the first recorded use in modern English (*OED* 4) is *Luc*, 1404. Shakespeare is also credited with the sense 'charm away' (*OED* 5) first cited from *Titus*, IV.i.35 and next from *TN*, III.iii.41.
430	**[touch . . . lute] ravish . . . human minds** cf. *PP*, 8.5–6 'touch . . . lute . . . ravish human sense'.
431	**style** (a) manner of writing (b) pen.
432	**sots the wise** makes the wise seem foolish; another aspect of antithesis.
433–4	**abstract . . . brief contains** legal terms, cf. *JN*, II.i.101–3 'abstract . . . contain . . . brief', *Ham*, II.ii.524 'abstract and brief', *R3*, IV.iv.28 'brief abstract'.
434	**contains** relative omitted, cf. Abbott 1869, 164.
435–6	**'Better than beautiful' . . . fair . . . fairer** cf. *LLL*, IV.i.62 'more fairer than fair, beautiful than beauteous'.
437	**ornament** bodily part, as in line 359 above (cheeks). This meaning remains unrecorded in the *OED*; but cf. *Sonn*, 142.6 'scarlet ornaments' (lips), *Titus*, II.iv.18 'lopped . . . those sweet ornaments' (hands), *EI*, 599 'lopped . . . those two ornaments' (hands).
437–42	**praise** (four times) deliberate rhetorical repetition.
438	**pitch** highest point in a falcon's flight; the first recorded use (*OED* sb² IV 18) is *1H6*, II.iv.11 (though *Titus*, II.i.14 is earlier on the *OED*'s own dating) and the second is *2H6*, II.i.12. Cf. also *EI*, 480.
438	**pitch . . . soar** cf. *R2*, I.i.109 'pitch . . . soars'.
438	**'Soar'** as a noun is also a technical term of falconry, a synonym for 'pitch' in the same line; this is its first recorded use (*OED* sb.1).
439	**flattery . . . convicted** here too flattery is considered a criminal offence, as throughout e.g. *1–3 H6* and *EI*.
440–41	**ten times more/ten times ten thousand more** cf. *3H6*, I.iv.155 'oh ten times more', *Titus*, V.i.44 'ten thousand more', *Ven*, 775 'twenty thousand', *Luc*, 963 'a thousand thousand', etc.
441–2	**worth . . . praise . . . praise's worth** chiasmus.
442	**thy** Q1 has 'their', presumably a compositorial misreading of the MS, as also in lines 556, 761 and 1152.
443	**I will to** I intend to.
445	**heart-sick** like Romeo, *Rom*, III.iii.72.
445	**languishment** mental pain (*OED* 2); the 1591 first recorded use is anticipated on the *OED*'s own dating by *Titus*, II.i.110, while the second is *1TR*, 38.

447–50 **Write I to a woman? ... love-lays ... praise a horse?** the same feigned confusion is jocularly introduced in *H5*, III.vii.39ff. 'sonnet ... praise ... mistress ... horse'.

451 **condition or estate** rank or wealth.

453–4 **throne ... footstool** cf. *3H6*, V.vii.1, 13–14 'throne ... seat ... footstool'.

456 **the proportion of her mightiness** the extent of her power (over the King).

459 **summer-leaping** a coinage that brightly evokes the ebullience of young love in country sunshine; cf. *Cym*, IV.ii.200 'leaping time' i.e. youth.

460 **sunburnt** tanned by the outdoor life, cf. *Tmp*, IV.i.134 'sunburn'd sicklemen'.

462 **nightingale ... wrong** in Ovid's *Metamorphoses* Book VI Philomela, raped by her brother-in-law Tereus, is changed into a nightingale.

462 **adulterate** adulterous; the first recorded use (*OED* 1) is *Err*, II.ii.140 and the second *R3*, IV.iv.69.

463 **satirical** ironic, as in line 1397.

464 **sin ... sin ... esteemed** the same distinction is drawn in *Sonn*, 121.1 ''tis better to be vile than vile esteemed'.

465 **virtue sin, sin virtue** antithesis and chiasmus together.

466 **silkworm** moth-caterpillar that spins a cocoon.

466 **softer ... silkworm's twist** cf. *Cor*, I.ix.45 'soft as ... silk', V.vi.95 'a twist of silk'.

467, 468 **flattering glass** cf. *R2*, IV.i.278 'flattering glass'.

469 **comes in too soon** the King, like the Countess and their creator, is a conscious stylist.

472 **burns my heart** cf. *Titus*, II.iv.37 'burn the heart', *EI*, 1461 'burn my heart'.

473–4 **descant makes ... ground** cf. *R3*, III.vii.49 'ground ... make ... descant', in the same image of treble and bass counterpoint.

474 **voluntary** word-play on the technical sense of spontaneity or improvisation, which thus antedates the earliest *OED* citations (sb I,2b). *Pace* other editors, a ground bass may well be improvised, so there is no suggestion here of musical unawareness – quite the contrary.

475 **turned thy ink to gold** an antithesis implied in *Sonn*, 65.14 'black ink ... shine bright'; for analogous contrasts cf. *LLL*, I.ii.242–3 'snow-white ... ebon-coloured ink', *2H4*, IV.i.50 'turning ... your ink to blood', *EI*, 1171 'fetch fire from heaven and mix it with thy ink'.

477 **gild** tinge with gold, like the sun; the first recorded use (*OED* 4) is *Titus*, II.i.6.

477 **gild thy paper** as if applied in gold leaf, a professional penman's technique.

477a **Read, lord, read!** vocative enclosed in repeated words, a 'special trick' of Shakespeare's early style (Hill 1957) and often found here (e.g. line 2241) and in *EI* as well as *Titus*.

478   **[nightingale] . . . hollows of mine ears** cf. *Rom*, III.v.2–3 'nightingale . . . hollow of thine ear'.

480   **period** full stop; after some 250 impassioned words from the King, Lodowick has not yet completed his first sentence. This gentle amused irony pervades the scene.

481   **praise . . . love . . . both infinite** cf. *Rom*, II.ii.133–5 'bounty . . . love . . . both are infinite'.

482   **apprehend** experience, feel the force of.

485   **more . . . most** the rhetorical repetitions begin with chiasmus. For less elaborate examples of 'more . . . most' cf. *2H6*, I.iii.71–2, *MM*, V.i.440, *EI*, 756.

486–7   **tell the sea by drops . . . earth by sands** cf. *R2*, II.ii.146 'numb'ring sands and drinking oceans dry'.

487   **drop the . . . earth by sands** this striking image envisages the whole earth crumbled through an hour-glass, grain by grain.

487   **sands** single grains of earth or soil; the first recorded use (*OED* sb² 1e) is drawn from this play (lines 1956–7) and the second is *Cym*, V.v.120, though *R2*, II.ii.146 is earlier. See also *3H6*, I.iv.25 'the sands are numbered' for another example of this idiosyncratic usage (which seems indistinguishable from *OED* 5 pl. where the first citation comes from *3H6*, I.iv.25 and the second from *Per*, V.ii.1).

488   **print them in memory** cf. *Ham*, I.iii.58–9 'in thy memory see thou character' (i.e. print or write).

492   **chaste . . . queen of shades** Diana, patroness of chastity and goddess of the moon; cf. *1H4*, I.ii.24–6 'Diana . . . shade . . . moon'.

493   **line** Q1 has 'loue'.

493–4   **gross and palpable . . . night** cf. *MND*, V.i.367–8 'palpable-gross . . . night' (where the epithet describes literary style, as here) and *1H4*, II.iv.226 'gross . . . palpable'.

494   **pale queen of night** i.e. the moon invoked as Diana; cf. *TGV*, IV.ii.100 'pale queen of night'.

496   **when the sun lifts up his head** cf. *Sonn*, 7.2–3 'when the [sun] lifts up his . . . head'.

498   **the eye of heaven** cf. *R2*, III.ii.37, *Sonn*, 18.5 'the eye of heaven'.

499   **[moon, chaste] . . . unmasked** the first recorded literal use of the transitive verb (*OED* 1) is *Ham*, I.iii.37 'unmask . . . moon', about chastity, the first figurative use (*OED* 2) is *Luc*, 1602, and the first absolute use is *MM*, V.i.206.

499   **outshine** this surely antedates the earliest citation (*OED* 1 trans.), from Spenser, *The Faerie Queene* V (1596).

503–4   **chastity . . . treasure** cf. *Ham*, I.iii.31 'chaste treasure'.

504   **ransack** cf. *WT*, IV.iv.349–50 'ransacked . . . treasury' and lines 1021 and 1311–2 below.

504   **treasure** Q1 has 'treason'.

507   **likened to the sun** introduces a series of metaphors, as in *EI*, 606f. 'likened to a tree'; and cf. *3H6*, V.ii.20f. 'likened oft to kingly sepulchres'.

508   **splendour . . . sun** cf. *Luc*, 25 'splendour . . . sun', *Sonn*, 33.9–10 'sun . . . splendour'.

509   **perfections emulates** noun-verb discord, see Abbott 1869, 235.
509   **emulates** rivals; the first recorded use (*OED* 2b) is *MWW*, III.iii.55.
510   **breeds ... sun** cf. *Ham*, II.ii.181 'sun breed', *Luc*, 1837 'sun that breeds'.
510   **sweets** fragrant flowers; the first recorded use (*OED* sb 7) is *Ham*, V.i.243.
510ff.   **sweets ... sun ... thaw cold ... cheer fresh** cf. *H5*, IV. Chorus 39–45 'freshly ... cheerful ... sweet ... sun ... thawing cold'; and see line 515 below.
511   **thaw** the first recorded use of the figurative sense 'liquefy' (*OED* 1b) is *TGV*, II.iv.200, of 'melt' (*OED* 2b) *Ham*, I.ii.130 and of 'unfreeze' (*OED* 4a) *Shr*, IV.i.9.
512   **cheer fresh ... sun [face]** cf. *Ven*, 483–6 'sun ... fresh ... cheers ... face'.
515   **free and general as the sun** cf. *H5*, IV. Chorus 43–4 'universal ... sun ... liberal ... everyone'; see also 510ff. above.
515   **general** this is the first recorded use in the sense 'affable to all' (*OED* a.6b).
516   **basest weed** cf. *Sonn*, 94.12 'basest weed', there too in antithesis with 'the summer's flower', i.e. the rose.
517   **fragrant rose** cf. *Sonn*, 95.2 'fragrant rose'.
519   **queen of shades** Q1 has 'lover of shades', but this must be a mistake, whether compositorial or authorial; Lodowick is repeating his line (492) as instructed.
522   **Judith** in the book of the Apocrypha thus named is a Jewish heroine who decapitated the Babylonian general Holofernes; also the name of Shakespeare's daughter, b. 1585.
525   **blot** delete by obliteration; the key-word of an image-cluster that permeates this passage.
526   **all that yet is done** Lodowick seems to have achieved the first two lines of a sonnet, after some 100 lines of detailed instruction.
528   **passing passing ill** worse than rather bad.
529   **boist'rous war** cf. *2H4*, IV.i.49 'boisterous ... war'.
530   **prisoner ... dark** cf. *Luc*, 379 'darksome prison'.
530   **immuréd ... constraint** this is the first recorded use of the verb, spelt 'emured' in Q1. The *OED* adds that this variant form is found in the 1623 Folio as both verb and noun, with first citations of the former from *LLL*, III.i.124 'emured, restrained' and of the latter from *Tro*, Prol. 8. Such instances *prima facie* exemplify the same rare word in the same idiosyncratic spelling.
532–4   **starves ... feast ... frozen ... fire ... grief ... happy opposite** the antitheses are announced as such by the speaker.
535   **sound well ... lovers' tongues** cf. *Rom*, II.ii.165 'silver-sweet sound lovers' tongues'.
538   **But soft** 'a common Shakespearean turn of speech' (Wilson 1948), also in lines 1080 and 1629.
539   **draw** make a diagram of; the King feigns to be discussing military strategy, a device which also serves to get Lodowick off stage.

540	**flankers** detachments of skirmishers placed on either side of the main army.
541	**discipline** training or experience in warfare, as in *JN*, II.i.39, etc.
543	**my thrice-gracious lords** as in *1H4*, III.ii.922; the Countess is fond of compounds in 'thrice-', as also in lines 555 and 572 below.
544	**intrusion** uninvited entrance; the first recorded use (*OED* 3) is *Rom*, I.v.91.
550	**thy gloomy consort, sullen melancholy** cf. *Per*, I.ii.2 'the sad companion, dull-eyed melancholy'.
550	**consort** spouse, queen; this far antedates the *OED* (sb.¹ 3) citation.
551	**straw** strew.
552	**ground** 'having reason to be ashamed' underlies the word-play.
555	**think . . . wrong** harbour ill-will.
556	**thy** Q1 has 'their'; see line 442 above.
566–7	**take thyself . . . tell thyself** for the idea of the self as divisible into quasi-independent components see e.g. *Err*, II.ii.120f., or *Ven*, 159 'woo thyself, be of thyself rejected'. See also lines 283–4, 704–5 and 1622.
568–71	**within thy power . . . happy . . . joy within thy power . . . happy** the chiasmus combines with repetition.
573	**power . . . power** (a) quantity (b) ability.
580	**store by giving doth augment** cf. *Sonn*, 64.8 'increasing store with loss', in the same paradoxical antithesis.
582, 585	**inherit . . . dispossess** legal metaphors.
583–4	**beauty . . . painted** cf. *Sonn*, 21.2 'painted beauty'.
583–4	**beauty . . . enjoy . . . wipe off** cf. *Tro*, II.ii.147–9 'beauty . . . pleasure . . . rape . . . wiped off'.
583	**enjoy** as in line 646.
588	**haunts** if this means 'like a ghost' the first recorded use (*OED* 5b) is *MND*, III.i.104 and the second *R2*, III.ii.158.
590	**intellectual soul** cf. *Err*, II.i.22 'intellectual . . . souls'.
590–2	**soul . . . body . . . body . . . soul** chiasmus combined with antithesis and repetition.
592–6	**palace to my soul . . . bower . . . court . . . abbey . . . house** cf. *3H6*, II.i.74 'my soul's palace', *Rom*, III.ii.81–2 'bower the spirit in . . . flesh', *JN*, V.vii.3 'soul's . . . dwelling-house', *Luc*, 719 'his soul's temple', *Sonn*, 146.1, 7 'soul . . . mansion'; and see also lines 2324–9 below.
595	**pure . . . unspotted** cf. *1H6*, V.iii.182 'pure unspotted'.
597	**I . . . my poor soul . . . my poor soul me** chiasmus with antithesis; for 'my poor soul' meaning the immortal part in contrast to the body cf. *Luc*, 1157.
604	Fails to scan; perhaps 'good my lord' was intended.
604–5	**sacred . . . profane . . . name** cf. *1H6*, IV.i.40–41 'sacred name . . . profaning'.
607, 613	**Caesar . . . tribute . . . image** cf. Matthew 22:17–20 'tribute . . . Caesar . . . image'.
609	**Sara** Parfitt (1985, 16) invokes Hebrews 11:11 and 1 Peter 3:6; but the intended reference here (as in *Shr*, V.i.136) is surely to the

slavish self-abnegation of Abraham's wife Sarai, Genesis 16:1–3,
who was later renamed Sarah and blessed by Jehovah (ibid. 17:15–
16).

610   **your stamp** i.e. the King's head on his coinage; death was the
penalty for clipping or forging.

610–13   **stamp . . . King of heaven . . . stamp his image . . . forbidden
metal** cf. *MM*, II.iv.45–50 'God's image . . . stamps . . . forbid . . .
metal . . . heaven' in the same context of illicit offspring.

613   **his image** cf. Genesis 1:26 'and God said, Let us make man in our
image'.

615   **marriage** perhaps an uninflected genitive, like 'highness' in line
623.

617   **younger house** second in precedence, subordinate; the cadet
branch.

619   **sole-reigning** this is the first and only recorded use (*OED* a. 10
comb. a) of an ingenious compound conflating Adam's 'dominion'
(Genesis 1.28) with the fact that he was 'alone' (ibid. 2.18).

619   **universe** i.e. the earth, far antedating *OED* 3.

620   **by God was honoured for a married man** cf. Genesis 2:22, 24 'The
Lord God . . . brought her unto the man . . . his wife'.

622   **[Adam] . . . penalty** crime, penal offence; this is the first and only
recorded use (*OED* 4); but cf. *AYLI*, II.i.5 'the penalty of Adam'
exemplifying the same usage in the same context.

624   **infringe the holy act** cf. *R3*, III.i.41 'infringe the holy privilege'.

626–8   **my husband's . . . doth loyal service . . . Salisbury** a deliberate
preparation for his later introduction on the stage.

632–6   **beauty . . . words . . . words . . . beauty . . . wind . . . sail . . .
sail . . . wind . . . words . . . beauties . . . beauty words** the repeti-
tive chiasmus is becoming obsessive.

634–41   see lines 1125–9 below.

635   **sail . . . unseen wind** cf. *H5*, III. Chorus 10–11 'sails . . .
invisible . . . wind', *LLL*, IV.iii.103–4 'wind . . . unseen'.

637   **honey-gathering** a coinage not recorded in the *OED*.

639–40   **poison-sucking envious spider . . . venom** the coined epithet is
again urecorded. Cf. also *R2*, III.ii.14 'spider . . . suck up . . .
venom', and see lines 1125–9 below.

640   **juice** Q1 has 'vice'.

640   **deadly venom** cf. *R3*, IV.i.61 'deadly venom'.

641–2   **Religion . . . weed** the scruples of the Countess are explained away
as religious prejudice; 'weed' may connote a nun's garment.

644–5   **when I would embrace her . . . catch nothing** cf. Ovid's *Metamorphoses* Book X, 58–9; Orpheus turned round and held out his arms
to embrace Eurydice, but touched nothing but air.

646–7   **I must enjoy her . . . beat . . . reason and reproof** cf. *Luc*, 489
'reproof and reason beat', 512 'I must enjoy thee', also in association with 'honey' (493), 'beauty' (496) and the Orpheus legend
(553).

646   **enjoy** physically; the first recorded use (*OED* 4b) is *MWW*,
II.ii.254, though it should have been *Luc*, 512 as cited above.

650   **bear my colours ... love** carry my banner, be my advocate; cf. *MWW*, III.iv.81 'I must advance the colours of my love', and see line 923 below.

653   **An** for 'an' = if, as often in the First Folio, see Abbott 1869, 73.

653   **old** great, plentiful; frequent in the canon and 'remains in midland dialect', according to Onions (*Glossary*).

657   **flattery** gratifying deception. The first recorded use in this Shakespearean sense (*OED* 2) is *Sonn*, 42.14 and the second *Oth*, IV.i.129. There are no others, but cf. *El*, 1464 and the plural usage first cited from *R2*, III.ii.216. Onions (*Glossary*) confirms the Shakespearean idiosyncrasy.

658   **tip ... with golden** cf. *Ado*, V.iv.44 'tip ... with gold', *Rom*, II.ii.108 'tips with silver'.

658   **peise [weigh down] ... lead** cf. *R3*, V.iii.105 'leaden ... peise'.

660   **performance ... promise** cf. *2H6*, I.iv.2 'performance ... promises', *H8*, IV.ii.41–2 'promises ... performance'.

662   **lavish tongue** cf. *1H6*, II.v.47 'lavish tongue', and see line 38 above.

663   **charactered** imprinted, written; the first recorded use of this special term, with its accent on the second syllable, is *TGV*, II.vii.4 in the literal sense (*OED* v. 1a) and *Ham*, I.iii.59 in the figurative (1b); 'not pre-Shakespeare' according to Onions (*Glossary*). See also line 2160 and cf. *Sonn*, 108.1.

666   **Age** the italics in Q1, presumably authorial, indicate a personification.

666   **cynic** this is the first recorded use in the sense of 'fault-finder' (*OED* B sb.2).

669   **my proper harm** my own harm.

670   **These** i.e. the contrasts between promise and performance mentioned by the King at line 658ff.

671   **duty** both moral and financial.

672   **stick** hesitate, as in *Sonn*, 10.6, *PP*, 18, 51.

674   **rash-disgorgéd** perhaps a coined compound; 'rash' may connote the Shakespearean sense (Onions, *Glossary*) of quick and strong function (*OED* A 2b) as in the first and only recorded uses of that component (*2H4*, IV.iv.48, *WT*, I.ii.319); cf also the first two recorded compounds (*OED* B 2) 'rash-levied' (*R3*, IV.iii.50) and 'rash-imbraced' (*MV*, III.ii.109).

674–5 **disgorged vomit ... thy word ... eat up again** cf. *2H4*, I.iii.97, 99 'disgorge ... eat thy ... vomit up'.

678   **grief ... medicinable** cf. *Cym*, III.ii.33 'griefs ... medicinable', IV.ii.242–3 'griefs ... medicine'.

679   **bruising** crushing, breaking.

680–1 **loss ... vantage** the thought underlying the antithesis is 'if injuring my honour is to your advantage then it is also to my own', cf. *Sonn*, 88, 11–12 'the injuries that to myself I do/doing thee vantage double-vantage me'.

681   **account** Q1 has 'accomplish', perhaps a misinterpretation of the authorial spelling 'accompt' as in *El*, 178, 658, 1492.

682   **unswear** this reading seems required, although Q1 has 'answer'.

The first recorded use of 'unswear' (*OED*) is *JN*, III.i.245 'unswear faith sworn'; this is the second.

686   **breaks the sacred warrant of an oath** cf. *R2*, IV.i.235 'cracking the strong warrant of an oath'.

689   **stands excommunicate** cf. *JN*, III.i.173 'stand . . . excommunicate', the only canonical use of the adjective.

694   **cancel . . . bonds** a legal metaphor; cf. *R3*, IV.iv.77, *Mac*, III.ii.49, *Cym*, V.iv.28.

703   **detestable** accented on first and third syllables, as in most canonical examples.

704   **tempt myself . . . wrong myself** separation of selves, as in lines 566–7 above; for the repetitions, cf. *R3*, IV.iv.420–2 'myself . . . myself . . . yourself . . . wrong yourself'. See also lines 283–4 and 1622.

705–6   Warwick's predicament here is paralleled in *2H6*, V.i.182–3 'It is great sin to swear unto a sin/but greater sin to keep a sinful oath'.

708   **cut this right hand off** cf. *3H6*, II.vi.81–2 'right hand . . . chop it off', V.i.50 'I had rather chop this hand off', *Titus*, III.i.72 'I'll chop off my hands too', *EI*, 686 'I'll sooner cut it off myself' and Matthew 18:8 'If thy hand . . . offend thee, cut [it] off'.

708–9   **better . . . profane . . . than confound** better violate than destroy. The underlying thought is that if an oath is exacted by an unfair authority, i.e. the King, it is better to break the oath than the authority.

709   **idol** means, on that interpretation, 'a person that is the object of excessive or supreme devotion, or that usurps the place of God in human affection', in which sense (*OED* 2b) the first recorded use is *TGV*, II.iv.144.

714   **remember** bear in mind, not the opposite of 'forget'; the insistence on antithesis sometimes takes precedence over the sense.

717–18   **true charity . . . love . . . true love . . . charitable** the same (line 714 above) applies to chiasmus.

719   **bear out** survive.

720   **buy out** discharge a liability by means of a payment. The first recorded use (*OED* II 8c) is *JN*, III.i.164 and the second *1H4*, IV.ii.22.

725   **embassage** ambassadorial duty.

728   **keep in promise of** keep your promise to.

730   **graceless** a strong expression: wicked.

730   **arrant** errand.

735   **endamagement** this may well antedate the first recorded use (Nashe 1593).

738   **attorney from . . . hell** an advocate (*OED* sb.¹ 4) as in *R3*, IV.iv.413 'be the attorney of my love to her', 418 'shall I be tempted of the devil thus?'

738–9   **[hell] housed my spirit in his form** i.e. I, Satan, have housed my spirit in his (Warwick's) form; cf. *Err*, IV.iv.54 'Satan, housed within this man'.

742–4   **life . . . honour . . . honour . . . life** yet more chiasmus.

744	**pawn thine honour** cf. *3H6*, III.iii.116, 'pawn . . . mine honour', *Luc*, 156 'pawning his honour'.
747	**sun . . . doth nourish** cf. *1H4*, IV.i.111–12 'sun . . . doth nourish', also in a country-proverb formulation.
748	**distain stain, defile, again** with the 'blot' image-cluster, as at line 525 above.
749	**the poets write** notably Shakespeare, in a play (*2H6*) which remained unpublished until the 1623 Folio (see next note); cf. also *TGV*, I.i.42, 45 'writers say' and the canonical references to the story of Lucrece (see lines 1020 and 1022 below).
749–50	**Achilles' spear . . . heal the wound it made** cf. *2H6*, V.i.100 'Achilles' spear . . . is able . . . to kill and cure'; there too the metaphor is appplied to the behaviour of a king. See also Ovid's *Metamorphoses* XIII. 171–2.
750	**the moral is** invented by the playwright; no such meaning was intended by Ovid.
750	**moral** import, meaning, signification; the first recorded use (*OED* 2c) is *Shr*, IV.iv.79.
752–3	**lion . . . being mild** the same implausible picture also appears in *LLL*, IV.i.88f. 'lion . . . from forage will incline to play'. Cf. also line 107 above.
752	**become** equivalent to 'grace' later in the line; the clement lion allegedly beautifies his bloody jaws. The only allied sense is *OED* 9c, to grace or adorn one's surroundings; its first recorded use is *Shr*, II.i.258 and its second *Tmp*, III.ii.104. See also line 2277 below.
753	**foragement** the taking of prey; this is the first and only recorded use of the word (*OED*) in any sense. Its inventor was thus familiar with, if not also the inventor of, the idea of foraging in the sense of glutting on prey; the first recorded use of that idiosyncratic application (*OED* v. 4) is *Ven*, 554 and the second is *H5*, I.ii.109–10 'beheld his lion's whelp forage in blood', which describes how King Edward III watched the Black Prince in battle. Further, the first recorded use of the noun 'forage' in the sense of 'a raging or ravening' (*OED* sb. 2b) is *LLL*, IV.i.88f.
754	**vassal fear** cf. *1H4*, III.ii.124 'vassal fear'. The first recorded use of 'vassal' as an epithet (*OED* a. 4) is *Luc*, 608; this (*E3*) is the second; the third is *Sonn*, 141.12.
758–65	These lines have been singled out by John Kerrigan (1986a) as self-evidently Shakespearean.
758–9	**drop . . . sea . . . hugey vastures** cf. the constant canonical insistence on the engulfing vastness of the seas, as in *Titus*, IV.ii.101 'all the water in the ocean', *Mac*, II.ii.57, 59 'all great Neptune's ocean . . . multitudinous seas'; and see lines 759 and 1973 below.
758–9	**poison . . . sea . . . can digest** cf. *Err*, II.ii.143 'digest the poison', *TN*, II.iv.100–1 'the sea . . . can digest'.
758, 763	**poison . . . sugared** cf. *R3*, III.i.13–14 'sugared . . . poison'.
759	**hugey vastures** cf. *Per*, III.i.i 'this great vast' (i.e. the sea), III.ii.58 'huge . . . billow', *AYLI*, II.vii.72 'as hugely as the sea', *Tim*, IV.iii.437 'vast sea', V.iv.78 'vast Neptune'. This is the first and

only recorded use (*OED*) of 'vasture'; but 'vasty' is twice first-cited from Shakespeare, *1H4*, III.i.52 and *H5*, II.iv.105.

760   **operation** effectiveness, as in *Ant*, IV.xv.26, also about poison.

761   **thy** Q1 has 'their'; see line 442.

765   **left undone** with overtones of the Book of Common Prayer, general confession.

767–8   **apparelled . . . suit** typical word-play, preceded by 'attorney' (738) and followed by 'solicitor' (774); cf. *AYLI*, IV.i.87–8 'apparel . . . suit', 94 'attorney'.

768   **answer . . . suit** also legal terminology.

771   **envired** surrounded, spelt 'inuierd' in Q1; this is the first recorded use (*OED* invier).

772, 781   **stain, blot** key-words of the 'blot' image-cluster, see line 525 above.

773   **the author of my blood** father, as in *R2*, I.iii.69 'the . . . author of my blood', a usage not noted in the *OED*.

774   **scandalous** a strong expression, meaning outrageous or grossly disgraceful; its first recorded use (*OED* 2) is *WT*, II.iii.121. See also lines 1492 and 1839 below.

774   **solicitor** playing on the bad sense of 'one who entices', which may thus antedate *OED* 5.

775   **No marvel though . . . then** cf. *Sonn*, 148.11 'no marvel then, though'.

775–6   **branches . . . root** cf. *R3*, II.ii.41 'why grow the branches now the root is gone?' for the same antithetical image and argument.

777–9   **[blood . . . vile . . . branches . . . root] leprous . . . die . . . envenometh . . . dug . . . sin** cf. *Ham*, I.v.59–76 'orchard . . . hebona [= poison] . . . leperous . . . blood . . . milk . . . sin' and *Rom*, I.iii.26 'wormwood . . . dug'.

779   **passport to offend** antedates the first recorded use (*OED* sb.5 fig d).

781   **law** with legal metaphor of 'cancel', as in line 694.

783–6   **offence . . . actor . . . [King's] graceless lust**, cf. *Luc*, 604–13 'vices . . . king . . . outrageous . . . actor . . . king's misdeeds . . . this deed [= rape] . . . monarchs . . . offenders . . . offences'.

786   **actor** performer of the given action; the first recorded use (*OED* 3) is *MM*, II.ii.37.

788   **unsay** not only retract but say the very opposite.

789   **honourable grave** cf. *Cor*, II.i.88 'so honourable a grave', *JC*, I.ii.138 'dishonourable graves'.

791–2   **[honourable] the greater man, the greater is the thing . . . good or bad** cf *Luc*, 1004–5 'the mightier man, the mightier is the thing/ that makes him honoured or begets him hate', in the same antithetical and proverbial form.

793   **unreputed** insignificant; this is the first and only recorded use (*OED* ppl.a.).

795–6   **summer's day . . . taint . . . carrion . . . kiss** cf. *Ham*, II.ii.181–2 'sun . . . maggots . . . kissing carrion', also in a context of concern for a dear daughter wooed by a royal personage, and *MM*, II.ii. 165–7 'sun . . . carrion . . . corrupt'.

797	**axe** implement and image recur at line 1655 below.
798	**aggravate** make more heinous; this is the first recorded use (*OED* 6b); cf. *R2*, I.i.43 'aggravate the note' (i.e. an accusation).
800	**by authority** on instruction.
800–3	**authority . . . Deck an ape . . . robe . . . scorn** cf. *MM*, II.ii.120–3 'ape . . . dressed . . . authority . . . laugh'.
802	**tissue** rich woven fabric.
804	**spacious** the first recorded use (*OED* 2b) is *Titus*, II.i.114.
805	**glory** Q1 has 'gloomie'.
806	**poison . . . golden cup** cf. Seneca *Thyestes*; 453 'venenum in auro bibitur' (poison is drunk from gold cups), with the same implied antithesis that humbler homes are safer.
807	**flash** the first recorded use of the noun in this sense (*OED* 1 sb.² 1a) is 'a flashe of lightening' from Painter's *Palace of Pleasure*, the source of this scene.
808	**lilies that fester smell far worse than weeds** cf. the same antithesis in the same words in *Sonn*, 94.14.
809	**inclines** accedes, submits.
810	**shame is treble . . . opposite** cf. *MM*, III.ii.269–70 'treble shame', also in a context of deliberate antithesis, including 'weed . . . grow'; and see line 1098 below.
813	**when thou convertest from** the verb should perhaps read 'converts' as in line 180 'thou wants'; that would help the scansion. This is the verb's first recorded use in modern English (*OED* II 8b intrans., turn aside from a course of conduct); the second (and only other) example is the analogous *Sonn*, 11.4 'when thou from . . . convertest'.
814	**bed-blotting** the *OED* fails to record this invention, of which this is no doubt the unique instance; but cf. *Luc*, 684–5 'lust . . . stain so pure a bed . . . spots'.
819	**well encountered here** cf. *2H4*, IV.ii.1 'well encountered here', also to begin a scene.
822	**sent me forth to muster men** a link with lines 145–6: 'Audley . . . go levy footmen'.
825, 828	**emperor . . . lieutenant-general** as in Froissart XXXII.
830	**via** onward: this is the first recorded use of this interjection (*OED* int. 1), though it was *prima facie* antedated by *TT* (1595), 710 and also appears in the corresponding passage of *3H6* (II.i.182), in the same spirit of martial enterprise, 'via, to London will we march'. Shakespeare is credited with the first use of two further senses (*OED* 2a, b): 'begone' (*MV*, II.ii.11) and 'in dismissal of an argument or subject' (*MWW*, II.ii.153).
830	**spacious** see line 804 above.
837	**underneath the brows** gloomy, preoccupied.
842–3	**wish . . . witch** surely deliberate word-play; perhaps the pronunciations were closer then.
849	**all but one is none** the word-play means that all love and all duty are as nothing without the Countess.

849   **what news with you?** a typical stage device, as in *MWW*, III.iii.23, *Shr*, IV.iii.62, *JN*, IV.ii.68, *2H6*, V.i.125, *Titus*, IV.iv.61, in each instance addressed to a character who has just entered, as also in *EI*, 735.

851   **charge** instruction, with a pun explicable by reference to *1H4*, II.iv.546 'a charge of foot', i.e. a levy of infantry.

852   **foot . . . trudge . . . horse** the King's fifth and sixth quibbles within ten lines.

854, 856   **Countess . . . I mean the emperor** the King has been thinking of the Countess ever since his entrance. His subconscious error and its ready acknowledgement recall Portia's Freudian slip in *MV*, III.ii.16–17 'one half of me is yours, the other half yours/mine own, I would say'.

859   **heart's abundance . . . tongue** cf. *R2*, I.iii.256–7 'tongue . . . abundant . . . heart'; both passages recall Matthew 12:34 'out of the abundance of the heart the mouth speaketh' and may well also imply or invite awareness of the continuation, 12:35, 'A good man out of the good treasure of the heart bringeth forth good things: and an evil man out of the evil treasure bringeth forth evil things'.

861   **imperator** absolute ruler; this is the second recorded example (*OED* b). The first is *LLL*, III.i.185, where it denotes Cupid (who will soon appear here, line 870 – 'love conquers all' is the shared thought).

865   **the more than Cleopatra's match** she who is more seductive than Cleopatra was to Julius Caesar; no doubt the playwright had read Plutarch's *Life* in North's translation.

868   **resolve** answer.

869–80   **drum . . . thunders . . . bosom . . . thundering . . . bosom . . . drum . . . drummer . . . drum** some of these repetitions may be inadvertent, as perhaps in *Titus* Act I, but there is also a deliberate striving after sonorous effect.

870   **start** startle.

871–2   **sheepskin . . . parchment** cf. *Ham*, V.i.114 'parchment . . . sheepskins'.

873   **conduct** convey.

873   **sweet lines** cf. *TGV*, I.iii.45 'sweet lines', also in a love-letter.

875   **writing-paper** this is the first recorded literary use (*OED* 1).

877   **counsel-bearer** a coined compound not recorded in the *OED*.

879   **touch** play.

880   **braces** a technical term for the thongs that control the tension of the drum's skin and hence its pitch. This is the first recorded use (*OED* sb.^{2} 10a,b).

881   **uncivil** impolite; the first recorded use (*OED* 3) is *TGV*, V.iv.60 and this is the second.

882   **trouble heaven with** cf. *Sonn*, 29.3 'trouble . . . heaven with'.

883   **quarrel** the first recorded literary use in this sense (*OED* sb.^{3} 4) is *MV*, V.i.238 and the second *Shr*, I.ii.27.

883   **arms** the King's obsessive word-play continues.

885   **deep** low in pitch, resonant; the first recorded use (*OED* a. 14) is *1H6*, II.iv.12 and the second *Tmp*, III.iii.98.

885   **penetrable** penetrating (*OED* 1), but perhaps also with the connotation 'susceptible' (*OED* 2b fig.), for which the first, second and third recorded uses are *Luc*, 539, *R3* III.vii.225, and *Ham*, III.iv.36 respectively; these are the only three canonical examples.

885–8 **groans . . . sighs . . . wind . . . whirl away** cf. *Luc*, 568, 588 'sighs like whirlwinds . . . sighs . . . groans'.

886   **my eyes shall be my arrows** cf. *1H6*, IV.vii.79 'o were mine eyeballs into bullets turned', *R3*, I.ii.150 'would [my eyes] were basilisks [cannon]'.

888   **sweetest** *sic*; but perhaps 'sweet's' i.e. the Countess's.

889   **wins the sun** no doubt the playwright recalled Froissart's account of such manoeuvring at the naval battle of Sluys.

891   **the wanton warrior** Cupid the archer; cf. *Tro*, III.iii.222 'the wanton Cupid'.

891–3 **blind . . . eyes . . . glory . . . dazzles** cf. *H5*, I.ii.278–80 'glory . . . dazzle . . . eyes . . . blind'.

896   **struck** Q1 has 'stroke'.

899–900 **his mother's face/modelled in his** cf. *Sonn*, 3.9 'thou art thy mother's glass'.

900   **modelled** this usage far antedates the *OED* examples.

904   **cloak itself on** plead the excuse of.

907   **choicest** most carefully selected; the first recorded use of 'choice' in this sense (*OED* a. 2a) is *LLL*, V.i.15 and the second *H8*, I.ii.162; cf. also *EI*, 917 'a choice company of arméd men' in the same context as here, namely élite troops.

907   **buds** young men; the first recorded use (*OED* sb.¹ 3b) is *JN*, III.iv.82.

910   **delineate** depicted, portrayed; this is the first recorded use (*OED* ppl.a.).

912   **looking wistly on me** intently; cf. *R2*, V.iv.7 'he wistly looked on me'.

913   **faults against themselves give evidence** legal metaphor: cf. *Ham*, III.iii.63–4 'faults . . . evidence'.

914   **Lust is a fire** cf. *MWW*, V.v.95 'lùst is . . . a . . . fire', II.i.68 'fire of lust'.

915   **light** (a) unchaste (b) burning.

916   **loose silks** with spaces between the threads.

917   **large limit** extensive territory.

919   **mansion** more body-imagery, as at lines 592 and 594.

920   **armour . . . eternal** cf. *Ham*, II.ii.490 'armour . . . eterne'.

923–4 **[love] advance . . . colours** cf. *MWW*, III.iv.81 'advance . . . colours . . . love' and cf. line 650 above.

924   **colours sweet the air** the flags are imagined as flowers as in lines 1115–16; cf. also line 1942 below and *EI*, 1342–3 'their flags and banners, yellow, blue and red/resembles. . . . weeds'. The same word-play as here occurs in e.g. *3H6*, II.v.98–7 'the red rose and the white . . . [our] colours'; the same association of fragrance and

colours in *Ven*, 1079 'flowers . . . sweet . . . colours' and *Sonn*, 99. 14–15 'flowers . . . sweet . . . colour'.

926   **cheer** expression, countenance.

930   **Dolphin** this spelling of Dauphin, found in the Fabian *Chronicles* of 1516 and *Mirror for Magistrates* of 1559, is also the preferred form (though often changed by editors) in e.g. *1H6* as well as *FV passim*.

932   **black** (a) dark-haired (b) foul; cf. *Sonn*, 131, 132.

935   **chase away . . . winter clouds** like the sun; weather imagery as in lines 511–12.

937   **hack and hew** i.e. by making war on France; cf. *1H6*, IV.vii.47 'hew . . . hack' on a French battlefield.

938   **embrace** sexually; the first recorded use (*OED* 1b) is *Ado*, IV.i.49.

938   **unlawful** adulterous; cf. the Shakespearean sense of 'illegitimate', first recorded (*OED* unlawful 2c) from *Ant*, III.vi.7–8 'all the unlawful issue that their lust/hath raised between them'.

939   **register** the Countess is pictured as an anthology or compendium of rare beauties; cf. *LC*, 52 'register of lies'.

939   **rarieties** invented by analogy with 'varieties'; this is the first recorded use (*OED*).

940   **leathern** another coinage meaning 'skin-clad' in reference to Genesis 3:21; again this is the first (and this time the only) recorded use (*OED* 1c).

945   **playfellow** with erotic overtones, as in *Per*, I. Chorus 34 'in marriage pleasures playfellow'.

947   **my objection in** my demand for.

949   **yield** (a) submit (b) render.

954   **sith** seeing that.

955   **unwillingness** the first recorded use (*OED* 1b) is *R2*, I.iii.149.

956   **no respect respected** no consideration, however highly esteemed.

957   **your mightiness** if a title of dignity, the first recorded use (*OED* 1b) is *Titus*, II.iii.126 'your mightiness'; cf. also the same phrase in *EI*, 769.

959   **discontent . . . content** cf. *Shr*, I.i.80 'content you in my discontent'.

960   The line means 'I'll force myself to say that I agree'.

961   **lets** hindrances.

969   **title in** entitlement to.

971   **opposition** antagonism; the first recorded use (*OED* 5a) is *LLL*, V.ii.733; Onions (*Glossary*) confirms 'not pre-Shakespeare'. Shakespeare is also credited with the first recorded use of *OED* 1a 'the action of setting opposite' (*Ham*, V.ii.171), 4d 'that which is opposite' (*1H4*, II.iii.14) and 5b 'combat' (*1H4*, I.iii.99).

978–82   **Hero . . . Leander . . . Hellespont . . . Sestos** cf. *AYLI*, IV.i.100–6 'Leander . . . Hero . . . Hellespont . . . Hero . . . Sestos'. The source is Ovid's *Heroides*, 17–18. Marlowe's *Hero and Leander c.* 1592 was not published until 1598, with a completion by George Chapman.

981   **throng** rush into.

981   **Hellespont** (Q1 has 'hellie spout') the first recorded use (*OED*) is *TGV*, I.i.22, 26.

981–4	For other rivers of blood, cf. *Luc*, 1437 and *EI*, 882–3.
986	**guilty of** deserving of.
990	**Star-Chamber** this powerful if anachronistic image for the night sky forms a fitting culmination for an extended legal metaphor. No doubt the dramatist was familiar with the dreaded Tudor court in the Palace of Westminster, so called because its ceiling was decorated with stars. This is the first recorded example of the allusive use (*OED* Star-Chamber 2b transf.).
991	**universal sessions** i.e. the Last Judgement.
991	**count** account.
992	**packing** conspiring; this adjectival usage far antedates the *OED* example.
993–4	**resolute . . . dissolved** determined to die; the word-play relies on a knowledge of Latin conjugation, as in re- or dis- solvo, -solutus. Cf. also *1H4*, I.ii.34 'resolutely . . . dissolutely' and *MWW*, I.i.254–5f. 'dissolved . . . dissolutely . . . resolutely'.
998ff.	This episode derives directly from Painter 1566–7, I, 361.
998	**[knives] doth hang** noun-verb discord; see Abbott 1869, 237.
998	**wedding-knives** this is the first and only recorded use (*OED* wedding vbl. sb. 4b).
1005	**more nimbler far** intensive comparative; see Abbott 1869, 22.
1006	**prevention** anticipation, forestalling.
1009	**most unholy suit** cf. *Ham*, I.iii.129 'unholy suits', i.e. illicit wooing, and *TGV*, IV.iii.30 'most unholy match', i.e. a bad marriage. On the latter passage, the New Penguin editor (Sanders 1958) comments: 'note the religious vocabulary used here in connection with love, as it is elsewhere in the play', and indeed in the canon *passim*.
1010	**solicit** in the sense of 'begging a woman's favour . . . with immoral intention' the first recorded use (*OED* 4b) is *TGV*, V.iv.40 'therefore begone, solicit me no more' and the second *Ado*, II.i.67, while the more general sense 'incite by some specious representation' (*OED* 4a) is first recorded from *1H6*, V.iii.190.
1011–13	**heaven . . . knife . . . stain . . . earth . . . stain . . . chaste blood** cf. *Luc*, 1836–40 'chaste blood . . . stainéd . . . heaven's . . . earth's . . . chaste . . . bloody knife', again with antitheses and repetitions. For the idea that blood is stained by rape or seduction cf. *Luc*, 1181 'my stainéd blood', 1655 'my blood stained', 1742–3 'blood . . . stained'. *Sonn*, 109.10–11 'blood . . . stained' is an analogous thought. See also the reference to Lucrece at lines 1021–2.
1011	**sharp-pointed** as in the Painter source (I.361); cf. *R3*, I.ii.174 'sharp-pointed sword', the first recorded use (*OED* a. 2) in the sense of having 'a fine point adapted for purposes of piercing or stabbing'.
1012	**stain** (a) discolour (b) dishonour.
1012	**stain thy earth** 'thy' because the land belongs to the King, as in *R2*, III.ii.10 'my earth'; ibid. V.v.110 'blood stained the king's own land' combines both ideas.
1015–16	**power** (a) divinity (b) ability. The first recorded use of the former meaning (*OED* sb.[1] 7), apart from an admittedly unclear example from Tindale 1526, is *MV*, IV.i.292 and the second *Tmp*, III.iii.73.

Both items overlook *R2*, III.ii.27–8 'the power that made you king hath power to keep you king' with the same word-play as here.

1018   **words . . . tends** noun-verb discord, see Abbott 1869, 235.

1019   **isle** i.e. England, as in the early histories and *EI*, 1889; see also line 2577 below.

1021   **her** Lucrece; cf. lines 1011–13 above.

1021   **ransacked treasury** cf. *WT*, IV.iv.349 'ransacked . . . treasury'. For the physical metaphor cf. *Titus*, II.i.131 'revel in Lavinia's treasury' and *Ham*, I.iii.31 'your chaste treasure open'. The words 'ransacked' and 'treasure' occur with the same connotations of rape in *Luc*, 836, 1056; cf. also lines 504 and 1311–12.

1021   **tasked** the first recorded use (*OED* task v. 3, to occupy or engage, to subject to severe trial) is *MWW*, IV.vi.30 and the second *H5*, I.ii.6.

1022   **so many pens** including those of Livy I.57, 58 and Ovid *Fasti* II.721ff. But the real reference, as the abundant quasi-quotation suggests, is surely to Shakespeare's poem *The Rape of Lucrece*, published in 1594.

1024   **after-ages** cf. *EI*, 766 'after-age' in the same sense of future historians apportioning praise or blame. The *OED* credits Shakespeare with its only other examples of such compounds with 'after-' (= subsequent): after-hours (*OED* a. 3a), *R3*, IV.iv.293, after-meeting (*OED* a. 3b), *Cor*, II.ii.39.

1024   **enrich thee with** praise you by crediting you with; this special sense is not separately recorded in the *OED*, but cf. *LLL*, IV.iii.320 'enriched you with', namely poetic praise, as here.

1025   **I am awakéd from this idle dream** as King Henry V says when he too rejects sin for virtue, *2H4*, V.v.51 'being awaked I do despise my dream'.

1025   **idle dream** as in *MM*, IV.i.63 'idle dream', *JN*, IV.ii.145 'idle dreams', IV.ii.153 'idle dreamer'.

1032   **through Flanders** as in Froissart L.

1034   **discover** dismantle.

1035   **siege** this metaphor links back to line 372, which in turn relates to the literal siege of lines 135 and 394 and the following battle scenes, thus unifying the two main themes of love and war.

1036   **sun . . . gild the eastern sky** i.e. with golden light, as in line 477; the first recorded use (*OED* gild 4) is *Titus*, II.i.6. See also lines 1939 and 2015 below, and cf. *Sonn*, 33.1,4 'morning . . . gilding'.

1042   **Enter . . . the Duke of Lorraine** brought back from Scotland, after line 217, in time to be historically present at this scene; cf. Froissart CXXV.

1043   **a thousand sail** Froissart records that the French fleet was very large, but its size is not specified.

1044   **a breakfast** i.e. news they won't relish, an ironic sense unknown to the *OED*, but cf. *2H6*, I.iv.74–5 'these news . . . a sorry breakfast for my Lord Protector'.

1045   **happy speed** safe arrival, as in *Oth*, II.i.67 'happy speed', there too with the connotation of safe landing from sea.

1048   **martial furniture for this exploit** military equipment for this expedition; the diction and word-order may be intended as Gallicisms.

1048   **exploit** scanned as an iamb not a trochee here as in the canon *passim.*

1049   **to lay aside** etc.; two otiose lines are devoted to protestations of urgency, as in *1–3 H6* and *EI.*

1049   **soothing** blandishments, as in *Cor*, I.ix.44.

1050   **circumstance** small-talk, irrelevance, as in *MV*, I.i.154.

1051   **bruited** reported.

1053   **subjects flock** cf. *1H4*, II.iv.138 'subjects . . . like a flock'.

1055   **harbour** perhaps suggested by 'navy', line 1043; cf. also 'anchorage', line 1064.

1055   **malcontents** this allusion to a divided England is surely as deliberately anachronistic and topical as in the early histories; cf. also *EI*, 377f.

1056   **bloodthirsty** perhaps because the Catiline conspirators reputedly drank human blood.

1056   **Catilines** as reported by Plutarch (*Cicero*) Lucius Catalina conspired and rebelled against the Roman state. His first recorded mention in English (*OED*) is from 1592; but this may well have been anticipated by *TT* (line 1366), the early Quarto of *3H6.*

1057   **spendthrifts** the first recorded use (*OED* sb. 1) is dated 1601, which overlooks this example; the first figurative use (*OED* 2) is *Tmp*, II.i.24.

1063   **never to sheathe his sword** cf. *Titus*, I.i.203–4 'your swords . . . sheathe them not'; see also line 2594 below.

1064   **anchorage** apart from 'anchorage dues' (*OED* 5) which is not in question here, the only usage recorded before 1611 is 'the set of anchors belonging to a ship' (*OED* 6), first cited from *Titus*, I.i.73 (the only canonical occurrence). This Shakespearean sense may well be the meaning here.

1066   **Netherland** a form not found in the *OED.*

1067   **ever-bibbing** an otherwise unknown coinage.

1068   **frothy** the first recorded use (*OED*) is *Ven*, 901, with 'mouth', as implied here.

1070   **aggravate** intensify.

1072   **stalls** installs.

1073   **the mightier** with the same thought as in *H5*, IV.iii.22 'the fewer men, the greater share of honour'.

1074   **the greater glory** cf. *MV*, V.i.93 'the greater glory'.

1074   **reaps . . . victory** verb and subject; the inversion may be deliberately stylistic, as in line 1048 etc.

1075   **domestic** Q1 has 'drum-strick'; but Capell's (1760) emendation has been generally accepted.

1075   **domestic power** cf. *Ant*, I.iii.47 'domestic powers'.

1076   **Polonian** a native of Poland; this antedates the first recorded use (*OED* B1), cited from 1599.

1077   **King of Bohemia** an ally named in Froissart CIII.

1079–80   **marching hither . . . but soft, I hear . . . their drums** a dramatic
               device also used in *3H6*, V.i.3, 11 'marching hitherward . . . I hear
               his drum', *EI*, 956–7 'soft, what drum . . . hearing', etc. See also
               line 538 above.

1086   **neighbourhood** neighbourly duty.

1089   **Moscow** (Musco in Q1) Muscovy, i.e. Russia.

1089   **fearful to** inspiring awe in, cf. *3H6*, II.ii.27; perhaps an anachro-
               nistic reference to Russo-Turkish relations at the time when these
               lines were written.

1090   **lofty Poland** the playwright apparently places Poland high up near
               the Arctic Circle; cf. *Err*, III.ii.99 'a Poland winter', i.e. a very long
               time, and *Ham*, I.i.63 where the Polacks are in sledges on the ice
               like Eskimos.

1090   **Poland, nurse of hardy men** cf. *R2*, II.i.51 'England . . . nurse . . .
               of royal kings'.

1091   **servitors** a class of soldiers, as in *1H6*, II.i.5.

1095   **crowns** a mild anachronism; these French coins were first issued by
               Philip of Valois in 1339 (*OED* sb. 8).

1098   **spoil** defeat.

1098   **treble gain** (Q1 has 'game') cf. *Titus*, V.i.8 'treble satisfaction'; see
               also line 810.

1100   **puissant** powerful; the French derivation is apt.

1101–3   **Agamemnon . . . Troy . . . Xerxes . . . drank up rivers . . . thirst**
               the same associations also appear in *EI*, 382 'Agamemnon . . .
               Troy', 864, 870 'Troy', 884–5 'thirst . . . suck . . . river dry'; each
               train of thought runs from one vast classical force to another,
               Greek navy to Persian army.

1104   **Bayard-like** Bayard was the legendary horse of Charlemagne; the
               name later came to typify blind recklessness.

1105   **reach at . . . diadem** cf. *2H6*, I.ii.7, 11 'diadem . . . reach at'.

1105   **imperial diadem** the crown of France; cf. *Titus*, I.i.6 'imperial
               diadem of Rome'.

1106   **swallowed of the waves** cf. *3H6*, V.vi.24–5 'sea . . . swallow', *Titus*,
               III.i.97 'brinish bowels swallow', etc.

1106–7   **swallowed . . . hacked** perhaps in allusion to the known fate of the
               Armada crews on the Irish coast.

1109ff.   the battle of Sluys is described, less vividly, in Froissart L.

1109   **described** discerned.

1111   **Armado** with obvious reference to the Spanish fleet of 1588, as in
               Err, III.ii.137, *JN*, III.iv.2, *LLL*, *passim*; in all such contexts the
               form 'Armado' is used.

1113   **withered pines** cf. *Luc*, 1167–8 'lofty pine . . . wither'.

1113–16   **pines . . . flowers** perhaps partly inspired by Froissart L, 'so great a
               number of ships that their masts seemed to be like a great wood'.
               For the double association of an invading force with both trees
               and flowers, as here, cf. *EI*, 1341–3 'a wood of pines . . . flags and
               banners . . . weeds in ripened corn'. See also lines 231 above and
               1939–40 below.

1115	**streaming ensigns . . . silks** cf. *R2*, IV.i.94 'streaming . . . ensign', *H5*, III. Chorus 5–6 'fleet with silken streamers' (also invading France).
1115–17	**ensigns . . . adorns** noun-verb discord, as in *EI*, 1342–3, 'flags . . . resembles', as if flags were a collective noun.
1115–16	**coloured . . . sundry flowers** cf. line 1942 'colours . . . sundry fruits'.
1117	**bosom of the earth** cf. *R2*, III.ii.147 'bosom of the earth', *JN*, IV.i.3 'bosom of the ground'.
1118	**majestical . . . course** cf. *H5*, III. Chorus 16–17 'majestical . . . course' (also invading France).
1119	**figuring** having the same shape as, congruent with, a meaning unknown to the *OED*. Senses 3 ('imagine') and 5 ('foreshow') of the verb are first recorded from *MM*, I.ii.53 and *3H6*, II.i.32 respectively.
1119	**hornéd circle of the moon** cf. *MND*, V.i.239, 244 'hornéd moon'; the Spanish Armada's battle formation was 'after the manner of a moon crescent' (Ubaldino 1590). See also line 1945 below.
1120	**admiral** the flagship.
1121	**handmaids** word-play on the technical sense of 'an accompanying ship', which thus antedates the first recorded use (*OED* sb. –1c), from Hakluyt 1599.
1122	**unite** united.
1123	**quartered equally by herald's art** the only 1590s dramatist known to have taken an intense interest in heraldry was Shakespeare, who in 1596 applied for a coat of arms on behalf of his father and in 1613 devised an emblem and motto for the Earl of Rutland at a tournament (Halliday 1964, 37 and 428). See also lines 1941–2 below.
1124	**tightly** effectively, vigorously; the first recorded use (*OED* 1) is *MWW*, I.iii.79, immediately followed by a metaphorical 'sail'.
1124	**merry** favouring, as in *Err*, IV.i.90 'merry wind', also about a voyage.
1125	**plough the ocean** the first recorded use of this metaphor (*OED* 4a) is *Tim*, V.i.50 'plough'st the foam', which overlooks this example; cf. also *H5*, III. Chorus 12 'the furrowed sea'.
1125	**hitherward** cf. *Per*, I.iv.60–61, 72 where a fleet is seen to 'make hitherward', also in association with 'descried', 'sail of ships' and 'white flags'. See also lines 1079–80 above.
1125	**amain** full speed ahead.
1125–9	**[Armado] . . . [bosom] . . . ocean . . . crop . . . fleur . . . honey . . . spider . . . suck . . . deadly venom** these associations become even more idiosyncratic when preceded by a description of a navy with flags streaming in the wind. This must surely be the same poet whose mind moved thus in lines 634–41 above: 'wind . . . sail . . . sail . . . wind . . . honey . . . bee . . . flower . . . poison-sucking . . . spider . . . deadly venom'; cf. also *R2*, III.ii.12ff. '[voyage] . . . earth . . . thy sweets [= flowers] . . . spiders, venom

... bosom ... pluck a flower ... death' and the further incorporation of bees and flowers into a seaborne invasion, *EI*, 1334f.

1131   **wing themselves** take flight, sail; the first recorded use in this sense (*OED* v. 2a) is *WT*, V.iii.133, 'wing me', also reflexive, overlooking the present example.

1131   **flight of ravens** i.e. the English ships, imagined as birds of prey and ill-omen, as in e.g. *JC*, V.i.84 'ravens ... fly o'er our heads'; see also lines 2110–11.

1135   **empty eagle** one that is hungry and seeks prey; the first recorded use of the epithet (*OED* a. 3 transf. b) is *2H6*, III.i.248, in the same vivid phrase 'empty eagle', which recurs in *3H6*, I.i.268.

1137   **These for thy news** so in Q1; the meaning 'these [coins]' seems acceptable enough to render such emendations as 'there's for' (Armstrong 1965) otiose.

1138   **bloody stroke of war** cf. *R3*, V.iii.90 'of bloody strokes ... war'.

1139   **survive** the first recorded use of this transitive sense (*OED* v. 2b) is *Titus*, V.iii.41 and the second *1H6*, III.ii.37.

1141   **Meanspace** meanwhile.

1144   **pitch your battles** align your forces in battle order, as in *3H6*, V.iv.66 'here pitch our battle'.

1146   **aid of** auxiliary force of, as in *3H6*, II.i.147 'aid of soldiers'.

1148   **coast** ground.

1149   **lodge** encamp.

1152   **thy** Q1 has 'their'; see line 442.

1152   **concept** considered opinion.

1155   **bring ... a pedigree** derive descent, as in *1H6*, II.v.77 'from John of Gaunt doth bring his pedigree'.

1156   **possession ... crown** in a technical legal sense (*OED* possession sb. 1b); cf. *EI*, 1822 'by possession you withhold my crown'.

1157   **the surest point of all the law** this far antedates the first recorded use of 'possession' (*OED* sb. 1d) in the proverbial sense.

1159   **a conduit ... blood** cf. *Titus*, II.iv.29–30 'blood ... a conduit'.

1159   **my dearest blood** cf. *1H6*, III.iv.40 'thy dearest blood', *3H6*, V.i.69 'the dearest blood'.

1160   **upstarts** the sole canonical usage is *1H6*, IV.vii.87; also in *EI*, 18.

1162   **repast** the taking of food or refreshment; the first recorded use (*OED* sb. 4a) is *LLL*, IV.ii.154.

1164   **the heavy day** cf. *R2*, III.iii.8 'alack the heavy day'.

1165   **field** category.

1165   **bears** their tenacious defence of their young is also cited in *3H6*, II.ii.13–14, also as an exhortation to defend the crown.

1166   **younglings** this is the first modern citation in the sense 'a young animal' (*OED* 1b); the word occurs only thrice in the canon (*Shr*, and twice in *Titus*).

1167   **Stir** move, direct; an alternative spelling of 'steer'.

1167   **Stir ... the happy helm** cf. *2H6*, I.iii.100 'steer the happy helm', in a context of vengeance.

1167   **Nemesis** goddess of vengeance, often represented as holding a helm; her only specific canonical mention is *1H6*, IV.vii.78.

1168	**sulphur** sulphurous: this is the second recorded use (*OED* sb. 9b).
1170	**echoing** this far antedates the first recorded use (*OED* ppl.a.).
1170	**cannon-shot** in *1H6*, III.iii.79, haughty words are compared to 'roaring cannon-shot', the only canonical occurrence of that compound and its first recorded use (*OED* 2) in the supposed sense of 'ammunition shot from a cannon'. But there too it surely means, as here, 'the shooting or discharge of a cannon' (*OED* 1, first cited from 1606 and antedated by both these examples); it is the discharge, not the projectile, that roars or thunders (line 1172).
1171	**disgests** an alternative form of 'digests', also found in *MV*, III.v.90, *Cor*, I.i.150 and *JC*, I.ii.301.
1172	**thund'ring terror** the epithet occurs only once in the canon, *R2*, III.iii.56, in the same spelling, and with 'terror' in the previous line.
1173	**buckle** put on armour, fight.
1175	**exhalations of the air** cf. *JC*, II.i.44 'exhalations whizzing in the air', surely terrestrial phenomena such as ball lightning in both contexts rather than 'meteors' as some editors explain.
1176	**lightning flash** the first recorded use of this phrase (*OED* lightning sb. 3) is *Titus*, II.i.3.
1178	**the rancour of their high-swoll'n hearts** cf. *R3* (Q1), II.ii.117 'the . . . rancour of your high-swoll'n hearts' and *Cont* (early Quarto of *2H6*), 117 'the big-swoll'n venom of thy hateful heart'.
1178	**high-swoll'n** the first and only recorded use of this compound (*OED* high III 10a) is *R3*, which is also the only canonical occurrence.
1180–81	**sweet Fortune turn . . . turning** cf. *1H4*, I.i.83 'sweet Fortune', also with personification, as again in *H5*, III.vi.32, 35 'Fortune . . . turning'.
1181	**forward** prevailing.
1183	**other** plural, as again in line 1198; cf. Abbott 1869, 24.
1185	**my heart misgives** cf. *MWW*, V.v.213, 'my heart misgives me', *3H6*, IV.vi.94 'so doth my heart misgive me'.
1185	**misgives** in this absolute or intransitive sense the first recorded use (*OED* v. 1b) is *Oth*, III.iv.89 'my mind misgives'.
1185	**mirror** the very model or image, as in *EI*, 250 'mirror of majesty', *1H6*, I.iv.74 'mirror of all martial men', *H5*, II. Chorus 6 'mirror of all Christian kings'. The *1H6* example should have been the first recorded use of this locution (*OED* sb. 5b), since it is readily distinguishable from the earlier Chaucer instance.
1185	**pale death** the bringer of bad tidings is white-faced at his news and for fear of his reception, like the servant in *Mac*, V.iii.11f.
1188	**sad discourse of this discomfiture** account of complete defeat, a strong expression; cf. *1H6*, I.i.58–9 'sad tiding of . . . discomfiture'.
1190	**France hath ta'en the foil** has lost the contest, a technical wrestling term; cf. *1H6*, V.iii.23 'England give the French the foil'.
1192	**iron-hearted** extremely cruel; this inventive compound far antedates the first recorded use (*OED*).

1194   **spleen** violent temper (*OED* sb. 6), first recorded from *R3*, II.iv.64; cf. also *EI*, 1801 and line 1200 below. Shakespeare is also credited with other senses of 'spleen': *OED* 3 'merriment' (*LLL*, V.ii.117), 4a 'sudden impulse' (*Ven*, 907, *1H4*, V.ii.19), 4b 'changeable temper' (*Shr*, III.ii.10, *1H4*, II.iii.78), 5a 'courage' (*Rom*, III.i.157), 5b 'impetuosity' (*JN*, II.i.448, V.vii.50), 8 with *the*, 'amusement' (*TN*, III.ii.68).

1198   **other** plural, as in line 1183 above.

1199   **earnest penny** a small sum paid as a pledge or deposit in advance of a larger transaction.

1200   [**spleen**] . . . **fiery dragons** . . . **flight**, cf. *R3*, V.iii.350 'spleen of fiery dragons', *JN*, II.i.68 'fierce dragons' spleens', *1H6*, I.i.11–12, 'dragon's wings . . . wrathful fire', all in a context of warfare.

1202–4   **death** . . . **gloomy night** . . . **darkness** cf. *1H6*, V.iv.89 'darkness . . . gloomy shade . . . death', which may well be earlier than the first recorded use of 'gloomy' (*OED* 1) namely *Titus*, IV.i.53. See also lines 550 above and 2411 below.

1203–5   **day** . . . **night** . . . **quick** . . . **reft of life** double antithesis.

1207   **the hideous noise** cf. Spurgeon, 1935, 76: 'war is clearly associated in Shakespeare's mind chiefly with noise'.

1209   **purple** this poetic epithet for the colour of blood is first cited (*OED* A 2d) from Spenser 1590. It is used parodistically in e.g. *MND* but seriously in the early canonical histories (*1–3H6, R2, R3, JN*) and in *EI*.

1212   **cranny** this adjectival usage is not recorded in the *OED*.

1212   **cleftures** this is the first and only recorded use (*OED*) in the sense of an actual cleft or fissure.

1214–18   **tossed** . . . **reeling** . . . **flood** [sea] cf. *EI*, 1439 'reeling sea . . . tossed'.

1218   **ruthless flood** cf. *3H6*, V.iv.25 'ruthless sea', 36 'ruthless waves'.

1222   **resolution** firmness of purpose; the first recorded use (*OED* 15) is *Titus*, III.i.238 and the second is *Luc*, 352.

1224   **laid about** fought, dealt blows.

1225   *Nonpareil* Q1 has *Nom per illa*; the emendation is Capell's (1760). See also *The Armada*. 164 below.

1226   *Black Snake of Bullen* i.e. of Boulogne, which sent a ship to the battle of Sluys, but none so named.

1241   **stuff** household goods, chattels.

1242   **quarter-day** when rents fell due.

1243   **bag and baggage** the first recorded use of the phrase (*OED* bag sb. 19) is this play's source, Froissart CCCXX, in the Berners translation.

1244   **quartering-day** a black pun – the day when we shall all be cut to pieces. The first and only recorded use of the epithet in this sense (*OED* ppl.a.) is *1H6*, IV.ii.11 'quartering steel' (as also in line 2387 below), in each context referring to the fate of French citizens at the hands of the invading English.

1250   **is't** the first recorded use of this abbreviation (*OED*) is *Tmp*,

	I.ii.245, overlooking scores of earlier canonical examples; and cf. *EI*, 1083, etc.
1251	**envy** evil, malignancy.
1253	**to their cost** the first recorded use of this expression (*OED* cost sb. 5d) in *2H4*, III.ii.17 which like *EI*, 919 is about an enemy in war; see also *EI*, 31, 726, 1560.
1256	**mirthful jollity** the epithet occurs only once in the canon, in the same context of apparent tautology; *3H6*, V.vii.43 'mirthful comic shows'.
1258	**nipped** the first recorded use (*OED* v.¹ 6b) is *LLL*, V.ii.802; cf. also *2H6*, II.iv.3, *Titus*, IV.iv.70 and *EI*, 742. In those last two contexts, as here, the nipping cold is an image of bad news.
1262	**washed** soaked, drenched.
1262	**suspects** expects.
1263	**charge and such a train as this** responsibility for such a convoy of refugees.
1264	**look . . . look for** (a) prepare (b) succour.
1266	**despair of ill** [*sic* in Q1] **success**; some editors amend to 'all success', but the Quarto phrase might mean 'you gave us hope that the English cause would miscarry'.
1272	**fearful** awe-inspiring, as in line 1089 above.
1272–4	**fearful . . . handful . . . rightful** these jingles may be evidence of hasty writing.
1274	**quarrel** see line 173 above.
1277	**prophecy** a notion apparently invented by the playwright, as in *1TR*, 1665f.
1278	**published** put about.
1279	**oracles** predictions, prognostications; this antedates the first recorded use (*OED* 9b).
1281	**lion rouséd** started from cover by the hunt; cf. *1H4*, I.iii.198 'rouse a lion'.
1287	**Sweet-flowering** the first recorded instance of this compound (*OED* a. and av. C2).
1288	**abandoned** banished from: a Shakespearean usage, according to the Chambers *20th Century Dictionary*; cf. *Shr*, Ind.ii.115.
1288	**expulsed the land** driven out of France; the only canonical instance of the verb is *1H6*, III.iii.25 'expulsed from France'.
1289	**ransacked** violated (i.e. peace).
1290	**ravens upon . . . houses** cf. *Oth*, IV.i.21 'the raven o'er the . . . house'.
1292	**unrestrained** in a special appositive sense 'without restraint', of which it is the first recorded use (*OED* ppl. a. 2b); the only canonical instance is *R2*, V.iii.7.
1293	The rest of this speech is strikingly paralleled in *JN*, II.i.227ff.
1294	**this fair mountain** cf. *Ham*, III.iv.66 'this fair mountain'.
1297–8	**burning like an oven . . . leaking vapour** [**smoke**] the vivid image evokes some mishap rather than an ordinary oven in domestic use; cf. Spurgeon, 1935, 122: 'among Shakespeare's images from

everyday life a stopped oven is especially noticeable, and the fierce burning, smoke and cinders which ensue', with examples from *Titus*, II.iv.36, *Ven*, 331.

1298–9   [smoke] vapour ... discern cf. *1H6*, II.ii.26–7 'discern ... smoke ... vapours'.

1302   dreadful ministers of wrath cf. *R3*, I.ii.46 'dreadful minister of hell'.

1302–3   dreadful ... measures ... march cf. *R3*, I.i.8 'dreadful marches ... measures'.

1304–6   right ... left ... midst the order of battle derives from Froissart CXXII.

1304   conquering the first recorded use (*OED* ppl.a.) is *1H6*, II.i.26; also in *EI*, 1022 and lines 1704 and 2072 below.

1305   hot unbridled son cf. *AWEW*, III.ii.28 'rash and unbridled boy'. The image is that of an untamed colt, as in line 1352; cf. also *R2*, II.i.70 'hot colts'.

1306   glittering host because of the sunlight on the armour, as in lines 230–1 and 1929f; cf. also *R2*, III.iii.116 'glittering arms', IV.i.51 'glittering helmets'.

1311–12   wives ... abused ... treasure shared for this association of ideas cf. *MWW*, II.ii.378 'my bed shall be abused, my coffers ransacked'. See also lines 504 and 1021 above.

1312   your treasure cf. *Ham*, I.iii.31 'your chaste treasure' and line 1021 above.

1312   your weeping eyes cf. *R3*, IV.iv.278 'her weeping eyes', also in a context of personal outrage.

1313   you yourselves perhaps intended to suggest a French reflexive verb.

1319   guide guidance, as in *Tim*, I.i.243.

1320   shallow shallow part or place, as in *JC*, IV.iii.221.

1320   Somme spelt Sone in Q1, as if the MS had contained that minim error and perhaps a superscribed abbreviation sign which had not been correctly understood.

1324   Gobin de Grey in Froissart LXXI–LXXIII his name is Gobin à Grace, who received 100 gold nobles for disclosing the ford at La Blanchetaque.

1326   enlarge set free, as in *H5*, II.ii.40, 57.

1340   Place-names as in Froissart CCXXII, but the first three are spelt Harslen, Lie and Crotag in Q1 instead of Harfleur, Lô and Crotay, which permits inferences about the *prima facie* authorial handwriting.

1341   wasted laid waste, sacked.

1342   apparent conspicuous.

1343   solitariness personified; this is the first recorded use (*OED* 2).

1343   progress make a ceremonial journey.

1345   refused our proffered peace cf. *EI*, 908 'refuse my proffered grace', *1H6*, IV.ii.9 'frown upon this proffered peace', *JN*, II.i.258 'pass our proffered offer' (about the resistance of besieged citizens, in all four contexts); cf. also *R3*, III.vii.202 'refuse not ... this proffered love' and lines 1738, 1765, 1810–11 and 1991 below.

1346	**sharp revenge** cf. *Titus*, I.i.37 'sharp revenge'; also in line 2518 below.
1347	**this** to such an extent, thus, as in *Ven*, 205.
1348	**kind embracement** cf. *Err*, I.i.43, *Shr*, Ind. i. 118, *Ven*, 312 'kind embracements'.
1349	**touch thy breast** the personification continues from lines 1117 and 1315.
1350	**mould** (a) earth (b) form.
1351	**disdainful pride** cf. *EI*, 905 'disdainful pride', again in the same siege context as line 1345 above; see also *Shr*, IV.ii.39, *AYLI*, III.iv.50 'proud disdainful', *Ant*, III.xiii.142 'proud and disdainful'.
1352	**skittish and untaméd colt** farm-animal imagery, cf. *MV*, V.i.72 'youthful and unhandled colts'; see also line 1305 above.
1353	**start** startle.
1359	**multitudes** see line 2230 below.
1361	**happily** haply, perchance, as in *TN*, IV.ii.52.
1361	**approach** hostile advance, as in *Tim*, V.i.164 and *EI*, 1537.
1364	**means to bid us battle presently** cf. *1H6*, V.ii.12–13 'means to give you battle presently', i.e. as soon as two armies are 'conjoined in one'; cf. line 1234 above, 'join our several forces all in one'.
1365	**he shall be welcome** cf. *JN*, II.i.83 'let them be welcome then', *EI*, 1919 'he is welcome', also said by bold commanders about their adversaries before a battle.
1368–70	**king . . . encroach . . . tyrannous** cf. *2H6*, IV.i.95–6 'king . . . encroaching tyranny'.
1369	**musing** marvelling, as in *Mac*, III.iv.84.
1371	**subvert** destroy, raze.
1371	**subvert his towns** cf. *1H6*, II.iii.65 'subverts your towns', in the same sense and context.
1372	**in this manner following** a legal formula; cf. *LLL*, I.i.205, 209 'in manner and form following'.
1373	**obraids** upbraids; cf. line 1448.
1373	**intrusion** in the sense (confirmed by line 1369) 'the action of thrusting oneself in, in an encroaching manner', the first recorded use (*OED* sb. 3) is *Rom*, I.v.91.
1374	**fugitive** in this sense of 'one who quits his country' the first recorded use (*OED* sb. B 1c) is *1H6*, III.iii.67.
1375	**mate** fellow.
1378	**fruitful** with the connotation of copious harvest as contrasted with barrenness; the first recorded use (*OED* a. 3) is *Ham*, I.ii.80, the second *MM*, IV.iii.154 and the third *Tim*, V.i.150.
1379	**pilfering** plundering, as in *H5*, I.ii.142.
1380	**insomuch** see line 2400 below.
1380	**infringed thy faith** violated it, as in *LLL*, IV.iii.144 'faith so infringed' and *3H6*, II.ii.8 'infringed my vow'.
1383–4	**cope with** come into contact with; the first recorded use (*OED* cope v.² 5) is *Luc*, 99, the second *Ham*, III.ii.55 and the third *WT*, IV.iv.424. Onions (*Glossary*) confirms 'not pre-Shakespeare'.

1384   **so much** Q1 has 'such'; Capell's emendation (1760) improves both the sense and the scansion.

1386   **feared . . . loved** cf. Spurgeon 1935, 154: 'the opposite of love in the Shakespeare canon is not hate but fear'.

1394–5   **gall . . . wormwood . . . pleasant taste . . . honey-sweet** cf. *Luc*, 889 'honey . . . gall', 893 'sugared . . . wormwood taste', etc.

1397   **satirical** ironic, as in line 463.

1398   **worthless** (also in line 2462) the first recorded use, of things (*OED* a. 1), is *Titus*, V.iii.117 and the second *TGV*, IV.ii.6; the first of persons (*OED* a. 2) is *1H6*, V.v.53.

1399   **soil** Q1 has 'foil'.

1399   **soil (my fame)** sully, tarnish cf. *R2*, IV.i.23 'mine honour soiled', which is the first recorded use in this sense of the verb (*OED* v.¹ 2c).

1400   **dim** a synonym for 'soil' above, as in *1H6*, I.i.79 'dim your honours', *2H6*, I.i.125 'dims the honour'.

1401   **thy wolfish barking** (i.e. speech), cf. *1H6*, III.iv.33 'the barking of thy . . . tongue'.

1402   **insinuate** ingratiate oneself; the first recorded use (*OED* v. 2b) is *Titus*, IV.ii.38.

1403–6   **strumpet . . . paint . . . vicious . . . deforméd . . . foul** cf. *Tim*, IV.iii.147–8 'whore . . . paint . . . mire', *Ham*, III.i.50, 52 'harlot . . . ugly . . . painted'; cf. Armstrong 1946, 67 'paint is mentioned with distaste by Shakespeare and . . . constantly brought into association with unpleasant ideas'.

1405   **counterfeit** the first recorded use 'of things abstract or immaterial' (*OED* sb. C 1b) is *Ado*, II.iii.104.

1408   **as who should say** a Shakespearean turn of phrase, according to J. Wilson (1948) citing *Titus*, IV.ii.121, *Ven*, 280, *Luc*, 320, etc.

1413   **securely** the first recorded use (*OED* 1) is *Titus*, III.i.3 and the second *R2*, II.i.266.

1413   **securely slept** (i.e. not waged war) cf. *Titus*, III.i.3 'dangerous wars . . . securely slept', *EI*, 307–9 '[the English are] up in arms . . . whilst Canute . . . securely sleeps', *1H6*, III.ii.19 'we'll sleep secure' (i.e. need not fight).

1419   **cross** quarrelsome, fractious; the first recorded use (*OED* a. 5a) is *Titus*, II.iii.53 and the second *R3*, III.i.216.

1419   **invectives** the sole canonical occurrence is *3H6*, I.iv.43.

1420   **execrations** the only two canonical occurrences are *2H6*, III.ii.305 and *Tro*, II.iii.7.

1421–2   **serpents . . . banks . . . sting** cf. *2H6*, III.i.228–9 'snake . . . bank sting' and *Ham*, I.v.39 'serpent . . . sting', also in contexts of contention for a crown.

1421   **hid** Q1 has 'hide'.

1421   **hid . . . hollow banks** cf. *1H4*, I.iii.106 'hid . . . hollow bank'.

1422   **sting with their tongues** as Shakespeare supposed, cf. *2H4*, IV.v.205 'their stings and teeth'; see also *EI*, 1651.

1422   **sting . . . swords** cf. *WT*, II.iii.86 'sting . . . sword'.

1422   **remorseless** cruel, pitiless; the first recorded adjectival use (*OED* adj. 1a) is *3H6*, I.iv.142, and the first recorded quasi-adverbial use is (*OED* 1b) *2H6*, III.i.213.

1422–3   **swords . . . plead** cf. *Titus*, I.i.4 'plead . . . swords', *3H6*, I.i.103 'swords shall plead', *EI*, 43 'plead . . . sword', again all about contention for a crown, as here.

1425   **immodest** arrogant; the first recorded literary use (*OED* a. 1) is *1H6*, IV.i.126.

1426   **scandalous** defamatory; the first recorded use (*OED* a. 3) is *MM*, V.1.122.

1426   **notorious lies** cf *AWEW*, I.i.100 'notorious liar'; in this strongly condemnatory sense, the first recorded use of the epithet in modern English (*OED* a. 4b) is *Err*, IV.i.84.

1427   **pretended** proposed.

1427   **quarrel** see line 173 above.

1430   **eternal shame** as in *LLL*, I.i.157, *H5*, IV.v.10.

1432   **his** i.e. the French king's.

1435   **enkindled . . . flame** for the same image of warfare in France cf. *JN*, V.ii.83, 85–6 'kindled . . . wars . . . fire . . . far too huge to be blown out'.

1438   **champion** champaign, open country; the French derivation is apt.

1440   **approves** proves.

1440–41   **tyrant . . . shepherd** the antithesis is recalled from lines 43–4.

1443   **thirsty tiger suckst . . . blood** cf. *3H6*, I.iv.137–8 'tiger . . . drain . . . blood' and *FI*, 1447–8 'devours . . . hungry . . . blood . . . lions'; in each context an enemy is accused of cruelty.

1446–7   **whom should they follow . . . but . . . their true-born sovereign?** cf. *3H6*, I.i.82 'whom should he follow but his natural king' in the same tone of sharp rebuke.

1446   **agéd impotent** etc.; for this unhistorical characterisation of Audley see lines 1609 below.

1447   **true-born** the first recorded use (*OED*) is *1H6*, II.iv.27 and the second *R2*, I.iii.309 (the only two canonical occurrences); cf. also *EI*, 853–4 'my king . . . a true-born prince'.

1448   **Obraidst** upbraidst, as in line 1373.

1448–9   **within his face/time hath engraved deep characters of age?** cf. *Luc*, 203 'engraven in my face', *Sonn*, 100. 9–10 'face . . . time . . . graven', 60.9–10 'time delves the parallels . . . brow', 19.5, 9–10, 'time . . . carve . . . brow . . . lines . . . pen', *TGV*, II.vii.4 'visibly charactered and engraved'. See also lines 2046 7, 2108 and 2303 below.

1449–50   **engraved . . . grave** deliberate word-play.

1449–50   **age . . . grave . . . experience** cf. *Titus*, V.iii.77–8 'age . . . grave . . . experience'.

1451   **stiff-grown** an invented compound unknown to the *OED*.

1451   **oaks . . . immovable** cf. *Cor*, V.ii.111 'the oak not to be windshaken'.

1456   **held the sceptre up** reigned, as in *2H6*, V.i.102 'hold a sceptre up', *Titus*, I.i.200 'upright he held [the sceptre]'.

1458   **true-born sovereign** repeated from line 1447 (q.v.).

1461   **unfought** without having to fight; this is the first recorded use
(*OED* ppl.a.1b).

1462   **now's** Q1 has 'knowes'.

1463   **intended** extended, drawn up.

1463   **must bide the touch** await the test, as a touchstone is used to test for
precious metals; cf. *1H4*, IV.iv.10 'must bide the touch', also in a
context of forthcoming battle.

1465   **your natural king** as in *3H6*, I.i.82, cited at lines 1446–7
above.

1466   **foreigner** the antithesis of 'natural', i.e. native-born, as in *EI*, 853–
4 'king . . . true-born . . . foreigner'.

1467–72   For this extended image of animal-training and government cf. *EI*,
150–62.

1468   **mild and gentle** cf. *2H6*, III.ii.392, *R3*, IV.iv.161 and *EI*, 214 'mild
and gentle'.

1470   **enthrone** the first recorded use in any sense, whether literal or
figurative (*OED* v. 1, 2), is *Ant*, III.vi.5, though the present instance
is far earlier.

1471   **a heavy hand** cf. *JN*, IV.iii.58 'a heavy hand', also about regal
tyranny.

1474   **haughty courage**, cf. *1H6*, IV.i.35 and *EI*, 905 'haughty courage'
('and disdainful pride', as in line 1351 above).

1475   **answer** correspond to.

1476   **fugitives** see line 1374 above.

1478   **belly-god** in the unprecedented sense, unknown to the *OED*, of
'one who makes a god of his own sexual appetite'. King John has
been well informed; this allusion is among the unobtrusive yet
effective devices designed to unify the two main plots of the play,
love and war, by means of succinct cross-reference. See also line
1507 below.

1478   **wantonness** (and in line 1676) personified, like a character in a
morality play; this is the first recorded use in any sense (*OED* 3b
trans.).

1481   **chines of beef** cf. *2H6*, IV.x.61 'chines of beef', the only canonical
occurrence of 'chines'. For the equation of these favourite cuts (ribs
or sirloin) with English martial valour, cf. *1H6*, I.ii.7–9 'the famished English . . . faintly besiege us . . . they want their fat bull-
beeves' and *H5*, III.vii.152–4 'these English are shrewdly out of
beef . . . they have only stomachs to eat and none to fight'. In all
these contexts the point is that the mocking French will have to eat
their words. See also lines 2125 and 2251 below.

1483   **resty-stiff** this is the first recorded use of this inventive compound
(*OED* resty a. 2, 'sluggish, lazy').

1484   **twere** see line 75.

1484   **a many** several, as e.g. in *AYLI*, I.i.115; see Abbott 1869, 63.

1484   **over-ridden jades** the epithet here is overlooked by the *OED*, where
its first recorded use, dated 1600, comes from *Edward IV* by
Thomas Heywood, in the same phrase; this, given Heywood's

tribute to *E3* (quoted on pp. 147–8 below) is surely more of a quotation than a coincidence.

1484   **jades** the first recorded use of the singular noun applied to a man (*OED* sb. 2c) is *Shr*, I.ii.247. See also line 1677 below.

1486   **captive bonds** the epithet is transferred, and means 'of a captive', as in *JC*, I.i.34 'captive bonds'.

1488   **Crécy** the battle is described in Froissart CXXX.

1490   **presently** soon.

1492   **scandalous** either 'grossly disgraceful' as in line 774 above and line 1839 below (q.v.), or else by transference 'defamatory' as in line 1426 (q.v.); see also line 1839.

1493   **entombéd** if this usage is figurative, its first recorded use (*OED* v. 2) is *Luc*, 679.

1495   **pitchéd field** ready for fighting in; cf *Tim*, I.ii.225 'pitched field'.

1496   **martialists** warriors.

1497   **type** distinguishing mark; the first recorded use (*OED* sb.¹ 2) is *3H6*, I.iv.121 and its second *H8*, I.iii.31; cf. also *Luc*, 1050 and *R3*, IV.iv.245. These are the only canonical occurrences, all used in 'the only Shakespearean senses' (Onions, *Glossary*, 234).

1499   **orderly** in correct sequence, as in *R2*, I.iii.9, also about a knightly ceremony.

1500   **attirement** accoutrements, first cited (*OED*) from Painter's *Palace of Pleasure*, a source book for this play.

1503–52   This solemn interlude, almost a masque within a play, recalls e.g. the parade of knights in *Per*, II.ii. Here too it is the dramatist's own interpolated invention.

1504   **impall** encircle.

1505–6   **unrelenting heart . . . flint** cf. *1H6*, V.iv. 59 'unrelenting hearts', *Titus*, II.iii.140–1 'heart . . . unrelenting flint'; the latter is the first recorded use of the epithet (*OED* 1a).

1507   **base affections** such as the speaker's for the Countess; dramatic irony.

1508   **conquer where thou comst . . .** [helmet 1511, lance 1517, **target** (= shield) 1523] cf. *Ven*, 100, 102–4 'conquers where he comes . . . Lance . . . shield. crest' [helmet]; see also line 1651 below.

1512   **the chamber of this brain** ventricle, brain-cavity.

1513   **Bellona** goddess of war, as in Ovid *Metamorphoses* V.155; her first recorded mention in English (*OED*) is *Mac*, I.ii.54.

1514   **laurel victory** the first recorded use of 'laurel' in this sense, as an adjective meaning 'renowned' (*OED* a.) is *Ant*, I.iii.100 'laurel victory'.

1518–19   **brazen pen . . . draw forth . . . stratagems** cf. lines 2046–7 below.

1518–19   **pen . . . draw** word-play.

1520   **[brazen] honour's book** cf. *Sonn*, 25.11 'the book of honour', *EI*, 749 'the brass-leaved book of . . . fame', both also said of warriors in battle.

1521   **vanquish** so in Q1; the variation from 'conquer' may be inadvertent.

1523   **target** a small round shield.

1524   **Perseus' shield** cf. Ovid *Metamorphoses* V.180f (immediately after Bellona, line 1513 above); but it was the Gorgon's head, not the shield, that petrified all beholders. See also line 2119 below.

1525   **astonish** paralyse; for similar phenomena see lines 2117–19 below.

1526   **meagre** fleshless.

1528   **Now wants there naught but knighthood** as we are reminded in line 1588 and shown in lines 1664–9.

1532   **green** strong, vital, as in line 414 above.

1532   **scarce-appearing** an inventive compound not found in the *OED*, where the first recorded use of such formations (scarce B adv. 2e) is *1H6*, IV.iii.50 'scarce-cold'.

1532   **appearing** the first recorded use in this sense of 'becoming visible' (*OED* ppl.a.1) is *2H4*, I.iii.39 'th'appearing buds', which is the latent thought here (cf. 'green').

1533   **comfortable** comforting.

1533   **good-presaging** this instance of such compounds in 'good-' antedates all the *OED* examples (good D Comb. 1c).

1533   **-presaging** the verb's first recorded use in the sense of 'give advance indication, by natural means' (*OED* v. 1b) is *1H6*, IV.i.191 and the second is at line 330 above; see also line 2102.

1534–5 **old Jacob's words . . . his blessing** cf. Genesis 49:1 'And Jacob called unto his sons, and said, Gather yourselves together', 28 'this is it that their father spake unto them, and blessed them'.

1535   **whenas** an already archaic form of 'when' chosen to fit the metre, as often in *Titus*, *1–3H6* and *EI* yet unaccountably omitted from Spevack 1973.

1535   **breathed** spoke softly. The first recorded use (*OED* v. 12a) is *JN*, IV.ii.36 'we breathed our council'; the extended application 'breathed his last' (like Jacob) is first recorded (*OED* v. 10c) from *3H6*, V.ii.40. Shakespeare is also credited with the first recorded use of the meanings 4b 'live' (*3H6*, III.i.82), 7 'sing' (*MWW*, IV.v.2, III.v.59), 8 'blow softly' (*Tmp*, IV.i.45), 9 'tarnish' (*TGV*, V.iv.131) and 11 'respire' (*LLL*, V.i.722). See also lines 2214–15.

1536   **hallowed . . . profane** antithesis with a touch of word-play in the latter component: (a) desecrate (b) prove unworthy of, put to wrong use.

1538   **patronage** defend, as in *1H6*, III.i.48 and III.iv.32, the only canonical instances, which should surely have furnished the first recorded use; their meaning is readily distinguishable from Greene's 1587 coinage (*OED* v. 1b = patronise).

1541   **wither . . . sapless tree** cf. *1H6*, II.v.11–12 'withered vine . . . sapless', also about senility.

1541   **sapless** the first recorded use (*OED* a. 1a) is *1H6*, II.v.12; its earliest figurative application to age, as here (*OED* a. 2b) is also *1H6*, IV.v.4.

1542   **[wither . . . tree] . . . remain the map of infamy**, no doubt recalling the withered fig tree in Matthew 21:19–20, which was to remain fruitless for ever.

1542	**map** the very picture or embodiment, cf. *R2*, V.i.12, *2H6*, III.i.203 'map of honour', *Titus*, III.ii.12 'map of woe'. The first recorded use in this sense (*OED* sb.¹ 2b) is cited from the year 1591, which on the *OED*'s own dating overlooks the *Titus* example.
1543	**steeléd** armed or protected with steel; this is the first recorded literal use (*OED* ppl.a.2). The first figurative uses (*OED* 5) are *H5*, II.ii.36 and *MM*, IV.ii.87.
1543	**battles** armies.
1544	**the leading of the vaward** (i.e. forefront), cf. *H5*, IV.iii.131 'the leading of the vaward', where the granting of this signal honour again makes an effective dramatic moment, as also in *EI*, 1402 'the leading of our army', 1404 'the leading of our forces' and again in *R3*, V.iii.297 'the leading of this foot and horse'.
1546	**gravity** sobriety, seriousness.
1548	**manage** conduct, handling of affairs.
1548	**second unto none** the first recorded modern use of the phrase (*OED* second a. and sb.² A 2a), and the earliest of all in this form, is *Err*, V.i.7 'second to none'.
1551	**ray** orderly array.
1558	**Genoese** (Q1 'Genoaes') for their defection see Froissart CXXX.
1560	**grudging to** this is the first recorded modern use (*OED* grudge v. 2a) of the infinitive construction. Shakespeare is credited with the special usage (*OED* 1d) 'to grudge a thought' (*1H6*, III.i.175).
1561–2	**no sooner . . . but straight** see lines 72–3 and 130–32 above.
1562	**straight retiring** cf. *EI*, 1051 'straight retire', in the same context of defection in battle.
1571	The King's withdrawal to a windmill-hill during the battle of Crécy is a detail found in Holinshed III as well as Froissart CXXX. Shakespeare thought it worth mentioning as an allusive aside in *H5*, I.ii.108: 'on a hill'.
1574	**Just-dooming** another inventive compound; the first recorded use of such a formation (*OED* just a. 13) is *JN*, II.i.345 'just-borne'.
1574	**dooming** the first recorded use of the verb in this sense of 'decreeing' (*OED* doom v. 5) is *Titus*, IV.ii.114. Shakespeare is also credited with the coinage of senses *OED* v. 2 'condemn' (*Titus*, III.i.47, *R2*, V.1.4) and v. 3 'consign' (*Ham*, I.v.10), as well as two senses of the noun: 4b 'death' (*Sonn*, 14.4) and 7b transf. 'one's last day', as in line 2066 (q.v.).
1575	**our gross judgement** our physical nature cannot comprehend the divine, as in *MV*, V.i.64–5, in association with 'grossly'.
1576	**wondrous works** a phrase frequent in the Bible (notably Psalms) and the Apocrypha (notably Ecclesiasticus).
1578	**the wicked stumble at themselves** cf. Proverbs 4:19 'the way of the wicked is as darkness: they know not at what they stumble'; the dramatist provides one explanation.
1580ff.	The predicament of the Prince and the requests for help are found in Froissart CXXX.
1580	**Enter Artois . . . Rescue, King Edward, rescue** cf. *R3*, V.iv.1 'enter Catesby . . . rescue, my lord of Norfolk, rescue'.

1585   **tis impossible that he should scape** cf. *3H6*, II.vi.38 'tis impossible
            he should escape'.

1590–2   **succour . . . close encompassed . . . a world of odds . . . honour** cf.
            1H6, IV.iv.20, 23, 25, 27 'honour . . . succours . . . a world of
            odds . . . compass him about', also said of an English hero sur-
            rounded by French forces.

1592   **redeem him** i.e. himself, a reflexive form; see line 1622 below.

1594   **what remedy** i.e. there's no help for it; the first recorded use in
            modern English (*OED* remedy sb. ?d) is *MWW*, V.v.236, though
            1H6, V.iii.132 may well be earlier.

1594–5   **we have more sons/than one** Régnier is similarly philosophical
            about the loss of his daughter, also after 'what remedy?' in *1H6*; and
            cf. the thoughts about the expendability of sons, also after 'Tut'
            (line 1587 here) in *EI*, 271f.

1595   **declining age** cf. *EI*, 803 'declining age'. This phrase is first cited
            (*OED* declining ppl.a.4b) from the year 1615; but it is surely
            synonymous with 4a, 'becoming weaker', first recorded from *R2*,
            II.i.240. Shakespeare is also credited with the *OED* 2 sense
            'drooping' (*Shr*, Ind. i.119).

1600   **snares** an image from bird-snaring, as in lines 1848–9 below.

1600   **emmets** ants.

1601   **muster** the first recorded use of this intransitive sense (*OED* v.¹ 4)
            is *MM*, II.iv.20; of the closely related transitive and figurative senses
            (*OED* 2c) the first recorded use is *Luc*, 442.

1603   **franticly** a form also found in *Titus*, III.ii.31 and *Ven*, 1039.

1603   **toil** net.

1604   **free himself** this reflexive sense (disengage, extricate) far antedates
            the first recorded use (*OED* free v. 3c). Shakespeare is also credited
            with senses 2c trans, 'grant immunity from' (*WT*, IV.iv.433) and 2e
            'absolve' (first *Luc*, 1208 and second *WT*, III.ii.111).

1605   **content** elliptical for 'be content', of which the first recorded use
            (*OED* 1b) is *R2*, V.ii.82, the second *JC*, IV.ii.41 and the third *Cym*,
            V.iv.102. No other instances are offered from any source. Onions
            (*Glossary*) confirms that 'be content' is recorded solely from Shake-
            speare; cf. also *EI*, 1951 and 1991. Further, the elliptical exclama-
            tion 'content!' for 'I am content' or 'very well' is first cited (*OED* 3b
            ellipt.) from *1H6*, IV.i.70 and then *Shr*, V.ii.70, with a third
            example dated as late as 1820.

1608–10   **season . . . savour** cf. Spurgeon 1935, 83–4: 'Shakespeare betrays
            again and again his appreciation of the value of flavouring and the
            necessity of seasoning . . . and does not hesitate to compare this to
            things of the highest import', here life and death.

1608   **season** in this special metaphorical sense ('qualify, temper') the first
            recorded use (*OED* v. 1d) is *R3*, III.vii.149 and the second *Ham*,
            I.ii.192.

1609   **Nestor** an aged Homeric hero, whose first recorded mention (*OED*)
            is *LLL*, IV.iii.167. One likely source for him and his 'years on
            earth', namely well over 200, is Ovid *Metamorphoses* XII, 169f.
            Perhaps the King is reminded of Nestor by the sight of Audley, who

is unflatteringly (and unhistorically) presented as the prototypical ancient warrior from line 1446 on.

1612   **epitaph** what posterity will say; posthumous reputation. This sense is not clearly defined in the *OED*; but cf. *Ham*, II.ii.526 'after your death . . . a bad epitaph'.

1615   **Exclaim no more** cf. *Oth*, II.iii.310 'exclaim no more'. The first recorded literary use of this sense 'cry out' (*OED* exclaim v. 1a) is *1H6*, IV.i.83; Shakespeare is also credited with coining sense 1b 'cry out [with quoted words]' (*1H6*, I.i.125) and 2a 'accuse' (*Luc*, 757).

1618–19   **falcon . . . haggard-like** a falcon dazed or distracted in its flight becomes wild and intractable; cf. Spurgeon 1935, 31: 'there is evidence of [Shakespeare's] personal experience' of falconry.

1622   **himself himself** cf. *Luc*, 157, 160 'himself himself'; see also lines 283–4, 566–7 and 704 above.

1622   **himself redeem from** the first recorded reflexive use of the verb in this sense of 'save' (*OED* 4a refl.) is *Tim*, IV.iii.500 and the first recorded construction with 'from' (*OED* 4b) is *Titus*, III.i.180. Shakespeare is also credited with the senses 'recover by payment' 2a fig. (*2H4*, II.iii.8) and the first recorded modern use of 3b 'ransom' (*1H4*, I.iii.86).

1623   **cheerful** adverb qualifying 'he'.

1629   **But soft** see line 538 above.

1630   **dismal** in a strong sense; if 'calamitous' (*OED* a. B3) the first recorded use is *Rom*, IV.iii,19, and if 'causing dismay' (*OED* a. B4; *OED* 4) the first is *Titus*, III.i.261 and the second *Mac*, V.v.12.

1630   **charge** summons.

1634   **shivered** splintered.

1640   **lords . . . you all . . . hearty thanks** cf. *EI*, 1023, 1027 'lords . . . hearty thanks to each of you', also immediately after a victory.

1640   **regreet** the first recorded use (*OED* v. 2a) is *R2*, I.iii.67.

1640–44   **regreet . . . fraught . . . port** cf. *Titus*, I.i.71–2, 75 'fraught . . . bay . . . resalute', with analogous word-coinage and victory metaphor of voyage and cargo; see also line 2431 below.

1643   **gulfs** whirlpools, as in *H5*, II.iv.10.

1643   **steely** resembling steel in hardness; this is the first recorded use (*OED* a. 2) and the second is *AWEW*, I.i.103.

1647   **first fruit** cf. *1H6*, V.iv.13 'first fruit'; on the *OED*'s own dating, both antedate the first recorded use (*OED* first-fruit 2), assigned to 1597.

1650   **whose thousands** Capell's ingenious emendation for the plainly erroneous 'Whom you sayd' in Q1. There are however other possibilities; thus the MS may have read 'when thousands'.

1651   **battered crest** the first recorded use of the epithet (*OED* ppl.a.) is *Ven*, 104 'battered shield and . . . crest [= helmet]'.

1652–3   **ponderous . . . marble** cf. *Ham*, I.iv.50 'ponderous and marble'.

1652   **glaives** heavy broadswords.

1653   **underprop** this is the first recorded use (*OED* v. 2 absol.).

1655   The axe is remembered from line 797 above.

1656   **a load of oaks** i.e. a great many; the first recorded use of this special
            sense (*OED* sb. load 6) is *Tro*, V.i.19. Shakespeare is also credited
            with sense 3a 'weight' (*2H6*, I.ii.2) and 4 fig. 'burden' (*2H6*,
            III.i.157).

1657   **recover** think of, recollect; this far antedates the first recorded
            use (*OED* v.[1] 8b). Shakespeare is also credited with sense 6d
            'get the wind of' (*Ham*, III.ii.346) and 9b 'restore' (*AWEW*,
            III.ii.20).

1660   **carved my passage forth** cf. *Mac*, I.ii.19 'carved out his passage'; for
            this idea of hewing a lane with a weapon through enemy troops see
            also *3H6*, I.iv.9 'make a lane', *EI*, 1666 'made a lane'.

1664   **knighthood** another invented ceremonial, like the bestowal of arms
            at 1498ff.

1666   **with blood of those that fought** cf. *EI*, 1657–8 'with blood/blood
            of myself and proudest Dane that fought'.

1670–4   **a note . . . foes . . . slain . . . princes . . . knights . . . common sol-
            diers** cf. *H5*, IV.viii.79–80, 89 'common men . . . note . . . French
            . . . slain . . . princes . . . barons . . . knights'. Both plays rely on
            their chronicle sources, here Froissart CXXXI.

1672–4   The 'note' seems to be in prose, which the Q1 compositor has
            unsuccessfully sought to versify.

1672   **of esteem** the first recorded use of this construction (not separately
            defined within *OED* sb. 4) is *1H6*, III.iv.8 and the second ibid.,
            V.v.27. Shakespeare is also credited with sense 2 'estimation' (*LLL*,
            III.i.4).

1676   **wantonness** see line 1478 above.

1677   **love-sick** the first recorded literary use is *Titus*, V.iii.82 and the
            second *Ant*, II.ii.194.

1677   **cockney** a spoilt child.

1677   **jades** again applied to soldiers, as in line 1484 above.

1682   **begirt** here (unlike line 135) the main verb, not a past participle; it
            antedates the first recorded use (*OED*).

1683   **upshot** a final shot in an archery contest.

1684   **wistly** silently, stealthily.

1684   **follow . . . the game's on foot** cf. *H5*, III.i.32–3 'the game's afoot:
            follow', also about a besieged haven town in France.

1684   **game** an image from deer-hunting.

1685–90   **What picture's this? A pelican . . . the motto** *sic et vos* another
            miniature masque, as in lines 1503ff. above, again evocative of *Per*,
            II.ii.17ff. 'who/what is [this]? . . . [description] . . . the [Latin]
            motto'. See also line 1941 below.

1686   **pelican** Lapides (1980) cites the punning pelican device of Sir John
            Pelham who captured John of France at Poitiers. But the prince's
            message here is surely more immediate and personal; his parent too
            should have been ready to shed blood for a child. John of Gaunt
            gratuitously alludes to Edward III and the Black Prince, and associ-
            ates them both with the wounded pelican in *R2*, II.i.124–7.

1691ff.   This Salisbury–Villiers episode and its later developments 1828ff.
            and 2140ff. are derived from the Froissart account (CXXXV) of the

agreement between Gualtier of Manny and a knight of Normandy, The introduction of a fictitious role for the Countess's husband is another unifying device.

1693ff. Note the striking contrast of style between this scene and its surroundings; simple plain speech is the apt medium here.

1695 I ... am ... possessed a usage unspecified in the *OED*, but cf. *1H6*, V.iv.138–9 'I am possessed/with more than half the Gallian territories'.

1695–6 possessed ... dukedom cf. *EI*, 286 'possess my dukedom'.

1699 in sign whereof cf. *1H6*, II.iv.58, *Shr*, I.ii.273.

1704 conquering the first recorded use (*OED* ppl.a.) is *1H6*, II.i.26; also in lines 1304 and 2072 below.

1708 that Capell's reading; both quartos have 'yet', which suggests a compositor's misreading of an author's abbreviation.

1717 and if thou wilt thyself if you agree.

1738–9 they refuse our proffered league ... ope their gates and 1747 it will repent them cf. *EI*, 887 'gates ... ope', 900 'you [will] repent it', 908 'refuse my proffered grace', *1H6*, IV.ii.5 'open your city-gates', 9 'frown upon this proffered peace'. See also lines 1345 above and 1811, 1991 below.

1742 accurséd detestable; the first recorded use (*OED* ppl. a.2) is *TGV*, V.iv.71.

1744 Enter six poor Frenchmen in Froissart CXXXIII there are 1,700 of them. Their dramatic treatment here recalls the 'poor Danes' episode in *EI*, 105–36.

1745 stand aloof this figurative usage (*OED* aloof adv. 5 fig.) is first recorded from *Ham*, V.ii.247, though *1H6*, V.ii.52 is earlier on the *OED*'s own dating.

1747 stubborn will cf. *EI*, 146–7 'stubborn ... wills'.

1752 gliding ghosts cf. *JC*, I.iii.63 'gliding ghosts'.

1754 breathe evince, display, far antedating the first recorded use (*OED* 12c).

1755 sleep of death cf. *Ham*, III.i.65 'sleep of death'.

1762 speed survive.

1765 proffered ... refused as in lines 1345 and 1738.

1772 lion scorns ... yielding prey recalling line 752; another link between the Countess scenes and the rest of the play.

1773 fresh refresh.

1777 here perhaps scanned as a disyllable; see Abbott 1869, 370f.

1779 this tidings singular, as in e.g. *R3*, IV.iii.22 'this tidings'; the usage is first recorded in modern English (*OED* 2b) from *JN*, IV.ii.115 'the tidings comes'.

1780 up in arms first cited from 1590 (*OED* up adv.[2] II 10b), but also in *EI*, 307.

1784–5 travail ... big with child word-play.

1786 subdued the first recorded use (*OED* ppl.a.1) is *Oth*, V.ii.348.

1789 Copeland (Q1 Copland) his story is found in Froissart CXXXIX.

1791 denies refuses, as Hotspur denied his prisoners, *1H4*, I.iii.29 and 77.

1796	**bring his prisoner king** preparing the unhistorical arrival of King David at Calais; see lines 2415 and 2599.
1803	**the burgesses of Calais** as in Froissart CXLVI.
1810–13	**refuse/our princely clemency . . . fire and sword** cf. *EI*, 907 'disdain your princely mercy', 878 'fire and sword', also at a siege.
1818	**prostrate . . . upon their knees** submissive, humbled; the first recorded use (*OED* prostrate a. 2) is *1H6*, I.ii.117.
1819	**afflicted** tortured.
1820	**masterships** applied ironically, as to servants in *TGV*, III.i.281 and *EI*, 1253.
1821	**a broken staff** perhaps a biblical echo, of e.g. Isaiah 14:5.
1825	**recall** the first recorded use in this sense (bring back a given state, etc., *OED* v. 4) is *2H6*, III.ii.61. Shakespeare is also credited with senses 1a 'call back, summon to return' (*TGV*, V.iv.155), 2a 'bring back from a given state' (*1H6*, I.i.65), 5b 'take back (a gift)' (*Per*, III.i.25); such examples constitute most of the verb's seven canonical occurrences.
1835	**advantage of** superiority over.
1838	**profit** the first recorded use (that which is to the advantage of someone, *OED* sb. 1b) is *MM*, I.iv.61 and the second *Oth*, III.iii.379; no others are cited. Onions (*Glossary*) confirms that this usage is 'only Shakespeare', who is also credited with sense 3 'progress, improvement' (*AYLI*, I.i.6).
1838	**commixed** this is the first recorded use (of things immaterial, *OED* v. 1b).
1839	**scandalous** grossly disgraceful; the first recorded use (*OED* a. 2) is *WT*, II.iii.121. See also lines 774 and 1492 above.
1841	**subscribe** sign, as in line 1875.
1848–9	**bird . . . escaped . . . beware** cf. *3H6*, V.vi.13–14 'bird . . . limed . . . misdoubteth'; both passages, like others cited by Spurgeon (1935, 27, 105) show the feeling for the trapped bird to which she finds no parallels outside Shakespeare. See also line 1600 above.
1849	**ensnared** the first recorded use (*OED* v. 1) is *R3*, I.iii.242 in the literal and *Luc*, 485 in the figurative sense; cf. also line 1912 below.
1850	**secure** over-confident.
1865	**quarrel** see line 173 above.
1867–9	**oath . . . infringe** cf. *LLL*, IV.iii.142 'infringe an oath'.
1869–70	**therefor./Therefore** a deliberate quibble.
1872	**honourable** upright, honest; the first recorded use of persons (*OED* a. 5a) is *JC*, III.ii.82 and of things (5b) is *Rom*, II.ii.143. Onions (*Glossary*) confirms that this meaning is 'not pre-Shakespeare'.
1872	**honourable mind** cf. *EI*, 634 'honourable minds', in the same (*OED* a. 5b) sense.
1876	**wheretofore** a coinage unknown to the *OED*, introduced here as an antithesis to 'hereafter'.
1896–1901	The stone-throwing is found in Holinshed's account of Poitiers, and the flight of birds in both his and Froissart's account of Crécy; but this prophecy seems to be a poetico-dramatic invention (as at lines 1277f.) here set out as a separate verse-stanza rhyming ababcc.
1897, 1904	**ray** array.

1909	**forage** ravage.
1910	**loss . . . less** deliberate word-play.
1911	**fancies** hallucinations, antedating the first recorded use (*OED* sb. 3).
1912	**ensnared** see line 1849 above.
1915–23	**death . . . clouds of [cannon] smoke . . . mouths . . . eyeless . . . all-ending night** components of the Shakespearean image-cluster described by Spurgeon 1935, 192; 'death, cannon, eye-ball, eye-socket of skull (a hollow thing), . . . mouth . . . and back to death again'.
1915	**the arms of death embrace us** cf. *EI*, 1450 'death hath seized him in his . . . arms'.
1918-21	**smoke . . . masking . . . sun** components of the 'blot' image-cluster.
1918-23	**smoke . . . burning sun . . . dark . . . night** cf. *JN*, V.iv.33–6 'night . . . black . . . smokes . . . burning . . . sun . . . night'.
1921	**twere** see line 75.
1922	**sullen** if this means 'dismal' the first recorded use (*OED* a. 3a) is *R2*, I.iii.265 and the second *Oth*, Q1, III.iv.51; if 'sombre' (*OED* a. 4), *1H4*, I.ii.212 is the second source cited. Shakespeare is also credited with *OED* a. 3b 'mournful in tone' (*Rom*, IV.v.88); cf. also *Sonn*, 71.2.
1923	**all-ending** the first recorded use (*OED* all E I 7) is *R3*, III.i.78. Shakespeare is also credited with the first substantive combination (E I 3) 'all-seer' and most adverbial combinations (E I 8), of which the first six are 'all-praised' (*1H4*, III.ii.140), 'all-watched' (*H5*, IV. Chorus 38), 'all-licensed' (*Lr*, I.iv.201), 'all-honoured' (*Ant*, II.vi.16), 'all-shunned' (*Tim*, IV.ii.14) and 'all-dreaded' (*Cym*, IV.ii.271), each unique in the canon.
1924	**expedient** expeditious, speedy; the first recorded use in modern English (*OED* a. A1) is *R2*, I.iv.39, the second *R3*, I.ii.216 and the third *JN*, II.i.60 ('his marches are expedient', in the same context as here). No further examples are given, and the usage is declared obsolete. Onions (*Glossary*) confirms 'a rare sense outside Shakespeare' and also classifies 'expedience' in the sense of 'speed' as 'only Shakespeare'.
1924	**head** advance. This antedates the first recorded use (*OED* sb.¹ 29); the second is *Ham*, IV.v.102. Shakespeare is also credited with sense 30 'a force raised' (first in *Titus*, IV.iv.63, next in *1H4*, I.iii.284), which is also implied here.
1928	**stronger-battled** more numerous. The *OED* offers no example of 'battled' in this sense, but cf. *Ant*, III.xiii.29 'high-battled Caesar', i.e. with great armies.
1929	**braving** defiant.
1930	**trimmed . . . up** decorated.
1931	**plate** precious metal objects, as in line 231 above.
1931	**the aspiring hill** cf. *Luc*, 548 'the aspiring mountains'.
1932	**quarry** here, in the context of 'shining plate', apparently *OED* sb.⁴ 'a candle(stick)'.
1932–3	**orb/aloft the which** in this context, perhaps 'the silver sphere of

imperial regalia, surmounted by a cross', although this sense (*OED* sb.¹ 11) is not recorded until the year 1702. The first recorded uses of 'orb' meaning 'sphere' in any sense (*OED* 8, 9a, 9b) are *LC*, 289, *MV*, V.i.60 and *TN*, III.i.38 respectively.

1933–5   **banners . . . cuff the air/and beat the winds** cf. *Mac*, I.ii.49 'banners flout the sky'.

1934   **new-replenished** unrecorded in the *OED*, which however notes (new adv. II 3, 4) that Shakespeare coined twenty compounds in 'new-'.

1934   **replenished** the first recorded use (*OED* ppl.a., described as 'rare') is *R3*, IV.iii.18 and the next *WT*, II.i.79; there is only one other canonical occurrence.

1934   **cuff** strike with the hand; the first recorded literary use (*OED* v.¹) is *1H6*, I.iii.48.

1935   **gaudiness** this antedates the first recorded use (*OED*).

1935–6   **the winds . . . kiss them** [banners] cf. *Ant*, II.ii.194 'winds . . . love-sick with them [sails]'.

1935–6   **winds . . . struggles** noun-verb discord.

1938   **coating** (Q1 coting) adorning.

1939   **gilded** i.e. by sunshine, as in lines 477 and 1036; the first recorded use (*OED* ppl.a.2) is *Ant*, I.iv.62.

1941   **device** heraldic emblem, perhaps in allusion to some actual coat of arms, like 'pelican' in line 1686 above.

1941–2   **heraldry/quartered** cf. line 1123 above 'quartered . . . herald's art'.

1942   **colours . . . sundry fruits** cf. lines 1115–16 'coloured . . . sundry flowers'.

1943   **Hesperides** where not only the tree's fruit but its leaves and branches were made of gold, according to a glancing reference in Ovid *Metamorphoses* IV, 637. The first recorded use in a transferred sense (*OED* 1b) is *Per*, I.i.27 'this fair Hesperides with golden fruit'. See also *LLL*, IV.iii.338 'climbing trees in the Hesperides'. All three contexts seem to incorporate the same misunderstanding; the name denotes the three daughters of Hesperus, not (*pace OED* 1c) a garden or location.

1945   **half-moon** cf. line 1119 above 'the hornéd circle of the moon'.

1947–8   **fatal crossbows . . . Chatillion** who recurs in line 1953. Why he is treated so prominently 'does not appear' (Armstrong 1965, 196). But the name no doubt derives from Holinshed (1587, 689 and 1692) where the 'master of the crossbows of France' is variously called Sir Guy, or Sir Hugh, de Chatellon. The form 'Chatillon' also appears in Holinshed. Shakespeare wrote 'Chatillion', as here, in *JN*, I.i.1 etc. and *H5*, III.v.43 etc.; that form is also preferred in *1TR*, 40 etc.

1949   **thus it stands** cf. *Shr*, I.i.179 'thus it stands', *EI*, 1403 'thus . . . it stands', introducing a summary of the situation.

1951   **royaliséd** rendered royal, i.e. by their princely presence; cf. *R3*, I.iii.124, the sole canonical use.

1952   **certain death** cf. *Cor*, III.i.287 'certain death', i.e. what will happen in the given circumstances.

1955	**parcelling** subdivision, introducing an antithesis between the general instance and its separate particulars. The first recorded use of 'parcelled' in any sense (*OED* addendum to 'parcel' v.¹) is *R3*, II.ii.81 'parcelled . . . general', with the same antithesis as here. Shakespeare is also credited with another more obscure sense (*OED* v.¹ 3) in *Ant*, V.ii.163.
1955	**power** army.
1956–8	These lines are here rearranged from Q1, where they stand in the order 1957, 1958, 1956.
1957–8	**sands . . . hands . . . handful . . . sands** the device of chiasmus is fully as contrived as the argument thus presented.
1957–61	**sands . . . sand by sand . . . number** see lines 486–7 above.
1964	**quarters** parts of an army. The first recorded use (*OED* sb. 14c) is *1H6*, II.i.63; this is the second. The third (and only other) example, Hakluyt 1599, is readily distinguishable. Shakespeare is also credited with the related sense 14d 'to keep good quarter' (*JN*, V.v.20) and perhaps also sense 8c 'fifteen minutes' (*Ado*, V.ii.83).
1968	**one self** one and the same, as in *TN*, I.i.38.
1971–2	**tells [= measures] . . . miles . . . steps** cf. *LLL*, V.ii.194–7; 'we measure . . . steps . . . miles . . . numbered in . . . one mile', with the same antithetical thought.
1972	**kills his heart** cf. *3H6*, II.v.87 'kills [my] heart'.
1978	**apprehend** fear; the first recorded use (*OED* v. 11) is *Tro*, III.ii.74. Shakespeare is also credited with senses 8c 'recognise' (*Ado*, II.i.81) and 10 'anticipate' (*MM*, IV.ii.142).
1979	**equality** the condition of being equal in power; the first recorded use (*OED* 2b) is *JN*, II.i.327, in the same context, 'armies, whose equality'. Cf. also *Ant*, I.iii.137, the only other canonical example.
1987	**his bloody colours** cf. *3H6*, II.ii.173 'our bloody colours'.
1989–90	**drink . . . blood . . . earth** cf. *3H6*, II.iii.15 'blood . . . earth . . . drunk' and Genesis 4:11 'earth . . . opened her mouth to receive . . . blood'; see also lines 2314–16 below.
1990	**our** *sic*; perhaps 'British' here means 'Brittany's'.
1991	**proffered mercy** cf. lines 1345, 1738 and 1765 above.
1992	**heaven . . . covers** arches over, a sense not clearly defined in the *OED*, but cf. *Cym*, V.v.350 'these covering heavens'.
1992	**the mercy** i.e. God's; mercy is a divine attribute in line 2392 also.
1993	**orisons** prayers.
1997	**tongue . . . steel . . . beg** a sword is seen as a long steel tongue skilled and active in pleading; cf. *Per*, II.v.64, 68 'sword . . . prove . . . tongue', *R2*, I.i.46 'tongue . . . sword . . .prove', *Titus*, II.i.35–6 'sword . . . approve . . . plead' and *EI*, 1830 'argue . . . sword . . . proof'; all five passages occur in contexts of challenge to single combat. See also lines 1422–3 above.
1998	**coward** this adjective far antedates its first recorded use (*OED* a. B1c).
1998	**burgonet** a light helmet; cf. the analogous threat in *2H6*, V.i.200 'and that I'll write upon thy burgonet'.
2001	**return** repay with something similar. The first recorded use (*OED*

v.¹ 21a) is *H5*, IV.vii.181; Onions (*Glossary*) says 'not recorded before Shakespeare', who is also credited with the cognate senses 18 'give back' (*Tim*, I.ii.6), 19a 'give answer' (*1H6*, II.v.20 and *TN*, I.i.24 – see also line 76 above), 19b 'say in answer' (*R2*, III.iii.121) and 20 'give thanks' (*1H6*, II.ii.51).

2001	**return him my defiance in his face** cf. *EI*, 719 'we do return defiance in thy face'; and see line 92 above.
2001	**defiance** with clear connotations of personal contempt and aversion. The first and only recorded use in that sense (*OED* sb. 5, described as 'obsolete' and 'rare') is *MM*, III.i.142; Onions (*Glossary*) specifies 'only Shakespeare'.
2002	**I go.** [**Exit**] as frequently in the canon, often with a message and on a separate line, e.g. *R3*, IV.iv.452.
2004–40	These episodes of the scornful gifts (horse, prayer-book) and defiant rejection run closely parallel to the Dauphin's bestowal of tennis-balls in *H5*, I.ii.254ff.
2007	**jennet** a small Spanish horse, as in *Ven*, 260 (the sole canonical occurrence).
2011	**beast** (a) horse (b) villain.
2015	**double gild** as in *2H4*, IV.v.128, the sole canonical occurrence. The first recorded use of 'gild' in this idiosyncratic sense of 'smeared with blood' (*OED* 1d) is *JN*, II.i.316 and the second *Mac*, II.ii.53; the other three are mere echoes of those examples. Shakespeare is also credited with senses 4a 'make golden, especially by the sun' (*Titus*, II.i.6), 5 fig. 'adorn' (*1H4*, V.iv.148), 6 'impart a flush' (*Tmp*, V.i.280) and 7 'conceal defects' (*2H4*, I.ii.149); and see lines 1036 and 1939 above.
2016	**capering** the first recorded use of the verb 'caper' (*OED* v.¹ 1a) is *LLL*, V.ii.113.
2020	**expired** (a) dead (b) out of date, as in *Rom*, I.iv.109–10 'expire the term of . . . life'; cf. also *Per*, III.iv.14 'till your date expire' and line 2365 below.
2025	**towards** in prospect, as in *Rom*, I.v.122.
2029	**unadviséd** thoughtless, as in *EI*, 695.
2030	**tendering** being solicitous about.
2032	**divine** priest, theologian.
2032	**extemporal** able to speak extempore; the second recorded use (*OED* a. 1b) is *LLL*, I.ii.183, and this (though published earlier) is the third.
2033	**commonplace** anthology, commonplace book.
2039	**courtly** in the bad sense of 'characterised by fair words or flattery' (*OED* a. 4), thus antedating the first recorded use in *Tim*, V.1.27.
2039	**wanton** spoilt child.
2040	**I go.** [**Exit**] as in line 2002 above.
2041	**confident** overbold, presumptuous; the first recorded use (*OED* a. 4) is *2H4*, II.i.111. See also line 255 above.
2041	**strength and number makes** noun-verb discord.
2042	**sound** try out.
2042	**those silver wings** i.e. the wise eloquence promised by your white

hairs; cf. *2H6*, V.ii.47 'the silver livery of adviséd age' and *Tro*, I.iii.65, where Nestor (with whom Audley is associated here, see line 1609 above) is linked with silver.

2043–4 **time . . . time's . . . time** (a) age (b) experience (c) moment.

2045 **bit** perhaps 'scarred'.

2046–7 **stratagems . . . iron pens . . . texted** printed, in large or capital letters, in one of the set formal hands used for legal documents. This (rather than Nashe 1599) should have been the first recorded use of the verb (*OED* v. 1 trans.); the second is *Ado*, V.i.183. Prince Edward echoes Audley's own language and imagery ('brazen pen . . . stratagems . . . print' in lines 1518–20 above); cf. also the King's earlier description of Audley ('face . . . time . . . engraved . . . characters' in lines 1448–9) and lines 2108 and 2303 below.

2048–9 **married man . . . blushing maid** cf. *EI*, 1153–4 'married men . . . blushing'.

2049 **blushing** the first recorded use (*OED* ppl.a.2) in any sense is *R2*, III.iii.63, though *1H6*, IV.i.93 may be earlier still. The present instance far antedates the example cited for the sense 'modest' (*OED* ppl.a.1).

2050 **an answer to** a defence against.

2051–66 Note the striking affinities between these sentiments and the Duke's more mature reflections on death in *MM*, III.i.11–13 and Claudio's rejoinder, 42–3.

2051 **to die is all as common as to live** cf. *Ham*, I.ii.72 ''tis common; all that lives must die'.

2052 **choice . . . chase** the word-play persists, even when the speaker is in deadly earnest.

2055 **bud . . . blow** cf. *TGV*, I.i.45–6 'bud . . . blow', also about the process of ageing; and see also line 2065.

2060 **follow it** Q1 has 'fear' yet again; but the pattern of thought surely requires the second half of the previous line to be repeated here as in lines 2058–9.

2063 **resolvéd proffer** deliberate action; the first recorded use of the epithet in this sense (*OED* ppl.a.3b) is *JN*, II.i.585.

2065 **ripe or rotten** cf. *AYLI*, II.vii.26–7 'ripe . . . ripe . . . rot . . . rot', III.ii.120 'rotten . . . ripe', again about ageing as in line 2055 above.

2066 **lottery** the first recorded figurative use (*OED* sb. 1b) is *MV*, I.ii.29, and the first of the sense 'something which comes to a person by lot or fortune' (*OED* sb. 3) is *Ant*, II.ii.242. Onions (*Glossary*) confirms the latter as 'Shakespeare only'.

2066 **lottery of our doom** cf. *MV*, II.i.15 'lottery of my destiny'.

2066 **our doom** our last day; the first recorded uses of this sense (*OED* sb. 7b) are *Titus*, II.iii.42, *R2*, III.ii.189, and *3H6*, V.vi.93.

2067–8 **armours . . . buckled on my back** cf. *R3*, III.vii.228 'buckle . . . on my back', V.iii.211 'buckle . . . armour', and for the figurative usage *JN*, II.i.564 'whose armour conscience buckled on'.

2069 **idiot . . . life** cf. *Mac*, V.v.24, 27 'life . . . idiot', *1H4*, V.iv.81 'life, time's fool'.

2072 **conquering** see line 1304 above.

2075   **grim death** the first recorded use 'of things personified, especially of death' (*OED* grim a. 4b) is *Err*, V.i.80 'grim . . . despair' and the second *Shr*, Ind.I.35 'grim death'. See also line 2301 below.

2076–7   **live . . . die . . . dying . . . life** chiastic antithesis.

2078   **he that rules it** i.e. Death.

2079   **indifferent** not mattering either way, as in *JC*, I.iii.115.

2082   **winds . . . their caves** cf. *2H6*, III.ii.88–9 'gusts . . . their caves'; the shared source may well be Ovid *Metamorphoses* I,262 'Aquilonem claudit in antris'. Jove imprisons the north wind in the caves of Aeolus, lord of the winds, who is named in the *2H6* passage loc.cit. 92.

2083   **hushed** this antedates the first recorded use (*OED* ppl.a.).

2085   **wonted** accustomed.

2093   **sleep . . . waking** antithesis combined with word-play; 'sleep' also means 'remain unsaid'.

2094   **But now** only a moment ago.

2094–5   **sun . . . looked . . . his golden coach** recalling the chariot of Phoebus, described in Ovid *Metamorphoses* II,107f.: 'aureus axis erat, temo aureus, aurea summa', etc., with golden axle, pole and wheels; cf. also *Titus*, II.i.5, 7–8 'golden sun . . . in his glistering coach . . . overlooks'.

2097   **[sun] . . . the under earth** cf. *Lr*, II.ii.162–3 'sun . . . this under globe'.

2098   **uncomfortable** disquieting; the first recorded use (*OED* a. 1) is *Rom*, IV.v.60, the sole canonical occurrence.

2101   **dismayed** appalled.

2102   **presage** see lines 330 and 1533 above.

2103–4   **flight** (a) flock (b) rout.

2108   **ghastly** 'frightfully . . . with a deathlike look' (*OED* adv. 1); the first recorded use is *2H6*, III.ii.170.

2108   **printed** cf. lines 1448–9, 1518–20, 2046–7 above and 2303 below.

2110–11   **flight of . . . ravens . . . o'er our . . . heads** cf. *JC*, V.i.84–5 'ravens . . . fly o'er our heads'.

2110   **ravens** huge flocks of crows were seen flying over both armies before the battle of Crécy, according to Froissart CXXX; here they serve to fulfil the dramatist's invented prophecy, line 1896.

2115   **the airy flower of heaven** i.e. the sun.

2119   **metamorphosed** this antedates the first recorded use (*OED* ppl.a.). It points to Ovid *Metamorphoses* (V. 180f.) as the source of these ideas, especially the warriors turned to stone by the Gorgon's head; cf. lines 1524f above.

2119–20   **like . . . images . . . pale, one gazing on another** cf. *R3*, III.vii.25–6 'like statues . . . stared on each other . . . pale'.

2119–20   **images . . . bloodless . . . gazing** cf. lines 1525–6 above 'gazing . . . senseless . . . images'.

2120   **bloodless** pale from diminished blood supply; the first recorded use (*OED* a. 1b) is *Ven*, 891 and the second is *2H6*, III.ii.162. Shakespeare is also credited with sense 2 'not attended with bloodshed' (*TN*, II.v.106).

2120	**bloodless and pale** (with 'meagre' in the corresponding passage at line 1526) cf. *2H6*, loc.cit. 'meagre, pale and bloodless'.
2121	**prophecy** i.e. lines 1896–1901. King John's explanation of the ravens characterises him (and his creator) as uncommonly astute.
2125	**a famished few** presumably missing their 'chines of beef' as in line 1481; cf. *1H6*, I.ii.7 'the famished English'. See also line 2251.
2128–30	**horse . . . [ravens] . . . sit watching** cf. *JN*, IV.iii.152–3 'waits/as doth a raven on a sick-fall'n beast'.
2129–31	**ravenous . . . ravens** another black pun.
2132	**marked to die** cf. *H5*, IV.iii.20 'marked to die' (also in a coming battle) and *Titus*, I.i.125 'marked [to] die'.
2143	**encompassed** surrounded.
2146	**disgrace** disfigure.
2153	**current** valid.
2158	**dash** destroy.
2158	**seal at arms** the impression of a signet ring engraved with heraldic bearings.
2159	**never-broken** this coinage is not recorded in the *OED*.
2159	**name** attestation by signature.
2160	**charactered** see line 663 above.
2162	**stable verdict** firm decision.
2164ff.	yet another dissertation on oath-taking and -breaking. The French king's clever arguments are in character; see line 2121.
2170	**to the utmost of** this is the first recorded use (*OED* utmost II sb. 7b). Shakespeare is also credited with sense II sb. 4 'the end, finish' (*MM*, II.1.36).
2171–3	**breach of faith . . . consent . . . consent . . . breach of faith** elaborate chiasmus.
2193	**pack** be off.
2198	**topless** having no summit; this is the first recorded use (*OED* a. 1). Shakespeare is also credited with sense 2b 'supreme, paramount' (*Tro*, I.iii.152, the only canonical occurrence).
2199	**azure** the first recorded use in modern English (*OED* B adj. 2a) is *Luc*, 419.
2204	**hooped . . . bond** cf. *2H4*, IV.iv.43 'hoop . . . bind'; and see p. 176 below.
2210	**bullets** cannon balls.
2214	**breath** opportunity for breathing. The first recorded use (*OED* sb. 8a) is *R3*, IV.ii.24 and the second *Tro*, II.iii.112. Shakespeare is also credited with sense 3c transf. 'the wind blown into a musical instrument' (*Mac*, V.vi.9), 3d fig. 'type of things insubstantial' (first *Luc*, 212 and then *MM*, III.i.8) and 7a 'power of breathing' (first *Err*, IV.i.57 and then *Ham*, V.ii.271).
2215	**breathe** take a rest; this precise sense (*OED* v. 5) is not clearly inferable from *JN*, IV.iii.137 as given in the *OED* (v. 5), but cf. *1H4*, V.iv.47 'breathe a while' and *EI*, 1978, 1985 'breathe awhile', also in between bouts of fighting. Shakespeare is credited with the coinage of seven new meanings of the verb (4b, 7, 8, 9, 10c, 11, 12a) as detailed at line 1535 above.

2216	**distract** distraught.
2220	**Courage** take heart; the first recorded use of this exclamation (*OED* sb. 4e) is *MV*, IV.i.111.
2221	**bandy** fight; the first recorded use (*OED* v. II 8 intrans.) is *Titus*, I.i.312. Shakespeare is also credited with sense 6c 'exchange one thing for another' (*3H6*, I.iv.49).
2223	**railing** scolding.
2223	**outscold** the first recorded use (*OED* v.) is *JN*, V.ii.160, the only canonical occurrence.
2225	**fire-containing** this compound is not recorded in the *OED* (fire sb. B comb. 2); it may well be the first as well as the only example.
2225	**bows** bowmen.
2226	**pretty-coloured** also unrecorded (*OED* pretty a. D comb.).
2227	**hurl away [bows] . . . and to it with stones** for the next stage cf. *1H6*, III.i.89–90 'nay, if we be forbidden stones we'll fall to it with our teeth'.
2228	**my soul doth prophesy** cf. *Ham*, I.v.40 'my prophetic soul'.
2230	**multitudes** hosts, i.e. armies, as in line 1359 above; the first recorded use of this plural sense (*OED* 2b) is *1H4*, III.ii.143; cf. also *EI*, 1333 'multitudes of Danes'.
2231	**distraught** mad with fear; the first recorded use (*OED* ppl. a. 2) is *Rom*, IV.iii.49 and the second *R3*, III.v.4; cf. also *EI*, 1052, which as here is about the trauma of battle.
2231	**Swift-starting** this is the first recorded use (*OED* swift a. C3).
2231–6	**fear . . . buzzed . . . fear . . . prophecy** cf. *3H6*, V.vi.86–8 'buzz . . . prophecies . . . fearful . . . fear'.
2233	**disadvantage** the first recorded literary use (*OED* sb. 1) is *2H4*, II.iii.36 and the second is *Cor*, I.vi.49 (the only two canonical occurrences); cf. also *EI*, 69. All four usages refer to warfare.
2234	**fear-possesséd** unrecorded in the *OED* (sb.¹ 6 comb. a); this is the fourth otherwise unknown compound word in ten lines.
2238	**attainted** infected.
2242	**let drive at** aim blows at, attack, as in *1H4*, II.iv.196.
2244	**retire** retreat.
2245–8	**fear . . . confusion . . . shame** (caused by a rout) cf. *2H6*, V.ii.31–2 'shame . . . . confusion . . . rout . . . fear'.
2248	**Pluck out your eyes** in allusion to Matthew 18:9 'if thine eye offend thee, pluck it out'.
2249	**arm** a species of weapon, i.e. the flint-stone, far antedating *OED* sb.² 2b.
2249	**arm . . . army** again the word-play is in grim earnest.
2249–50	**David . . . with a stone . . . Goliahs** in allusion to 1 Samuel 17.
2250	**foiled** defeated.
2250	**Goliahs** the first recorded use (a giant, *OED* Goliath 1) is *1H6*, I.ii.33, in the form 'Goliasses'; cf. also *EI*, 1953 'Golias'. All three contexts illustrate contrasting opponents in combat. The form 'Goliah', as here, occurs in *MWW*, V.i.22.
2251	**naked starvelings** again the motif of the famished English, as in lines 1481 and 2125; cf. also *1H6*, I.ii.35 'lean raw-boned rascals' as the French élite call the English soldiers.

2252	**a puissant host** cf. *3H6*, II.i.207 'a puissant host'.
2253	**accomplements** first recorded (*OED*) from Fleming's 1587 continuation of Holinshed 1579, where the dramatist may well have found it. There it seems to connote 'accomplishments', here 'accoutrements'; both are subsumed in the vague *OED* definition 'anything that completes' for which the present example figures as the first recorded use, described as '*Edward III* (?Shakespeare)', an attribution omitted from later citations.
2254	*Mortdieu!* the first recorded use of this strong oath (*OED* int.) is Marlowe, *The Massacre at Paris* 1593, though on the *OED*'s own dating *2H6*, I.i.123 had at least an equal claim to priority.
2254	**quait** so in Q1; a form (*OED* dial. var.) of 'quoit', i.e. throw missiles at; the first recorded use of the transitive verb (*OED* v. 2) is *2H4*, II.iv.192 'quoit him down'.
2255	**wicked elders** a reference to the story of Susanna and the elders in the Apocryphal book 'The History of Susanna' also obliquely alluded to in *MV*, IV.i.223 'a Daniel'.
2259	**blurt . . . at** make a contemptuous puffing noise with the lips. This is the first recorded use (*OED* v. intrans. 2a); the second is *Per*, IV.ii.34 'blurted at', the only other construction with 'at' and the sole canonical occurrence.
2261	**bury up** the first recorded use of 'bury' ('up' has been added merely to help the metre) in this sense of 'consign to oblivion' (*OED* v. 2b) is *3H6*, IV.i.55 and the second is *JC*, IV.iii.159 'bury unkindness', as also in *EI*, 604 and 1725. Onions (*Glossary*) confirms 'not pre-Shakespeare'.
2262	**Make up** unite our remaining forces; the transitive sense (collect a company) is first recorded (*OED* v.¹ make up 96f (e)) from *2H6*, II.i.39. Shakespeare is also credited with the related senses 96h (b) 'form the components of' (first *Rom*, V.i.48, then *3H6*, I.iv.25), 96k (a) 'make up one's mind' (first *JN*, II.i.541 then *Tro*, II.ii.170), 96k (b) 'come to a decision' (*Lr*, I.i.206), 96n (a) 'draw near to' (first *JN*, III.ii.5, next the present example, although this latter surely means 'unite' intransitively, as stated above).
2263	**quail** overcome.
2264	**adverse part** the enemy, as in *R3*, V.iii.13 'adverse party'.
2269	**How fares my lord?** cf. *2H6*, III.ii.33 and III.iii.1 'how fares my lord?', also spoken solicitously to an apparently dying man, the latter instance also at the beginning of a scene.
2271	**bloody feast** cf. *Titus*, V.ii.203 'bloody . . . feast', there with explicit and here with implicit reference to the bloody battle at the marriage feast to which the Lapithae invited the Centaurs, as described in Ovid *Metamorphoses* XII, 210ff. The tale is there told by the ancient hero Nestor, the role-model for Audley; see lines 1609 and 2042.
2272, 2278	**scar** fresh wound, a sense unknown to the *OED* (sb. 2); but cf. *2H6*, I.i.87 'received deep scars', i.e. in battle, and *EI*, 1712 and 1714, where the context entails recent wounding. See also line 116 above and 2579 below.
2273	**the count is cast** the reckoning is complete, an image from bookkeeping.

2276   **crimson . . . blood** the adjective's reference to blood is first recorded (*OED* a. 2) from the year 1681, which also overlooks e.g. *2H6*, III.ii.200, *Rom*, V.iii.95 and *Luc*, 1738.

2276   **bravery** (a) finery (b) courage.

2277   **become** grace, pay homage to; see line 752 above.

2284   **captive** as in Froissart CLXIV.

2285   **high-vaunting** yet another compound unknown to the *OED* (a. III 10a); but cf. the analogous 'high-reaching' of which the first recorded use (*OED* high-reaching) is *R3*, IV.ii.31, and also *2H6*, III.i.50 'high vaunts'.

2289   **early** young; this far antedates the first recorded use (*OED* a. 3a).

2295   **counsel-giver** a compound (*OED* counsel 9 comb.) found in the Coverdale Bible (2 Chronicles 22:4); the first recorded use of 'counsel-keeper' is *2H4*, II.iv.267 and of 'counsel-keeping' *Titus*, II.iii.24.

2298   **the proverb verified** cf. *3H6*, I.iv.126 'the adage . . . verified', *2H6*, III.i.170 'the proverb . . . effected', *EI*, 1634 'the proverb is' etc., in each instance introducing and quoting the relevant proverb in question. See also line 750.

2299   **'too bright a morning breeds a lowring day'** the 'proverb' itself adapts weather lore to warfare; cf. the converse claim in *EI*, 1059 'a louring morning proves a fairer day'.

2301   **grim discouragement** a quasi-personification; see line 2075 above.

2303   **writ . . . face** Audley's face is still an open book, as in lines 1449, 2047 and 2108.

2303   **note** record, account.

2304   **wooest death** cf. *JN*, III.iv.35 'buss [death] as my wife', *H5*, IV.vi.26 'espoused to death'.

2309   **bemoaning** this far antedates the first recorded use (*OED* ppl.a.).

2311   **tongue ring** cf. *JN*, III.iii.36–7 'bell . . . tongue', etc.

2311   **ring out thy end** the first recorded use (*OED* ring v.[1] 10a fig.) is *1H6*, IV.ii.41 'ring thy dire departure out'; cf. also *EI*, 728.

2312   **my arms . . . the grave** cf. *EI*, 1506–7 'my lap . . . your sepulchres and your graves', *3H6*, II.iv.115 'my heart . . . thy sepulchre'.

2314–16   **drink . . . blood . . . blood . . . drink** this notion (cf. line 1989 above) is now rearranged in the equally characteristic chiastic pattern.

2314, 2321   **captive kings . . . kings' captivity** the chiastic pattern itself is also ingrained.

2315   **restorative** medicinal, therapeutic.

2316   **a health** the first recorded use (*OED* sb. 6) is *Shr*, III.ii.170 'a health'; cf. also *EI*, 416. Onions (*Glossary*) confirms the Shakespearean origin.

2317   **dispense with** come to some arrangement with, a legal expression; cf. *2H6*, V.i.181 'canst thou dispense with heaven for such an oath?' The verb occurs only twelve times in the canon, and always in this same 'with' construction, as Onions (*Glossary*) points out.

2318   **never-dying honour** the first recorded (and sole canonical) use of the compound epithet (*OED* never-dying) is *1H4*, III.ii.106 'never-dying honour'.

2321   **a Caesar's fame in kings' captivity** the fifth allusion to Julius, in a variety of contexts. He was famed for his capture of Vercingetorix, king of Gaul, 'a prisoner reserved for the triumph', as Plutarch describes him.

2322   **hold ... at a bay** a deer-hunting image, as in *Shr*, V.ii.56 'hold ... at a bay'.

2322   **dim death** cf. *Luc*, 403 'death's dim look'.

2324   **soul ... castle** cf. the Countess's imagery 'palace ... soul ... bower ... court ... abbey' at lines 592–4 above.

2324–9   **soul ... yield this castle of my flesh ... worms ... soul ... city ... earthly** cf. *Sonn*, 146.1–2, 4, 6–7 'soul ... earth ... rebel powers ... walls ... mansion ... worms', *R2*, III.ii.167, 170 '[death] flesh ... walls ... castle wall' with the same siege imagery.

2326   **consummation** death; the first recorded use (*OED* sb. 2, as distinct though not distinguished from vaguer fifteenth-century applications) is *Cym*, IV.ii.280. Shakespeare is also credited with sense 4 'crowning or fitting end' (*Ham*, III.i.62).

2327   **Cheerly** as an expression of 'encouragement among sailors' (*OED* adv. B1b) the first recorded use is *Tmp*, I.i.5; but this overlooks the same expression (though among soldiers) in *1H4*, V.iv.44 and *H5*, II.ii.192 (there linked by 'cheerly to sea').

2327–9   So in Q1, but the syntax is unclear. Perhaps a line has been omitted.

2329–30   **divorcéd ... [i.e. of soul from body] by ... sword** cf. *H8*, II.i.76 'divorce of steel' (i.e. of soul from body, by axe).

2338   **bequeath** bequest.

2344   **easy** comfortable.

2344   **litter** as in Froissart CLXIV.

2344–5   **march ... towards Calais with triumphant pace** cf. *3H6*, II.vi.87 'now to London with triumphant march'.

2349   The story of the burghers of Calais is found in Froissart CXLVI.

2351   **pacify yourself** this reflexive form is unrecorded in the *OED* (v. pacify), but cf. *2H4*, II.iv.80 'pacify yourself', the sole canonical occurrence, and *EI*, 133 'pacify yourselves'.

2353   **written in our looks** continuing the running image noted at line 2303 above; cf. *MM*, IV.ii.153 'written in your brow'.

2354   **this ... resisting town** cf. *JN*, II.i.38 'this resisting town', the only canonical use of that epithet.

2359   **Contemptuous** the first recorded use (*OED*) is *JN*, II.1.384, in the same siege context as here, 'contemptuous city'.

2360   **ears are stopped ... bootless cries** cf. *Sonn*, 29.3 'deaf ... bootless cries'.

2361   **threatening swords** cf. *Tim*, V.i.166 'threatening sword', also to menace a city.

2365   **expired** the first recorded use (*OED* ppl.a.2) is far antedated by *Luc*, 26 'expired date', in the same legal sense as here.

2367   **torturing death** cf. *Titus*, II.iii.285 'torturing pain', i.e. a death sentence. Both contexts far antedate the first recorded use of the

epithet (*OED* ppl.a.); cf. also *EI*, 1276 'torturing pain' in the same
sense. The verb 'torture' in its two main meanings (*OED* 1 and 2)
is also credited as a Shakespeare coinage in *2H6*, III.i.376 and *LLL*,
V.ii.60; so is the noun 'torturer' (*R2*, III.ii.198).

2372   **servile** low-class; the first recorded literary use in this sense (*OED* a.
2b) is *Titus*, V.ii.55. Shakespeare is also credited with sense 3
'cringing' (*Lr*, III.ii.21).

2373   **felonious robbers** cf. *2H6*, III.i.129 'felonious thief', the only
canonical occurrence of that epithet.

2375   **albeit severity lay dead** even if I were disposed to be merciful.

2376   **overreach** outwit, cheat; the first recorded use in that bad sense
(*OED* v. 6b) is dated 1596, although such connotations are surely
implicit in e.g. *Titus*, V.ii.143.

2377–81   A hyperbolic confirmation of the citizens' wealth and importance.

2378   **low-brought** unknown to the *OED* (low adv. 5 comb. a or a. 22);
the first recorded use of such a compound with 'low-' (*OED* a. 22)
is *Cym*, V.iv.103 'low-laid'.

2386   **your bodies shall be dragged** (i.e. by horses) cf. *2H6*, IV.iii.12 'the
bodies shall be dragged at my horse heels'.

2387   **quartering steel** the first recorded (and sole canonical) use of the
epithet (*OED* ppl.a.) is *1H6*, IV.ii.11 'quartering steel', also at a
siege in France.

2390   **stablish peace** the first recorded (and sole canonical) use (*OED*
stablish v. 4) is *1H6*, V.i.10 'stablish quietness', also about peace in
France.

2391–2   **kings approach the nearest unto God/by** (showing mercy); cf. *MV*,
IV.i.196–7 'earthly power doth then show likest God's/when mercy
seasons justice' and *Titus*, I.i.117–18 'wilt thou draw near the
nature of the gods?/draw near them then in being merciful'.

2399   **abuses** injuries, wrongs; the first recorded use (*OED* sb. 5) is *3H6*,
III.iii.188 and the second is *MWW*, V.iii.7.

2400   **insomuch** as in line 1380 above: the first recorded (and sole
canonical) use of this construction (*OED* adv. 4 with ellipsis of 'as')
is *AYLI*, V.ii.55.

2402   **other** plural, as in lines 1183 and 1198.

2402   **dint of sword** as in *2H4*, IV.i.126, the only canonical occurrence.

2406   **Two** so in Q1, but this line should surely be chorused by all the
citizens.

2411   **gloomy** see lines 1203–4 above.

2411   **o'erspent** over, past; this usage is overlooked by the *OED* (over-
spend, v.).

2415   **David, King of Scots** the playwright's mind has been dwelling on
captive kings in lines 2314 and 2321; but he had no authority in
historical fact for bringing King David to France from captivity
in England. The reason for doing so in this play was however
known to Shakespeare, although it is far from self-evident; he
explains it in *H5*, I.ii.162 thus: 'to fill King Edward's fame with
prisoner kings'.

2416   **proud presumptuous** cf. *3H6*, I.i.157 'presumptuous and proud'.

2416	**esquire** country gentleman, squire; the first recorded use (*OED* sb. 2b) is *2H4*, III.ii.57, which overlooks *2H6*, IV.x.43 and V.i.75; see also line 2446 below.
2423	**wilful disobedience** cf. *1H6*, IV.i.142 'wilful disobedience'; the noun occurs only eight times in the canon.
2425	**single fight** the first recorded use of the epithet in this context (*OED* a. 15) is dated 1592, which on the *OED*'s own chronology overlooks *1H6*, I.ii.95 and *2H6*, I.iii.208 'single combat' and *3H6*, IV.vii.75 'single fight', as also in *EI*, 1910.
2427	**pre-eminence** real distinction, as in *Err*, II.i.23; the only other canonical occurrence is *Lr*, I.i.131.
2430	**vail** doff, as a mark of respect.
2430	**bonnet of ... victory** for the symbolism of headgear cf. *3H6*, V.iii.2, *Per*, II.iii.10, *JC*, V.iii.82 'wreath(s) ... of ... victory' and line 2549 below 'wreath of conquest'; the homelier bonnet better befits the lowlier squire.
2431	**custom** due tribute.
2431	**fraught** with the same metaphor and humble duty as in lines 1640–4 above and *Titus*, I.i.70–1; the noun occurs only thrice in the canon.
2441	**I like his words** the King continues to be characterised as emotional and impressionable; the Queen's objection at lines 2435–6 is unanswerable.
2443	**ensues** results from.
2444	**all rivers ... sea** recalls Ecclesiastes 1:7 'all rivers run into the sea'.
2445	**faith ... king** is drawn to the sovereign, like a river to the sea.
2446–8	**[esquire] Kneel ... down ... rise ... knight ... maintain ... freely give ... marks** cf. *Cont* (the early version of *2H6*) 2106–11 'kneel down ... esquire ... rise ... knight ... maintenance ... freely give ... marks'. See also line 2416 above.
2459	**sing** speak solemnly; this usage, unrecorded in the *OED*, antedates its nearest approximation (v.[1] 12 c). Shakespeare is also credited with the related sense 13b 'force with singing' (*Oth*, IV.i.189).
2459	**accidents** events.
2462	**my worthless self** cf. *MV*, II.ix.18 'my worthless self'. The first recorded use of the epithet as applied to persons (*OED* 2) is *1H6*, V.v.53; see also line 1398. Shakespeare is also credited with sense 1, of things (*Titus*, V.iii.117).
2464	**safe conduct** as in *H5*, I.ii.297 and *Tro*, III.iii.276 and 287, the only three canonical occurrences of the phrase.
2475	**cut his thread of life** like the Fate Atropos, in classical mythology; cf. *1H6*, I.i.34 'his thread of life', *2H6*, IV.ii.29 'their thread of life', *H5*, III.vi.47 'vital thread cut'.
2477	**quittance** requite.
2479	**diffused** confused.
2487	**barricado's open front** cf. *TN*, IV.ii.37 'transparent as barricadoes' (one of only two canonical occurrences). These usages clearly correspond; yet neither is readily identifiable as the *OED*'s 'hastily-erected barrier' (sb. 1); both seem rather to employ the same

forgotten technical term of warfare, which perhaps also appears as *OED* sb. 2 'any barrier' (*WT*, I.ii.204).

2488   **thick embossed** bulging, bristling; perhaps a compound word, though not cited as such in the *OED* (thick adv. 7).

2488   **ordinance** ordnance. cannon.

2489   **battle** army.

2490   **in quadrant wise** in a square.

2491   **deadly-wounding** the *OED* records no such present-participial compound (deadly a.9 comb. or adv.); but cf. *Titus*, II.iii.32 'deadly-standing'. The first recorded use of any compound in 'deadly-' is *2H6*, V.ii.9 'deadly-handed', also about the use of a weapon; those two are the only canonical occurrences.

2492   **point** perhaps the needle-point of a mariner's compass.

2493   **horizon** also stressed on the first and last syllables in *3H6*, IV.vii.81, the only canonical occurrence.

2494   **twere** see line 75 above.

2494   **rising bubble in the sea** the context suggests the meaning 'water-spout'.

2495   **wand** sapling.

2495   **wood of pines** cf. *EI*, 1341 'wood of pines', in the same context of battle-forces; the imagery here continues from line 231 above 'wood of pikes', 1113 'grove of . . . pines' and 1939–40 'pikes . . . trees'.

2496–8   **fast-chained . . . fasten** again, serious word-play. The compound is not recorded in the *OED* (fast adv. 8 comb.).

2496, 2498   **bear . . . chained unto a stake . . . dogs** cf. *2H6*, V.i.203 'bear chained to the staff', *3H6*, II.i.15 'as a bear, encompassed round with dogs', *Mac*, V.vii.1–2 'tied . . . stake . . . bear-like', *JC*, IV.i.48–9 'stake . . . bayed about', *Lr*, V.ii.54 'tied . . . stake'.

2499   **death-procuring** yet another coined compound unrecorded in the *OED* (death sb. 18b).

2502   **clangour** the first recorded use (*OED* sb.) is *3H6*, II.iii.18, the only canonical occurrence, where the 'dismal clangour' surely refers to the sound of the trumpets as here. Onions (*Glossary*) confirms 'not pre-Shakespeare'.

2505   **intricate** entangled; the only canonical occurrence is *Err*, V.i.270.

2506–7   **sighs . . . black . . . smoke** for the idea that sighs darken the atmosphere cf. *Titus*, III.i.211–12 'our sighs . . . stain the sun with fog', *EI*, 1503–4 'sighs . . . cast a misty fog upon the air', *Rom*, I.i.133 'adding . . . clouds with . . .. sighs'.

2507   **powder** gunpowder.

2507   **[cannon] . . . fuming . . . smoke** the first recorded use of the verb in this sense (*OED* fume v. 3) is *Luc*, 1043, 'as smoke which from dischargéd cannon fumes', also in a context of sighs, tears and death. Shakespeare is also credited with the related sense 5 'be clouded' (*Ant*, II.i.24)

2518   **sharp . . . revenge** cf. *Titus*, I.i.137 'sharp revenge'; also in line 1346 above.

2518	**unheard-of . . . revenge** cf. *EI*, 709–10 'vengeance . . . unheard' and *Titus*, II.iii.285, *EI*, 1276 'never-heard-of' (describing revenge).
2521	**weep out bloody tears** shed drops of blood.
2522	**empty veins . . . dry** cf. *1H4*, I.iii.133–4 'empty . . . veins . . . blood . . . drop by drop', *R3*, I.ii.59 'empty veins . . . no blood', *EI*, 131 'veins . . . shed . . . drop by drop'.
2523	**hearse** a metal or wooden framework for memorial candles.
2523	**their** Q1 has 'his'.
2524	**city** the first such adjectival use (*OED* II 7 attrib.) in any phrase other than the fourteenth-century 'city town' is *Cor*, I.x.31 and the second *Tim*, III.vi.67.
2537	**in captive bonds** cf. *JC*, I.i.34 'in captive bonds', with the same transferred epithet in the same context of being led prisoner in a triumph; see also line 1486.
2543–4	**lost . . . found . . . son rejoice** the antithesis is embellished by biblical allusion to Luke 15:6, 'Rejoice . . . found . . . lost' (cf. also *EI*, 371 'lost . . . rejoice . . . find) and the following parable of the prodigal son, Luke 15:23–4 'be merry . . . son . . . lost'.
2549	**wreath of conquest** see line 2430 above.
2558–9	**had . . . had** subjunctive mood in a final speech of formal lamentation, as in *3H6*, V.vi.35–6 'hadst . . . hadst', *EI*, 1922–3 'had . . . had', etc.
2559	**civil** if this means 'consisting of citizens dwelling together in a community', the first recorded use (*OED* a. A I 1) is *Rom*, Prol.4. Shakespeare is also credited with the sense 7 'well-governed' (first *TGV*, V.iv.156, then *H5*, I.ii.199).
2570	**of this I was foretold** namely in lines 1900–1.
2577	**that little isle** England, as distinct from Scotland and Wales; cf. *EI*, 1897 'this little isle', *R2*, II.i.45 'this little world'.
2579	**bloody scars** see lines 116, 2272, 2278.
2580–3	**weary nights that I have watched in field . . . cold** themes of campaigning; cf. *EI*, 414 'weary watchful night', *TGV*, I.i.31 'watchful weary . . . nights', *H5*, IV.Prol.38 'weary and all-watched night', *3H6*, V.vii.17 'in our armours watched the winter's night', *Titus*, III.i.5 'the frosty nights that I have watched', etc. A common canonical contrast is the idea of sleeping secure; cf. line 1413 above 'securely slept' and *EI*, 309 'securely sleeps'.
2585	**hereafter ages** the first recorded use of the adjectival sense (*OED* hereafter B, as adj.) is *1H6*, II.ii.10 'hereafter ages; cf. *R3*, IV.iv.390 'hereafter time', which is the only other such canonical usage; cf. also *EI*, 766 'after age', i.e. posterity.
2587	**resolve** if this means firmness of purpose, the first recorded use (*OED* sb. 2) is *1H6*, V.v.75; if determination or resolution (*OED* sb. 1) then *Rom*, IV.i.123.
2589	**Spain, Turkey** no doubt topical (and hence anachronistic) references.
2591	**retire** retreat, as in line 1562.
2593	**intercession** intermission.

2594   **Sheathe up . . . swords, refresh . . . wearied limbs** cf. *EI*, 1864 'sheathe up . . . sword', 2015 'refreshing . . . wearied limbs', at the conclusion of hostilities and of the play, respectively.

2595   **peruse** inspect, review.

2599   **three kings** namely of England, France and (unhistorically, see lines 1796 and 2415) Scotland.

V

Early Commentary, up to 1760

England first emerged as a world power in Tudor times. Concomitantly, the patriotic note of past conquests was sounded in Tudor drama, an entirely new and immensely popular art-form. As Thomas Nashe wrote in *Pierce Penniless*, 1592: 'How would it haue ioyed braue *Talbot* (the terror of the French) to thinke that after he had lyne two hundred yeares in his Tombe, hee should triumphe againe on the Stage and haue his bones newe embalmed with the teares of ten thousand spectators at least (at seuerall times), who, in the Tragedian that represents his person, imagine they behold him fresh bleeding.'

Prima facie, this describes an early version of Shakespeare's *1 Henry VI*,* written a few years earlier. There was no need to specify its author; Nashe's readers would already know. No text of it was published until 1623; but this still contains the quoted phrase 'the terror of the French' (I.iv.42). Nashe was also right about the rich receipts, as other documents demonstrate. So Shakespeare would naturally soon seek, in the late 1580s or early 1590s, to repeat that striking success with another patriotic drama about English triumphs abroad. All his plays are difficult to date and indeed to define, because he was so thoroughgoing a reviser. But at least *Edward III* has a *terminus a quo* in the 1588 Armada, to which it clearly refers (1111, 1119); so it was presumably begun *c.* 1589.† After the customary time-lag it would become available for printing; plays were profitable in that format also. And just such a success was indeed duly noted by the playwright and critic Thomas Heywood, in terms very similar to Nashe's, thus: 'What English prince, should hee behold the true portrature of that famous King Edward the Third, foraging France, taking so great a king captive in his own country, quartering the English lyons with the French flower-delyce, and would not be

---

* *Pace* the Oxford editors' notions of collaboration by 'Nashe', 'X', 'Y' and perhaps others (Taylor 1988, 217).
† There is however no discernible justification for the claim inferred from Herz (1903, 5–6) by T. Baldwin (1959, 233) and continued by Lapides (1980, 37, 39, 41), Limon (1985, 160) and Taylor (1988, 136–7) that English actors had performed a play about Edward III on tour in Danzig by 1591. Philip Waimer's 1591 *Knittelvers* play about Edward's love for the Countess of Salisbury was avowedly drawn independently from Bandello 1554.

suddenly inflamed with so royale a spectacle, being made apt and fit for the like achievement?'

Edward III was entered in the Stationers' Register on 1 December 1595 and published by Cuthbert Burby in 1596; a second edition appeared in 1599. The play was presumably still popular as late as 1612, when Heywood published those admiring words. They further resemble Nashe's earlier tribute in recalling the actual text. Edward vauntingly unites the two nations' emblems 'quartered equally' on all the flags of his invading fleet (lines 1122–3) sent to 'forage' France (line 1909); and King John of France is brought back to England as a prisoner (line 2599). After 'the like achievement', Heywood proceeds to stipulate 'So of Henry the Fift', thus praising another play on that same theme of English conquest in France. In neither case need he name the playwright, who would be even more familiar to Heywood's readers in 1612 than to Nashe's twenty years before.

Indeed, Shakespeare was already well known to the Tudor theatre world by 1589, three years earlier still (Sams 1995a, 68–70, 121–4), again on the authority of Nashe. Of course Shakespeare's devotees would be familiar with his style and oeuvre, from his earliest days. The modern notion that Tudor theatre enthusiasts were uninstructed in literary matters may safely be discounted; playgoers and readers were at least as enthusiastic and perceptive then as they are now, and many of them would have been innately scholarly and analytical.

They could have seen Edward III 'sundrie times plaied about the Citie of London', as the 1596 and 1599 title-pages tell us. No company is named; but a play so dominated by one kingly larger-than-life figure would be a natural starring vehicle wherein the great actor Edward Alleyn could ride in triumph through the City playhouses, following his famous success in the title role of Marlowe's Tamburlaine. Further, according to an analyst of Tudor casting and acting records, 'Edward III was built on the same formula as the plays for the Admiral's Men about 1589, whatever this fact may mean' (T. Baldwin 1959, 235). If this is indeed a fact, then it means, discounting academic coyness, that a first version of Edward III was written c. 1589 for the Admiral's Men, with their star actor-manager Alleyn in the name part. This role is some 300 lines longer than any other, an unusual and striking disproportion; and the play is also notable for the absence of any major comedian or clown, which was also true of the Admiral's Men (Baldwin 1959, 235).

Historians and literati who attended the first performances of Edward III could soon recognise the Chroniques of Froissart (available in English since 1525) as one source-book and Painter's Palace of Pleasure (1566–75) as another. Shakespeare's indebtedness to both was already apparent. In the surviving text of 1 Henry VI (I.ii.29–31) a Frenchman says that:

> Froissart, a countryman of ours, records
> England all Olivers and Rolands [i.e. warrior-heroes] bred
> during the time Edward the Third did reign.

Such allusive cross-reference is entirely typical of Shakespeare (Sams 1995a, XV). No one would be surprised to note that the 1596 first edition of *Edward III* was published anonymously, in the fashion of the times (like *Titus Andronicus* 1594), or that its publisher Burby had already issued, again anonymously, *The Taming of a Shrew* 1594 – surely (Sams 1995a, 136f.) Shakespeare's own first version of his far more famous Shrew play which remained unpublished until 1623. Burby's name would soon also appear on the second edition of *Romeo and Juliet* 1597 and the first of *Love's Labour's Lost* 1598, which was printed from Shakespeare's own working manuscript (Kerrigan 1982, 242) and which incorporated his own emendations ('newly corrected and augmented by W. Shakespeare', as the title-page records). Similarly Simon Stafford, who may well have printed the first edition of *Edward III* and whose name was added to the second in 1599, also printed *1 Henry IV* in that same year. Many readers and playgoers would notice such close connections. Those who had read *Venus and Adonis* and *The Rape of Lucrece*, published in 1593 and 1594 respectively, would be well placed to appreciate the plain parallels between both those poems and the text of *Edward III*; for example, their red–white contrasts, also found in *1 Henry VI*, reappear in the Countess scenes. *Venus* was reprinted twelve times up to 1636; it was the most famous and popular narrative poem of its day. *Lucrece* ran it close, with eight editions up to 1655. They would both have joined *Edward III* in many libraries and bookshelves; they are singled out for comment and parody in *Willobie his Avisa* 1594, which apparently alludes to *Edward III*, and in the *Parnassus* plays *c.* 1598, which burlesqued red–white contrasts among other aspects of Shakespeare's early style (Sams 1995a, 88, 101). As Latinists, educated Elizabethans would also know that 'The Argument' prefixed to *Lucrece* was drawn in some detail from Painter's translation of the Livy source (Roe 1992, 35); the poet and the dramatist used the same material. *Edward III* actually refers to the poem, with becoming modesty; the story of Lucrece 'hath tasked/the vain endeavour of so many pens' (1021–2). Again such cross-reference is characteristic (Sams 1995a, XV).

Those two great narrative poems were both inscribed to the Earl of Southampton, the addressee of Shakespeare's contemporary sonnets (Sams 1995a, 103f.), one of which (76.6) says that their author's poetic style was universally known and recognised. Though they remained unpublished until 1609, some of them certainly circulated in manuscript; of course their lyric genius would be recognised and acknowledged by all the many connoisseurs. So the presence in *Edward III* (line 808) of the sonnet line 'lilies that fester smell far worse than weeds' (94.14) would occasion no surprise or comment; the usual explanation of self-reference would already have been perfectly

apparent in the 1590s, just as in 1609 when the *Sonnets* were first published
and 1640 when they were reprinted. Indeed, the 'private friends' among
whom certain sonnets had circulated (Meres 1598) would also know that
Shakespeare was in Southampton's service; so the *Edward III* episode where
a poet-secretary is commissioned to write a love poem for his lord's use would
command special attention. Only the first two lines of the poem are heard,
because they were 'all that yet is done', as their author explains (526).
But they already sound like the exordium of a sonnet, in the 1590s fashion:
'More fair and chaste than is the queen of shades, /more bold in constancy
. . . than Judith was' (492, 520–22). Not only the private friends but the
enemies too (and both Southampton and Shakespeare had already made
many, separately) would have taken an interest in *Edward III* and its
authorship.

There was good reason for its lasting anonymity. It may well have been
the play described in a complaint to Lord Burghley from an Edinburgh
correspondent on 15 April 1598: 'that the comedians of London should
scorn the king and people of [Scotland] in their play; and it is wished that
the matter should be speedily amended lest the king and the country should
be stirred to anger' (Chambers 1923, i.323). The king in question was James
VI who only five years later would become James I of England and rule both
realms until his death in 1625. No wonder that *Edward III* was never
published under Shakespeare's name, not even posthumously in the 1623
First Folio, although by then the correspondences among that play, the
poems and sonnets, and the works in general had become complete, manifest,
and quantifiable. Already in 1605 King James had decreed that George
Chapman should be imprisoned for his part in the play *Eastward Ho*, which
was also uncomplimentary about the Scots (Halliday 1964, 147). But printed
play-texts continued to be cherished by the general public, even despite the
later suppression of the theatres in Puritan England; and the creative
and critical geniuses of succeeding generations included such supremely
insightful commentators as John Dryden, Alexander Pope and Samuel
Johnson. Had they studied *Edward III* they could readily have discerned its
stylistic development from the earliest popular plays to the lyric eloquence of
the sonnets.

Theirs was also the age of the great Shakespeare scholar Edward Capell
(1713–81). His ten-volume edition of 1768 was the first to study and collate
the Quartos, and concentrate on other contemporary sources including the
Stationers' Register. In 1760, at the height of his powers, he published
Edward III as 'a Play thought to be writ by Shakespeare', by which he meant
that the ascription relied on processes of rational inference from internal
evidence rather than external documentation. He himself had no doubt of its
authenticity. But later commentators lacked his nonpareil knowledge and
insight, and relied instead on their own opinions and feelings. That practice
still prevails; so ever since Capell 'the question of Shakespearean authorship
has been batted to and fro by editors and critics. Some have maintained that

the whole of the play is by Shakespeare, and some that none of it is. Others to whom parts or the whole have been attributed include Drayton, Greene, Lodge and Peele. No general agreement has yet been reached. The balance of opinion has tended to favour divided authorship, the Countess scenes in particular being allotted to Shakespeare' (Slater 1988, 1–2). Marlowe has also often been mentioned (e.g. by Merriam 1993); but otherwise this sad summary is unassailable. The only certainty is the universal neglect of *Edward III*. How has this happened?

VI

The Evolution of the Current Consensus

Romantic subjectivism supervened. It still prevails, among both the opponents and the supporters of a Shakespearean *Edward III*; it has hardened into a rigid mind-set among an entire profession. How does one *feel?* How did one's distinguished predecessors *feel?* These are the current criteria. Yet they were cogently rejected thirty years ago, as follows, in a book about Elizabethan dramatic authorship: 'Rule 7. Intuitions, convictions and subjective judgements generally, carry no weight as evidence. This no matter how learned, respected or confident the authority' (Schoenbaum 1966, 178). The only possible reservation is that this should perhaps have been Rule One. Let it now be called Schoenbaum's Law. Had it been heeded by all concerned, including its proponent, Shakespeare studies would still stand secure. Instead, it has been steadfastly ignored, and the whole edifice has collapsed (Sams 1995a, *passim*). *Edward III* represents only one casualty among very many.

Infallible feeling about that play began with Swinburne, who was moved and thrilled by a misprint in Shelley (Housman 1911, 306) but nauseated by an even more obvious misprint in *Edward III* (Muir 1960, 12). At least Swinburne reacted passionately, like a poet. But even a sober prose commentator, even eighty years later, and even in the act of rejecting such subjectivity, can topple into exactly the same pitfall, thus: '[Swinburne] has argued most persuasively against the attribution of the play to Shakespeare [although he] relied entirely on aesthetic arguments' (Muir 1960, 11). But this makes the selfsame subconscious assumption, namely that personal opinions (which is what 'aesthetic arguments' means) have their own validity. By Schoenbaum's Law, they have none. The same applies to all such personal judgements as 'un-Shakespearean' (Brooke 1908, xxii), 'by no means up to Shakespeare's level' (R. Smith 1911, 103), and so forth, which still typify twentieth-century Academia. So do the analogous assumptions made by Professor Muir himself; for example 'Swinburne's intimate knowledge of Elizabethan drama gives more weight to his opinion than Tennyson's;* but, as so frequently with his criticism, [his view] appears to be coloured by personal animosity' (1960, 12).

---

* Which was that the Countess scenes were by Shakespeare.

The eighteenth century had already adumbrated a much more objective approach (Whiter 1794) based on the classical philosophy of John Locke. Whiter (ibid., 147–52) cites lines 795–6 from *Edward III* and compares them to parallel passages from *Hamlet* and *Measure for Measure*, reaching the conclusion that the unity of thought thus demonstrated is readily distinguishable from mere imitation and hence provides evidence of shared authorship. The method is validated thus: by the term *association*, Locke understands 'the combination of those ideas which have *no* natural alliance or relation to each other, but which have been united only by chance or by custom . . . the mind is . . . often totally unconscious of the force and principle of their union' (ibid., 65). But no two poets, or people, can share the same unconscious mind; so such associations are evidence of individual identity. This actually is an argument, acceptable or not. The same method was applied by R. Chambers (1923, 1939) to *Sir Thomas More*, by Caroline Spurgeon (1935) and E. Armstrong (1946) to Shakespeare in general, and by E. Everitt (1954) to other apocrypha including *Edmund Ironside* (cf. also Sams 1985d, 1986d) and *Edward III*. That last-named play has now become generally accepted as entirely or partly Shakespearean, on Lockean grounds of resemblances too close for coincidence; the alternative of 'plagiarism from Shakespeare' is ruled out by known dates. This commonsense conclusion is reinforced by the wide variety of sources and systems chosen for comparison, all of which afforded the same answer to each one of many specialist researchers, as follows, without any reasoned opposition on any grounds from any quarter:

Deep and close parallels to *Measure for Measure* etc. (Collier 1874), *Henry V* (Phipson 1889, Everitt 1954, Ribner 1957), nature imagery (Phipson 1889, Madden 1897), characterisation, especially of the Countess (Moorman 1910), parallels from *Venus and Adonis* and *The Rape of Lucrece* (Østerberg 1929, O'Connor 1948), parallels from the *Sonnets* (E. Chambers 1930, O'Connor 1948, Schaar 1962, Kerrigan 1986b), versification (Timberlake 1931), diction and vocabulary (Hart 1934, Bell 1959, Slater 1982, 1988, Sams 1985d, 346–8, Calvert 1987), parallels from *Richard II* and *Richard III* (O'Connor 1948), use of historical sources (Ribner 1957), parallels from *1–3 Henry VI* (Bell 1959), the detailed analysis of mental process in all its aspects (Muir 1953, 1960, Wentersdorf 1960), general themes and imagery (Koskenniemi 1964, Broadbent 1987, Mills 1987), and particular image-clusters (Muir 1960, Hobday 1965, 1969). Two dissertations (Lapides 1966, Horn 1969) included texts of *Edward III*; both favoured Shakespeare as sole author. The former, published in book form in 1980, offers a useful summary of earlier commentary.

But many of these enthusiasts were amateurs, and much professional work (notably the magisterial Wentersdorf thesis of 1960) remained unpublished as too specialised. Where convictions lack authority, the authorities lack conviction. Nothing has ever moved in modern Shakespeare studies without the sworn affidavit of leading experts. But their contributions, now to be considered in detail, had the desolating effect of halting *Edward III* at the frontier of the Shakespeare canon, where it has been officially held for questioning during most of this century.

Ironically, its present predicament has been as much occasioned by its chief academic advocates, such as Kenneth Muir (1960), MacDonald Jackson (1963) and John Kerrigan (1986a) as by its sole academic adversaries, namely Stanley Wells (1986c) and Gary Taylor (1988) throughout their Oxford edition and commentary. Thus the assurance that some of *Edward III* was by Shakespeare and the rest by a 'collaborator' calls both hypotheses into question; the latter is plainly derived from mere unevidenced opinion, and so perhaps, therefore, is the former. Sadly, this dilemma undermines all Muir's otherwise excellent and original work. He certainly paid due tribute (1960, ix–xi) to the work of Whiter, Spurgeon, R. Chambers and Armstrong; and he reinforced their Lockean conclusion that personal and private associations are identificatory, because 'an imitator is quite unlikely to have had precisely the same associations'. But Muir's own mind is already closed before his case opens. His first essay on *Edward III* (1953, 47) suggested that the play resulted from Shakespeare's revision of someone's else work, an uneconomical and unevidenced thesis later expanded into a book actually called *Shakespeare as Collaborator* (1960, 1–55). Muir adjudges the evidence of *Henry VI* parallels 'ambiguous, since [*sic*] some critics still believe that *Henry VI* is not wholly Shakespearean' (ibid., 14). Further, certain image-clusters 'appear in scenes which are not generally ascribed to Shakespeare, and one therefore [*sic*] tends to be suspicious of their validity' (ibid., 22). Such deference damages the scholarly ideals it seeks to subserve. By Schoenbaum's Law, opinions don't count, not even one's own. But this instantly puts paid to Muir's unevidenced 'collaborator', whose sole function is to contribute those lines that Muir considers un-Shakespearean. This chimera is then hailed as a probability. 'The blank verse of [lines 1–175] is monotonous, and nearly all end-stopped' (ibid., 33); so 'it seems probable that the play was written by Shakespeare in collaboration, for some scenes one would be unwilling to ascribe to him at any stage of his career – not because they are bad, but because their badness is unlike Shakespeare's' (ibid., 32–3). This subjective criterion is supported by an admired academic consensus, which for most of this century has also invented 'actors', 'pirates', 'reporters' and similar needless entities for exactly the same purpose of denying to Shakespeare whatever one is unwilling to ascribe to him, regardless of any evidence, whether external or internal, and in defiance of printed dates. Such attitudes render Professor Muir susceptible to all theories of dual authorship and impervious to the far more rational alternative of single authorship, throughout his otherwise perceptive exegesis. As a direct result, he begins with a false step in the wrong direction by dividing *Edward III* 'into two parts – (A) the possibly Shakespearean scenes [and] (B) the rest of the play'.*

---

* i.e. lines 178–1037 and 1915–2079 of this edition are assigned, while 1–177, 1038–914 and 2080–600 are denied, to Shakespeare *a priori*.

This procedure is doubly impermissible. It not only creates unevidenced agencies and circumstances but also helplessly begs the question at issue. Nothing that Professor Muir says about the dual authorship of *Edward III* ever follows from any other premiss than his own assumption of a 'Part A' and a 'Part B'. Thus (ibid., 13): 'The incidence of new words [i.e. those not used before in Shakespeare's plays] in A is twice as frequent as in B. This would seem to suggest that the play was not written by a single author.' Again (ibid., 29) 'the test of the incidence of new words appears to support the view of double authorship'. But these data are at least equally apt to suggest or support the view that the play's single author was more inventive at some times than at others.

Again: as to the argument that the occurrence of compound words in *Edward III* provides evidence of single authorship, because 'the proportion in each part of the play conforms reasonably to the number of lines, and, in addition, there are inspired and original formations in each section' (Bell 1959, 112), Professor Muir comments (1960, 14) that 'while all the "-like" compounds appear in part B, all the six "thrice-" formations are in part A', with the implication that this somehow speaks for dual authorship. But a single hand might well distribute thus; why not?

Next, the evidence of known Shakespearean rare words and an image-cluster in the supposedly non-Shakespearean section is rejected as 'ambiguous' or unproven because of the unargued opinions of unnamed critics (ibid., 14, 20). Again, the same image-cluster evidence is rejected on the shaky ground (ibid., 21) that *Edward III* in lines 98–9 apparently accepts a belief (about drones in an eagle's nest) which Shakespeare had expressly repudiated, in *2 Henry VI*. 'Shakespeare might of course have put into the mouth of one of his characters something he knew to be absurd, but it seems more likely that he did not write this scene' (i.e. lines 1–175). But no such conclusion follows. For example, Shakespeare might have learned better before he wrote *2 Henry VI*, which remained unknown in performance or print until the 1623 First Folio. Further, quasi-clusters of admittedly Shakespearean imagery 'appear in scenes which are not generally ascribed to Shakespeare' (ibid., 22, 30); so out they go, for no real reason at all. 'There is, moreover, always the possibility that an anonymous author, steeped . . . in the early works of Shakespeare, would unconsciously pick up the same associations'. But this not only invokes a new series of invented entities but denies what was earlier asserted (ibid., xi), as the *raison d'être* of Muir's entire enterprise: an unconscious association, even in feeble lines, is as authenticatory 'as the signature Vincent on a Van Gogh painting'. Similarly, when a part B image 'happens to fit in with' a group which is 'characteristic of the Shakespearean parts of the play' (ibid., 33), 'this is probably accidental'. Here again, and *passim*, is the same self-validating assumption; some parts are Shakespearean and others are not, and experts can distinguish gems from paste. So even when 'it would be difficult to tell from the verse alone that this [lines 178–273] was not by the same author as the later part of the scene [273–349], it might be argued that the characterisation of the Countess as undaunted does not harmonise with Warwick's description of her a few lines later [278–80]' (ibid., 34). But only a convinced believer in dual authorship could argue thus.

The same preconviction appears yet again in the argument that because the Earl of Salisbury makes no reference to his Countess in any of his lines, this is 'a slight indication that the scenes in which he appears were not by the same author' (ibid., 47). But as before, there is no such indication, save to an A and B allocator who speaks consistently of 'the Shakespearean parts', defined solely by personal feeling, yet chides a fellow-professor for affirming a mere 'matter of opinion' (ibid., 39). Finally, the B author is identified as a 'young poet, "able to bombast out a blank verse as the best" of the University Wits, as Greene said of Shakespeare, but liable to strange lapses; one whose sense of situation was superior to his power of characterisation' (ibid., 53). This would serve so suitably as the description of the young Shakespeare himself that only a dualist could miss the single most obvious inference. But Muir's *a priori* preconvictions are presented as their own proof *passim.* Thus the unfortunate imaginary author of the so-called 'Part B' is ceaselessly castigated for 'stiff' and 'unvaried' blank verse, 'conventional' imagery, an 'inappropriate' simile, 'undistinguished' writing, 'disappointing' poetry, 'feeble' lines and so forth (ibid., 46–53). He cannot therefore conceivably be the young Shakespeare. This possibility – given weight in quite the wrong sense – cannot surface from the depths to which it has been consigned. Indeed, no such idea is ever mentioned.

Only three years later, *Edward III* took another hard knock from another of its ostensible advocates. Professor MacDonald Jackson (1963, 331–2) noticed that one of its image-clusters, included by Muir among his evidence for part-Shakespearean authorship (1960, 22), also clearly occurred in the anonymous *Edmund Ironside.* But the obvious inference – namely that *Ironside* too was a Shakespeare play – was ignored in favour of 'doubts as to the validity of this sort of evidence'. The doubts were based solely on the admitted coincidence that four words of a quite different Shakespeare cluster, identified by a different analyst (Armstrong 1946, 24), occurred in a poem by Shelley. Those words were *beetle, bat, death* and *night.* Jackson, without arguing that either Muir's or Armstrong's work on Shakespeare was invalid in this or any other respect, nevertheless felt that 'one's faith in image-clusters tends to be diminished by such a coincidence'. In his own terms, therefore, mere coincidence detracts from actual evidence. So undue weight must have been attached to the coincidence pan of the scales by some underlying assumption. Consciously or not, Jackson assumes that *Ironside* is not Shakespeare's, with the inference that Muir's image-cluster may also be misleading about *Edward III.*

The same sequence of *non sequitur* was explicitly avowed by Samuel Schoenbaum in his influential monograph *Internal Evidence and Elizabethan Dramatic Authorship* (1966), thus: 'The blot-cluster that Muir cites as evidence for Shakespeare's hand in *Edward III* has recently been discovered in the anonymous *Edmund Ironside*, which (*pace* Everitt) Shakespeare is most unlikely to have written' (Schoenbaum 1966, 147). This alleged lack of likelihood fatally blighted the blot-cluster and infected all others. Like Jackson's contribution, it killed off not only Everitt (1954) but Muir (1960) and hence not only *Edmund Ironside* but *Edward III*; two whole books and two whole plays with one brickbat. There was no mention of Everitt's detailed reasons for attributing both plays to Shakespeare in their entirety, or of his independent arguments (1954, 74–8) for assigning them both to the same author. As to Muir's pioneer work on *Edward III*, 'we should know more than at present we do' about image-clusters, in which 'confidence is shaken' (Schoenbaum 1966, 188). Once again personal feelings are promoted into decisive criteria. Schoenbaum then proceeds to draw a 'simple moral . . . it behooves the investigator to proceed with extreme caution' (ibid., 189); except apparently about *Edmund Ironside* and other anonymous Tudor plays, about which Schoenbaum was recklessly subjective. Further, he not only strained at Shakespeare's authorship of unfamiliar texts but swallowed such fantasies as 'Bad Quarto' lore and regurgitated them as fact. Thus, in this same book (174), *The Contention of York and Lancaster* 1594 and *The True Tragedy of Richard, Duke of York* 1595 had already been dismissed as 'nonexistent plays', just because Schoenbaum then believed them to be 'Bad Quartos', i.e. the hypothetical result of the 'memories' of 'actors' in 'performances' of the 'pre-existing' 1623 Folio counterparts *2–3 Henry VI*. In the 1590s, to judge by actual evidence and rational inference, the latter pair were the nonexistent plays, whereas their earlier versions named above were Shakespeare's own extant work which he later revised (Sams 1995a, 154–62). So if *Edmund Ironside*, written *c.* 1588, and hence *Edward III*, begun *c.* 1589, could be shown to share the same style with each other and with *Contention* and *True Tragedy*, both *c.* 1590, the only outcome would be the rejection of all four by authorities who, then as now, classified the last two as 'Bad Quartos' or 'memorial reconstructions' on no evidence at all. For having the nerve to deny the 'Bad Quarto' delusion, the unfortunate Everitt was denounced by Schoenbaum as the promulgator of theories that were not just 'implausible' but even 'eccentric' (1966, 143). In reality, any argued theory would far outweigh the opinions of Schoenbaum, which are often demonstrably wrong (Sams 1993a). Yet they possess massive gravitational force, which can be observed and calculated from his distortions of what Alfred Hart (1934, 219–41) says about *Edward III*. At least Hart's words (ibid., 241) are correctly quoted, thus: 'The other possibility is to accept the facts, confess our ignorance, and permit the play to remain authorless.' Incredibly, Schoenbaum selects this sentence to typify Hart's considered conclusion about *Edward III*, whereas in fact it relates solely to participial adjectival compounds, and is part of an argument for Shakespeare's single authorship. One has only to read five lines further on to arrive at Hart's own firm conclusion to that effect, on the basis of the facts and arguments he has adduced.

More recently, Professor George Parfitt (1985, iii), in an edition notable chiefly for 'grossly inaccurate text' (Proudfoot 1986a, 185) which however indicts R. Armstrong 1965 for 'dubious text' and Lapides 1980 for textual errors, insists that *Edward III* 'must continue to be seen as anonymous' in the absence of external evidence. But of course internal evidence such as the blot-cluster (analysed in detail at pp. 177–8 and 209–12 below) can always be just as conclusive as any other; hence the acceptance of Shakespeare's hand in *Sir Thomas More*. Rejection of all such evidence by the judge before the trial, therefore, like *a priori* acceptance of theories and opinions, damages or destroys the scholarship it seeks to preserve.

No other academic contributions to the debate were quite so negative; but many were neutral or passive. Thus Professor Muriel Bradbrook (1951; 1964, 186–7) was content to record the deep and detailed indebtedness of *Henry V* to the supposedly 'pseudo-Shakespearean' *Edward III*, without further reflection. Professor Richard Proudfoot, who had supervised the pioneering work of Eliot Slater on *Edward III*, chose that play as the topic of his 1985 British Academy lecture, which neither supported Slater's new approach to the authorship question nor reached any independent conclusion of its own. Its most daring claim was that research was 'far on the way to demonstrating' that the author was either Shakespeare or 'some person unknown' (Proudfoot 1986a, 184). But at least there was just one person. The lecture made no mention of Muir's assumptions about collaboration; the principle of economy was rightly respected. Indeed, the play's integrity and unity were repeatedly stressed, and a 'forthcoming edition' of it was promised (ibid., 161).

Meanwhile Toby Robertson produced *Edward III* at the Theatr Clwyd in Mold, and later on tour, with a programme note by Professor Proudfoot broadly hinting that some of its lines may have been written by Shakespeare. The Cambridge audience of 31 July 1987 quite agreed; the line 'Lilies that fester smell far worse than weeds' was not only spoken simultaneously by two characters on the stage, as a directorial device, but audibly echoed in the auditorium. Professor Lois Potter (1987) drew attention to the excellence of Annabel Leventon's performance as the Countess and commented 'I don't feel strongly about the authorship question, but it would not distress me to find [*Edward III*] included in the Shakespeare canon'. Other reviewers (Brown, Hoyle, Proudfoot, Shorter, Williams, all 1987) expressed similar sentiments of benevolent detachment.

But one commentator (Kerrigan 1986a) had already seen far further, albeit with a double vision that made out a shadowy collaborator who used the word 'but' in supposedly un-Shakespearean senses (unspecified, but perhaps as in line 2209 for example). This phantom was still unexorcised four years later, when *Edward III* though a 'fine play' was perhaps only partly authentic (Kerrigan 1990, 47). But that authenticity had been announced in ringing tones:

Reading the Countess of Salisbury scenes . . . I'm overwhelmed by the quality of the writing. Every word doth almost tell his name, and if this [i.e. lines 759–

65] isn't early Shakespeare, I'll eat my mortarboard. . . . Thus, burning with enthusiasm, I ring the Oxford Shakespeare. But no, their edition won't include Act II, because the computer doesn't approve. I imagine something like a fruit machine, whirring mindlessly in the OUP cellars. Such tests are worse than unreliable, because inveigling . . . [*Edward III* is] a central if collaborative document. . . . Oh best and wisest OUP editors, who think even *Timon* collaborative, reconsider this play, and do not leave it outside the canon, doomed to be read only by dons. (Kerrigan 1986a)

The Oxford Shakespeare editor-in-chief replied austerely thus: 'Sir: Gathering material, as it emerges, for his "friendly, informal" column, John Kerrigan rang me up in a friendly, informal way and asked me, among other things, why we should not be including the anonymously published *Edward III* – for which he displays so touching an affection – in the forthcoming Complete Oxford Shakespeare. My friendly, informal reply may have made him think that the decision is based on the mindless whirrings of a computer, but in fact it depends upon the cogitations of a human brain whose thought processes will be concisely revealed when the edition is published' (Wells 1986b).

In the Oxford *Complete Works* the thought processes were indeed revealed, as follows: 'In modern times, the most plausible case has been made for parts, or all, of *Edward III*. . . . It was first ascribed to Shakespeare in 1656. Certainly it displays links with some of his writings, but authorship problems are particularly acute during the part of his career when the play seems to have been written, and we cannot feel confident of the attribution' (Wells, with Taylor, 1986c, xxi). Yet the same volume confidently attributed *1 Henry VI* to 'Shakespeare and others' (ibid., 173), *Timon of Athens* to 'Shakespeare and Middleton' (p. 997), *Henry VIII* to 'Shakespeare and Fletcher' (p. 1343), *Pericles* to 'Shakespeare and Wilkins' (p. 1167) and the poem 'Shall I die?' to Shakespeare (p. 881), on no real evidence at all; and indeed, in the first three instances, in defiance of the First Folio's express assurances of authenticity and integrity. The self-contradictions continued; thus in the *Textual Companion to the Oxford Shakespeare* Taylor (1988, 78) repeatedly rejected his earlier opinion of *Edward III*, thus: 'Such [vocabulary] criteria tend to confirm [*sic*] Shakespeare's authorship of . . . *Edward III*. . . . Such [image] clusters confirm [*sic*] Shakespeare's authorship of *Edward III*.' Under the heading 'Works excluded from this edition' we learn that this play 'of all the non-canonical plays has the strongest claim to inclusion in the *Complete Works*. . . . It was once generally thought that Shakespeare was responsible only for the Countess scenes, but most recently studies of vocabulary and imagery conclude that the play is of single authorship. . . . In some ways the dispute over whether Shakespeare was sole or part author is irrelevant, and has served to obscure the consensus of investigators that *Edward III* deserves a place in Shakespeare canon.' So why was it excluded? 'In part because of uncertainties about date, in part because Shakespeare's share of the early plays is itself problematical: for instance, Slater's rare vocabulary test links *Edward*

III most closely to *1 Henry VI*, of which Shakespeare wrote only about 20 per cent' (Taylor 1988, 136–7). Here subjectivism returns with a vengeance. Muir had already claimed (1960, 14) that the large number of rare words shared by *Edward III* and the Henry VI trilogy was 'ambiguous' evidence, because of the opinions of 'some critics'. Thirty years later, Gary Taylor paradoxically presented his own opinion about *1 Henry VI* as evidence against the authenticity of *Edward III*, in which however he believes. His confident claim of only about one-fifth Shakespeare for the former is merely one Oxford theory among many others, not a fact at all; in reality there is no reason to doubt that Shakespeare wrote *1 Henry VI* 1623 in its entirety, just as its Folio editors testify. No doubt its compositional dates are debatable, as always within the *oeuvre* of any revising writer. But such doubts apply throughout the misdated Oxford edition (Sams 1992a); there was never any reason to exclude *Edward III* on any such grounds.

On the contrary; the Cambridge thesis and the Oxford antithesis can readily be reconciled. In part by Shakespeare, says the former; from the same hand throughout, says the latter; therefore by Shakespeare throughout. As a so far unconceded consequence, all those Oxford opinions about *1–3 Henry VI* are just wrong; the obvious reason why the unique or rare vocabulary of those plays also appears in *Edward III* is the shared Shakespearean origin of all four. Yet the baseless invention of multiple authorship in *Edward III* still prevails, freely creating 'authors', and even 'Shakespeare and his collaborators' (Melchiori 1994, 124, 129).

Modern stylometric analyses, however, for whatever they are worth (see Sams 1994c; and 1995a, 189–92) all agree with their predecessors Hart (1934) and Slater (1982, 1988) about the authorship of *Edward III*. Slater's adversaries claim that his approach is fundamentally flawed (Ule 1983) and that his results are at best helpful in determining chronology within a given *oeuvre* (Smith 1986, 1988a, 1988b), not authorship. However, this purported proof rests solely on Smith's assumptions and methods, whereas the latter have never been independently tested and the former are sometimes demonstrably wrong (Sams 1994c, 1996b). Besides, Smith himself freely concedes (1993, 204) that *Edward III* may well be by Shakespeare. One of Smith's long-standing adversaries, Thomas Merriam, has abandoned his own elaborate advocacy of Marlowe (1993) and conceded the case for Shakespeare (Matthews and Merriam 1994, 27). The latest statistical findings offer no 'serious challenge to the status of *Edward III* as the best candidate from the apocryphal plays for inclusion in the [Shakespeare] canon' (Hope 1994, 137, 154).

What made it the best candidate is not stated; but its credentials and qualifications either remain unexamined or have proved far from self-evident. The case now needs to be reopened and its contents redisplayed for a new generation of readers.

VII

The Case for Shakespeare

General

No doubt *Edward III* itself is its own best advocate. But before the trial begins, some preliminary points are proposed. First, the standard of proof required should be that of civil cases, namely a preponderance of probability. Questions of attribution are all too commonly considered as criminal charges against which Shakespeare needs to be defended, with a concomitant insistence on proof beyond reasonable doubt or else a verdict of innocent. Given such assumptions, the best is not only the enemy of the good but of everything else. In the real world, where Shakespeare belongs, a strong probability is as much as anyone can reasonably expect; and it should suffice, in principle as in practice. Secondly, the procedure should also resemble a court of law in admitting circumstantial evidence, whence accurate inference 'tends to become easier as the number of established facts grows and as they point, ineluctably, to the same conclusion' (Curzon 1978, 15). Thus the first of the following sections, 'Alliteration', does not seek to imply that only Shakespeare uses such devices; each such item is meant to serve as one single strand of a cord which when complete will sustain a massive weight of evidence. Thirdly, the jurors' mind-set needs to be neutral, or they cannot properly address themselves to the matters of fact that they are required to consider. So any *a priori* bias in favour of such modern theories as 'late start', 'late development', 'lost years', 'memorial reconstruction' or 'collaboration' is a disqualification.

In particular that last-named canard needs to be shot down and silenced. It was flown by the Oxford Shakespeare thus: 'Certainly, it would have been difficult for any young playwright, trying to establish himself in the professional public theatre of the late 1580s and early 1590s, to avoid writing collaborative plays. . . . It therefore seems likely that some of Shakespeare's earliest works, like some of his latest, were written in collaboration' (Taylor 1988, 73). On the evidence (Sams 1995a), he was already active if not indeed established in the earlier 1580s; and there is no record that he ever collaborated with anyone until *The Two Noble Kinsmen c.* 1613, which was registered and published posthumously, in 1634, as the work of 'Mr. John Fletcher and Mr. William Shakespeare, Gent.'. There is thus no *a priori* reason for providing *Edward III* with a second author, and not even the Oxford proponent of collaboration does so; on the contrary, its 'single authorship' is mentioned with apparent approbation (Taylor 1988, 78). Further, it is unlikely, on any hypothesis, that Shakespeare shared his creative writing with another dramatist whose style happened to coincide with his own in dozens of identifiable particulars. In fact almost all the characteristics analysed in the following separate sections are exemplified throughout the play. The application of Muir's misleading categories (1960, 13) to the textual facts analysed below strongly suggests that the author (A) of lines thought possibly good enough for Shakespeare (lines 178–1037 and 1915–2079 of this edition) is the same person as the writer (B) of lines thought certainly too bad for Shakespeare (1–177, 1038–914 and 2080–600). Thus in line 136 B looks over A's shoulder at the Painter source of the love scenes, while the copy of Holinshed consulted by B would also come in handy for A in lines 626–8 and 889. Similarly A's bee and spider (637–40) behave in the same bizarre ways as B's (1127–9), though no two dramatists could possibly have observed any such phenomena even in shared nature rambles. Their joint identity extends to wielding the same axe (797, 1655–6), counting sand by grains (486–7, 1957ff.), or comparing banners with flowers (924, 115–16). There are a dozen other links between the two main themes of love and war, and the two main plots of failed seduction and successful invasion.

Finally, the evidence for textual unity and integrity is corroborated by detailed analysis of the canonical links listed in the notes above, which verifiably occur in constant and consistent profusion throughout the entire play.

So any supposed disparities of style need some explanation other than dual authorship. One possible answer is that the key scenes of love (178–1037) and war (1915–2079) were deliberately written in heightened and enhanced language, which now seems more Shakespearean. Another is that a rapidly developing artist revised his own early work some years later, with the predictable and observed result that some sections are stylistically more advanced than others. This has the further advantage of explaining analogous discontinuities in many other Shakespeare plays (Sams 1995a). It also corresponds with known parallels in other art-forms; thus the piano trio Op. 8 by Brahms (1833–97) audibly contains stylistic components that tally with the known dates of 1854 for the first version and 1889 for radical revision. Even the Oxford Shakespeare editors concede that Shakespeare revised such a masterpiece as *King Lear* 1608, and also that certain other passages, e.g. in the first Quarto of *Hamlet*, 'could only be attributed to Shakespeare at all if they were written earlier than any of his acknowledged work' (Taylor 1988, 398). So the notion of collaboration could, and therefore should, be more economically restated in terms of authorial revision. This in turn would resolve the apparent contradiction among various compositional dates from *c.* 1589 to *c.* 1594, propounded for *Edward III*, after careful study. Each period separately, and both together, may well be right. The editor of the first

Quarto facsimile (Farmer 1910) offers the confident pronouncement: 'From internal evidence it is clearly shown that the play was written early in 1589 and produced on the stage immediately.' Unfortunately the evidence in question is not mentioned; but it is reasonable to suppose, given Shakespeare's penchant for topical reference (Sams 1995a, xv), that the Armada allusions (e.g. lines 1111 and 1119) were written in 1588 or soon after. The same conclusion has been reached in other studies (notably Wentersdorf 1965), and it is corroborated by inferences from theatre company records (T. Baldwin 1959, 235).

A new piece of evidence (Godshalk 1995) indicates a date before March 1593, the registration date of Thomas Deloney's ballad 'Of King Edward the Third, and the fair Countess of Salisbury', which was based on the play among other sources (Mann 1912).

Recent research into the association of the play with Shakespeare's patron Lord Hunsdon suggests a date of 1594 for first performance, and this in turn is confirmed by 'textual references to the war between Austria and Turkey, which broke out openly in June of 1593' (Prior 1993/4). Nevertheless, this dual dating is also entirely compatible with the single authorship of a Shakespeare who wrote popular plays in the 1580s, became a great poet in the early 1590s with the *Sonnets*, and incorporated that poetry into his plays thereafter. The proposed identifications and linkages that now follow are presented in alphabetical order of subject-matter.

Alliteration

This feature of the early Shakespeare style (Sams 1995a, 89–90) is exemplified *passim*, e.g. succour...sovereign should send (179), hot hounds...hardy...heels (275), fair...famished few (2125), hide his high head (2199).

Allusion, Personal or Topical

This neglected but indubitable trait helps with dating-termini as well as identification.

SUSANNA AND JUDITH SHAKESPEARE, 1583–5

There are only two *Edward III* references to the Apocrypha, i.e. the non-canonical books of the Old Testament commonly omitted from Protestant Bibles but included in the Catholic Vulgate or Latin Bible of Tudor times. The resolute heroine Judith (522) is named; a mention of 'wicked elders' stoned to death (2255) suggests the story of Susanna and the perjured elders, against whom the people rose up. Both stories were familiar to Shakespeare; thus a character in *Love's Labour's Lost* (IV.ii.8, 53) shares the name of

Judith's adversary Holofernes, while Susanna's saviour Daniel is repeatedly saluted in *The Merchant of Venice* (IV.i.223 etc.). The names Susanna and Judith were more familiar still, in every sense. Not only are they fully conformable with Shakespeare's Catholic background (Sams 1995a, 11–16, 32–5 etc.); they had been bestowed in baptism upon his only two daughters, in 1583 and 1585 respectively.

MARLOWE, *c.* 1587

The much-mentioned Marlowe style, which has encouraged some stylometrists to offer that ascription (Merriam 1993, soon retracted in favour of a Marlowe-influenced Shakespeare: Matthews and Merriam 1994, 27) entails a familiarity with *Tamburlaine c.* 1587; so that cruel hero, described in that play's prologue as 'the Scythian' may well be the 'flint-heart Scythian' here (423).

THE ARMADA, 1588

'The proud Armado of King Edward's ships' and the imaginative descriptions of an invading navy (1111ff.) and a sea-fight (1192ff.), with its anachronistic use of artillery, together with the half-moon formation of the French army (1945–6), are no doubt intended to evoke the Armada of 1588. So perhaps is the reference to 'tyrant's fear' (278), or the fate of being drowned or 'hacked apieces' before reaching the shore (1106), like many a Spanish mariner wrecked off the Irish and other coasts, while English 'malcontents' (1055) may well be an equally typical anachronistic allusion to Tudor times. The Quarto's '*Nom per illa* [*sic*], that brave ship' (1225) was no doubt a misreading for *Nonpariglia*, as in Ubaldino's account of the Armada *c.* 1589 and its English translation of 1590; the *Nonpareil* fought with distinction in that encounter. The same pamphlet describes the Spanish fleet as 'placed in Battle Aray after the Manner of a Moon crescent, being ready with her Horns and her inward Circumference, to receive either all, or so many of the *English* Navy, as should give her the Assault'; this may well have been in the dramatist's mind in imagining the French land forces at Poitiers as arrayed on a hill which 'like a half moon, opening but one way . . . rounds us in' (1945–6).

SPENSER, BEFORE 1590

If *The Faerie Queene* is recalled in lines 227 or 413, the reminiscence may derive from the manuscript circulation which that epic is known to have enjoyed (Honigmann 1982, 74–5).

PERSONAL CROSS-REFERENCE, EARLY 1590s

Sly cross-reference to one work in another is characteristic of Shakespeare (Sams 1995a, xv). Among the best-known examples are his canonical allusions to *The Rape of Lucrece*, which are worth recording: 'Lucrece was not

more chaste than this Lavinia' (*Titus Andronicus* 1594, II.i.108–9);
'Tarquin . . . That left the camp to sin in Lucrece' bed' (ibid. IV.i.63–4);
'swear with me, as with the . . . father of that chaste dishonour'd dame Lord
Junius Brutus sware for Lucrece' rape' (ibid. IV.i.89–91, referring to 'that
deep vow which Brutus made' in the poem, 1840–1, 1847); 'sad Lucretia's
modesty' (*As You Like It*, III.ii.148, also mentioned in the poem, 401);
'silence, like a Lucrece knife with bloodless stroke my heart doth gore'
(*Twelfth Night*, II.v.105–6, again in allusion to the poem, 1723–4 and 1735–
6, where the blood does not flow until the knife is withdrawn); 'Roman
Lucrece for her chastity' (*The Taming of the Shrew*, II.i.296, another poetic
theme, 692, 808); 'with Tarquin's ravishing strides, towards his design/
moves like a ghost' (*Macbeth*, II.i.55–6; cf. 'marcheth . . . wickedly he
stalks . . . night-waking', etc., *passim*, in the poem). The *Edward III* comment about how the Lucrece story 'hath tasked/the vain endeavour of so
many pens' (1021–2), including Shakespeare's own, fits comfortably into this
sequence. The literary world was talking about his narrative poem in 1594,
the year of its publication, as attested by the specific reference to it (the first
such allusion ever recorded) in the anonymous satire of the same year,
Willobie his Avisa (see Sams 1995a, 95–102).

This *Edward III* mention of Lucrece is also clearly congruent with the
ironic detachment in the lines 'writers say . . . in the sweetest bud the eating
canker dwells . . . The most forward bud is eaten by the canker ere it blow'
(*The Two Gentlemen of Verona*, I.i.42–3, 45–6); the writer who says this, in
the same characteristic phrasing, is Shakespeare, in the *Sonnets* and elsewhere
(Rowse 1989, 61–4). So when in *Edward III* we learn something else that
'poets write', namely that 'Achilles' spear/could heal the wound it made'
(749–50), the natural inference is that here is yet another self-quotation, this
time from *2 Henry VI*, where the same point is invoked in much the same
words: 'Achilles' spear [could] kill and cure' (V.i.100). It had already been
advanced by Ovid. But the reference is to its English formulation and hence
to Shakespeare; and hence also *prima facie by* Shakespeare. Further, the poet
employed as a sonnet-writing secretary by the obsessed King Edward (350–
547) surely has a strongly ironic autobiographical flavour. It is worth quoting
Professor Tillyard on the author of *Edward III*: 'an intellectual, probably
young, a University man, in the Southampton circle, intimate with Shakespeare and deeply under his influence, writing in his idiom' (1944, 121–2).
Or, less fancifully, Shakespeare himself, during the period of his intimate
acquaintance with the young Earl of Southampton (Sams 1995a, 103–13).
That identification would lend added significance to the play's frequent
reference to ideas and imagery which recur in the *Sonnets*, including the
actual line 'lilies that fester smell far worse than weeds' (808; Sonnet 94, 14).

OTHER TOPICAL ALLUSIONS *c.* 1593

As Roger Prior has pointed out (1990), the play apparently contains 'a series
of topical allusions to the war between Turkey and the Habsburg empire

which was declared in 1593'. These are said to include the 'surprising arrival of Poles and Muscovites at Crécy' (1076, 1082, 1089–90) as well as the mention of Turkey (2589–90), which also lies far beyond the explicit plot of the play. Such anachronistic references are entirely typical of Shakespeare (cf. the Earl of Essex in *Henry V*, V. Chorus 30–4; Sams 1995a, xv), and they serve to confirm his hand even in those parts of the play not normally assigned to him (see p. 155n above). Their dating relevance is less clear in the work of a revising writer who would naturally insert topical allusion to please patrons and the public. Students are also indebted to Roger Prior for his work on the relation of *Edward III* to Lord Hunsdon, the patron of Shakespeare's own acting company, with evidence of performance in 1594; see pp. 173–4 below.

Antithesis

In line after line of *Edward III*, for page after page, a word is sharply contrasted with its opposite; and the writer's thoughts flow from that contradiction. Of course the dramatic form itself essentially consists of confrontations; but their constant permeation of the play at all its levels from its basic structure to the fine grain of the language, whether in imagery or vocabulary, is surely identificatory. No other known Tudor dramatist wrote thus, throughout each of his known works. But 'the foundation of Shakespeare's imaginative thought . . . is the realisation and expression of life's dualism. His mind was dominated by the warring opposites disclosed by experience . . . Life and Death, Good and Evil, Day and Night. . . . To a remarkable extent Shakespeare's imagery can be ranged into contrasts according to such antitheses' (Armstrong 1946, 107). Or again: 'Throughout his working life, Shakespeare displayed a marked predilection for analysing situations by way of contraries or antitheses. Dualities and polar opposites are a striking feature of his style, superimposed upon the individual verbal habits of particular characters: darkness and light, frost and fire, summer and winter, love and hate . . . certain words seem to summon up their opposites almost automatically, as the result of an ingrained habit of mind more than from the requirements of a particular situation or rhetorical pattern. This is the case especially with the true–false antithesis, as even a quick glance at the two words in the Shakespeare concordance will reveal. They are surprisingly constant companions' (Barton 1980, 144–5). Similarly Caroline Spurgeon, though concerned solely with Shakespeare's imagery, notes his special feeling for colour contrasts such as facial red and white and their surprising association with the rising sun (1935, 61ff.). These are just three such testimonies among hundreds; and each one of their various different examples is represented in the following *Edward III* conspectus, arranged in alphabetical order of the positive aspect. In particular the true/false dichotomy, though stipulated only once, is the focus and pivot of all the ceaseless meditation on oath-taking and -breaking.

Augment/giving (580), begun/end (124–5), blessing/curse (811–12), body/soul (816), charge/discharge (851, 853), conqueror/servilely (78–9), conquest/overthrow (190), content/discontent (959), day/night (1203), deeds/words (658–9, 2441–2), defence/hurt (1220), feast/starves (532), fight/fly (237–8), fire/frozen (533), found/lost (2542), friends/foes (770–1, 2504), friend/enemy (922), fruitful/barren (1377–8), gall/sweet (1394–5), glory/shame (755, 805), golden/black (813–14), golden/lead (658–9), good/ bad (792), hallowed/profane (1536), happy/grief (534), heat/cold (2583), heaven/earth (936, 1011–12, 1927), hill/vale (2197, 2201), honour/shame (813–14), hope/fear (1194), inner/outward (326–7), life/dying (2077), law-ful/lawless (1861–2), light/dark (495), lightning/dark (807), lilies/weeds (808), live/dead (361), live/die (2051, 2053–4, 2076, 2079, 2341), living/ death (969–70), living/expired (2020), loved/feared (1386), love/hate (36–7, 299–300, 952–3), modest/immodest (363–5), noon/night (2116), nourish/ withers (747), particular/general (1955–64), peace/war (296–7, 1386–7), pleasure/displeasure (863), quick/reft of life (1204–5), red–white (355–70), remember/forget (713–14), resolution/cowardice (1222), rich/poverty (902–4), right/left (1304–5, 1930/1936), right/wrong (36–7, 952–3), ripe/rotten (2065), sacred/profane (604–5), shepherd/tyrant (43–4, 1440–1), steel/lead (2235), summer/winter (392–3, 1641–5), sunshine/shadow (587–8), sweet/ bitter (762–3), sweet/wormwood (1394–5), sweeter/sour (1917), true/false (122), vantage/loss (680–1), virtue/sin (465), waking/sleep (2093), wisdom/ foolishness (390), wise/sots (432), won/lost (1232). Further, the diction is often deliberately derived from contradiction, whether in single phrases, consecutive contrasts (lines 328f., 350f., 390f., 532–4), or entire speeches, such as the elaborate saying and unsaying at 788ff. These family features are self-replicating; they create many other modes of diction such as chiasmus and words beginning with '-un' (as discussed under those headings below).

There are far too many such examples to analyse in detail; but even these single words speak for the known Shakespeare. Thus his red–white contrasts were plainly apparent to his contemporaries (Sams 1995a, 88, 119), as well as his commentators; in *Edward III* they are indeed overtly associated with faces and allusively with the rising sun ('oriental red', 360), just as Caroline Spurgeon says. In addition, her painstaking analyses point to his clear but equally unusual and characteristic contrast between love and fear (1935, 154–8), and this too is duly exemplified. The French king, desperate to denounce his English counterpart, can hardly imagine any graver accusation than that Edward seeks to be feared rather than loved (1386).

The Bible

Spurgeon suggests (ibid., 155) that this striking contrast may have been unconsciously influenced by the biblical dictum that 'There is no fear in love;

but perfect love casteth out fear' (1 John 4:18). And it is surely true that Shakespeare towers over all Tudor dramatists in the amount and nature of his scriptural knowledge and the number of his allusions. His surprising affinity with Genesis and Matthew has often been noted. Of the former, the standard authority avers that 'it is only when we assemble all the references to Adam and Eve that we realize how intimately he knew that narrative . . . there is hardly a phase of the story as narrated in the first three chapters of Genesis that has been missed' (Noble 1935, 42). Short of imagining some other dramatist, now unknown, who shared that same trait, this fact surely serves to identify the writer who knew why Adam might be called 'sole-reigning' (619) and 'leathern' (940). The influence of other Genesis chapters and other books including Matthew is equally apparent *passim,* e.g. in lines 31–2, 609, 613, 620, 707–8, 859, 1534–5, 1578, 1989–90, 2248, 2249–50, 2444 and 2543–4. See also Marriage, p. 179 below.

Bodily Action and Personification

'Pictures drawn from the body and bodily action form the largest single section of all Shakespeare's images . . . , and this apart from his very large number of personifications, which two groups it is difficult always clearly to separate.' Not only the quantity but the samples are typical. Their chief characteristic is pictorial vividness; the actions are quick and nimble, 'such as jumping, leaping, diving, running, sliding, climbing and dancing' (Spurgeon 1935, 49–50), while 'entities and abstractions are seen by Shakespeare – many of them repeatedly – as *persons*; angry, proud, contemptuous, saucy, indignant, smooth-faced, surly and wanton; sinning, suffering, repenting, kissing, winking, wrestling, resisting, whirling, hurrying, feasting, drinking, bragging, frowning and grinning' (ibid., 246). The two groups together total 'seventy-one listed images' in *King John* (ibid.). The tally is well over 100 in *Edward III*: it contains exactly such ideas, in just such profusion, which defeats detailed analysis. But the degree of verbatim correspondence with Spurgeon's findings offers a clear illustration; even excluding synonyms, there is profuse literal parallelism in quick and nimble images of climbing (40) and leaping (459), while the personifications are variously depicted as angry (1167), proud (111, 2354), wanton (891, 1478), sinning (779), kissing (796, 1936), resisting (2354), whirling (888), feasting (2271) and drinking (351), among many other such imagined attributes and activities. In this context, Spurgeon adds, one of Shakespeare's 'outstanding characteristics is the way in which by introducing verbs of movement about things which are motionless, or rather which are abstractions and cannot have physical movement, he gives life to the whole phrase'. The attentive reader of *Edward III* will notice how truth *pulls* a mask off (81), defiance or reflection *rebound* (93, 471), fear *turns his back* (258), and so forth.

Chiasmus

This stylistic device, known to Puttenham (1589) as Antimetabole, arranges words or ideas in the pattern ABBA. It is conveniently combined with Antithesis (q.v.) when A and B are opposites. The figure was 'a favourite with Shakespeare and there is a steady increase in his tragic writing from two examples in *2 Henry VI* to seventeen in *Richard II*' (Hill 1957, 66). It also proliferates in the two narrative poems and the *Sonnets*. In *Edward III* it is frequent and deliberate, sometimes to the point of overworked contrivance. Examples are found at 265–6 (welcome . . . com'st well; also a pun), 318–19 (contemplative desire . . . desire . . . contemplation), 441–2 (worth . . . praise . . . praise's worth), 465 (virtue sin, sin virtue), 485 (more . . . most . . . most . . . more), 568–70 (within thy power . . . happy . . . joy . . . within thy power), 590–2 (soul . . . body . . . body . . . soul), 597 (I . . . poor soul . . . poor soul me), 633–4 (words . . . beautify, beauties words), 717–18 (charity . . . love . . . love . . . charitable), 742–4 (life . . . honour . . . honour . . . life), 1957–8 (sands . . . hands . . . handful . . . sands), 2076–7 (live . . . die . . . dying . . . life), 2171–3 (breach of faith . . . consent . . . consent . . . breach of faith), 2314–16 (drink . . . blood of . . . kings . . . king's blood . . . drink).

As it happens, all these instances except the last fall within the accepted Shakespearean section. However, the final 'non-Shakespearean' sample looks equally characteristic. The explanation of the disparity, if any is needed, is surely that the device is essentially poetic and hence better suited to lyrical contexts than to passages embodying plot or action.

Compound Words

Shakespeare's originality is often expressed in his use of compound words, which still awaits serious study. The following samples occur in *Edward III*: after-ages* (1024), all-ending* (1923), bed-blotting (814), belly-god (1477) boisterous-boasting (255), cannon-shot* (1170), cheerful-sounding (166), counsel-bearer (877), counsel-giver (2295), day-stars (316), dead-sick (2310), deadly-wounding (2491), death-procuring (2499), double-gild (2015), ever-bibbing (1067), fast-chained (2496), fear-possessèd (2234), fire-containing (2225), flint-heart (423), good-presaging (1533), hare-brained* (1097), heart-bloods (984), heart-sick* (445), high-swoll'n* (1178), high-vaunting (2285), honey-gathering (637), iron-hearted (1192), just-dooming (1574), love-lays (449), light-borne (206), low-brought (2378), milk-white* (2043), never-broken (2159), never-dying* (2318), new-replenished (1934), nimble-jointed (2007), over-ridden (1484), parti-coloured* (336), poison-sucking (639), pre-eminence* (2427), pretty-coloured (2226), resty-stiff (1483), sharp-pointed* (1011), slaughter-house* (1439), scarce-appearing

(1532), stiff-grown (1451), stronger-battled (1928), such-like* (1283), summer-leaping (459), sweet-flowering (1287), swift-starting (2231), thorny-pricking (115), thrice-dread (572), thrice-gentle* (555), thrice-gracious* (543), thrice-loving (967), thrice-valiant* (898), tongue-tied* (2092), top-gallant* (1120), through-shot (1212), under-garnished (342), wedding-knives (998), writing-paper (875). There may well be other examples less readily classifiable, such as 'all-too-long' (339).

Of these hyphenated words, those marked with an asterisk occur verbatim in the canon, no more than a few times each and mostly just once, usually in plays dated later than *Edward III*. Almost all the rest, despite their unfamiliar look, contain at least one component used by Shakespeare in his characteristic practice of hyphenated word-coinage; the only exceptions are 'boistrous-boasting', 'poison-sucking' and 'resty-stiff'.

First Recorded Usage

The great *Oxford English Dictionary* (*OED*) published in the late nineteenth and early twentieth centuries by Sir James Murray and his successors was furnished with illustrative quotations, which 'are not merely examples of the fully developed use of the word or special sense under which they are cited; they have also to illustrate its origin, its gradual separation from allied words or senses, or even, by negative evidence, its non-existence at the given date'. This claim is repeated verbatim in the second edition (1989, xxix). Its final phrase has crucial significance for Shakespeare dating and attribution; it plainly implies that the canonical citations of first recorded usage are his own coinages. If so, here is vital evidence of authorship. Thus any previously unknown usage first recorded from *Edward III* 1596 which also occurs in a Shakespeare play not then published or performed, or indeed (so far as is known) written, offers some evidence that he minted the expression in question and later reused it, i.e. that he wrote the *Edward III* line. In other words, he spent his own coinage without stealing anyone else's. Of course anyone concerned can (and, in an age where theories take precedence over facts, many will) freely hypothesise that Shakespeare was filching words from plays he had seen or read or acted in. But an economical explanation is always more rational, especially when the examples are copious, as in *Edward III*; and these surely provide powerful evidence of its Shakespearean authorship. Sample words concerned are therefore listed here, in alphabetical order with *OED* categories and references.

aggravate, v. 6b (798), blurt, v. 2a (2259), brace, n. 10 (880), clefture, n. [the 1545 example differs] (1212), commix, v. 1b (1838), constraint (530), conventicle, n. II.6 (414), cynic n. B2 (666), delineate, ppl. a. (910), Dutchman n. 2 (1068), en- prefix 1, as in encouch (420), faceless, a. a [the 1567 example differs] (258), foragement, n. (753), general, a. 6b (515), gimmaled, ppl. a. [gymould in Q1] (207), immuréd ppl.a. [emured in Q1]

(530), envier, v. [invier in Q1] (771), leathern, a. 1c (940), naught, a. [nought in Q1] (175), penalty, n. 4 (622), rariety, n. (939), regenerate, ppl.a. 3 (109), resty-stiff, resty a. 2a comb. (1483), sand n. 1e (1960), snaily, a. 1 (144), soar, n. 1 (438), sole-reigning, a. sole 10 comb. (619), solitariness, n. 2 personif. (1343), Star-Chamber, n. 2b transf. (990), steeled, ppl.a. 2 (1543), steely, a. 2 (1643), sweet-flowering, sweet a. C2 (1287), swift-starting, swift a. C3 (2231), thorny-pricking, a. 5 comb. (115), topless, a. 1 (2198), undecked, ppl. a. 1 [the 1570 example differs] (333), under-garnished, ppl.a. (342), underprop, v. 2 fig. absol. (1653), unfertile, a. a (334), unfought, ppl. a. 1b (1461), unpolished, ppl. a. (80), unreputed ppl. a. (793), unrestrained, ppl. a. 2b (1292), utmost, n. 7b (2170), vasture, n. (759), via, int. 1 (830), viper, n. 3b (109), wantonness, n. 3b transf. (1478), wedding-knives, wedding n. 4 attrib. b (998), winning, ppl. a. 3 (323).

Further, at least fifty *Edward III* words have been overlooked by the *OED*, which for example first records its compound adjective 'iron-hearted' (1192) from a 1618 source. An even larger category of misdatings is comprised in those words which appear in *Edward III* 1596 but are first recorded in the *Oxford English Dictionary* from canonical Shakespeare plays, whether by oversight or on the misconceived assumption that those plays were actually written earlier. In fact, however, only *Titus Andronicus* 1594 was published before *Edward III*, which nevertheless contains well over *two hundred* words the first recorded usage of which is assigned by the *OED* to a later, and often a much later, canonical work. The dictionary was thus doubly fallible, in the completeness of its references to *Edward III* and above all in its Shakespeare dating, which is all too often derived from outmoded literary theory (such as '1588' for *Love's Labour's Lost*). These admittedly wrong dates remain unchanged in the second edition, to the continuing detriment of sound scholarship. However, the forthcoming third edition, ambitiously planned for the year 2005, will incorporate a thoroughgoing revision. In particular, Shakespeare plays will at last be factually dated, by the year of first publication considered as a *terminus ad quem*; thus *Love's Labour's Lost* will be assigned to 1598, not 1588. Even then, another serious obstacle to research is likely to remain insuperable, namely the often quite different and incompatible but equally baseless and sometimes self-contradictory datings proffered by the Oxford Shakespeare editors (Wells 1986c, Taylor 1988). These too are based on literary theory, though of the early twentieth century instead of the *OED*'s late nineteenth century; thus *2–3 Henry VI*, *The Taming of the Shrew* and *The Two Gentlemen of Verona*, all four entirely unknown in print before 1623, are announced as Shakespeare's earliest works *c.* 1590 – notions underpinned solely by the personal opinions of Peter Alexander (1929) for the first three of those plays and of Stanley Wells (1963) for the fourth. Protests (Sams 1982–95) have gone entirely unanswered; there is apparently no present prospect of any revised Oxford Shakespeare.

Despite all these difficulties of detail, however, the general evidence is surely as clear as it is copious. Scores of unusual words and ideas first recorded

from Shakespeare and universally accepted as his typical coinages are in fact
found *earlier*, throughout *Edward III*, long before there is any evidence that
the canonical play concerned was written or performed, let alone published.
All this vocabulary is recorded and glossed in section IV above (pp. 78–146).
To avoid confusion, the following selection of usages first recorded by the
OED from Shakespeare is confined to canonical works which *on the OED's
own dating* are later, and often much later, than 1596, which is itself a
terminal date; much or all of *Edward III* may well have been written up to
eight years earlier still – accent (380), actor (786), [stand] aloof (1745),
Bellona (1513), confident (255, 2041), cost (1253), counterfeit (1405),
courtly (2039), defiance (2001), disadvantage (2233), dismiss (211), embrace
(938), emulate (509), enclose (136), enjoy (583, 646), enthrone (1470),
entreat (57), epithet (380), esquire (2417, 2419), fruitful (1378), increasing
(167), insomuch (1380), is't (1250), lineal (39), misgive (1185), muster
(1601), niggard (306), plough (1125), profit (1838), scandalous (774, 1426,
1492, 1839), servile (2372), sully (280), sweets (510), task (1021), tightly
(1124), twas (363, 365), twere (75, 452, 1484, 1921). These 37 usages in 47
occurrences soon become another hundred and more when the *OED* Shakespeare dates are corrected from literary theory to historical fact, for example
by reverting to the date of first printing considered as a *terminus ad quem*.

Pending the third *OED* edition, there is little to be done save to regret the
blunting of so potentially powerful a dating tool. However, the specialised
lexicographers for whom this section is intended may thereby be enabled
to reach clearer conclusions. An essential prerequisite is a thorough objective
reappraisal of the facts and problems, including the assumptions made by
the author of the only relevant monograph (Schäfer 1980, on *OED* first
citations) and his readers and reviewers (e.g. Proudfoot 1981) as well as the
earlier *OED* and other modern Shakespeare series editors. Thus Schäfer
investigated main lemmas only, on the admittedly fallible basis of *OED*
dating (1980, 9–1), which also often conflicts with *SOED* dating (ibid., 77).
Proudfoot, as a believer in 'memorial reconstruction', is disposed to credit
some hapax legomena to an imaginary 'reporter' (1981, 61). Other editors
have their own theories about the dates and provenance of Shakespeare texts,
including a plethora of 'collaborators' as well as 'reporters'. Finally the *OED*
itself is inconsistent in its treatment of many word-categories (Schäfer 1980,
12–34). All such defects are in urgent need of remedy.

Meanwhile however it is irrational to suppose that any of the *OED* first
citations from Shakespeare are unreliable or negligible. The sole credible
criterion of error is factual knowledge, for example of an actual earlier use, in
some known non-Shakespearean source, of the same word or usage in the
same defined sense. In the absence of such corrections, the *OED's* data must
prevail; and every single instance of the hundreds noted anywhere in this
volume has been reprinted as recently as the *OED's* 1989 second edition,
entirely unchanged after nearly a century. The reason why the specialised

vocabulary of *Edward III* remains so extensively comparable with that of canonical Shakespeare as recorded in the *OED* is *prima facie* identity of authorship, in complete conformity with the findings of Hart (1934), Everitt (1954) and Slater (1988).

Flora and Fauna

One clear sign of Shakespeare is his obsession (hardly too strong a word) with ideas and imagery derived from plants and animals. As Caroline Spurgeon says (1935, 86) 'One occupation, one point of view, above all others, is naturally his, that of a gardener'; more generally, nature and animals are among his main sources of imagery (ibid., 13). The two narrative poems and the early plays teem with such life, as if they were also herbals and bestiaries. *The Rape of Lucrece* for example names some seventy types some ninety times, an average of one every twenty or so lines. None of them need have been mentioned at all. *Edward III* is entirely comparable. Thus it specifies ape, ash, barking, Bayard (= horse), beak, bears, beast (3 times), bee, bird, birds (2), black (= horse), blossom, blow, bough, branches, bud, buds, buzz, canker, carrion, cherry, comb, coral, corn, cornfields, crop, cropped (2), crows (2), dogs, dragons, drone, eagle (2), earth, emmets, falcon, feathered, field (?), flight, fleur-de-lis (2), flower (3), flowering, flowers (2), fowl (2), fowls, foxes, fragrant, fruit, fruitful, fruits, game, garden, grain, grass, grasshopper, ground, grove, growth, haggard (= hawk), hare, harvest, hazel, herb, horse (13), hounds, jade, jades (2), jennet, laurel, leaves (3), lilies, lion (6), lop, meadow, nest, nightingale (4), oaks (2), orchard, ordure, pelican, pine, pines (2), planting, prey, ravens (6), reap, ripe, root, rose, rotten, sapless, seed, serpents, sheepskin, sickle, silkworm, snail, snake, spider (2), thorny, tiger, tree (2), trees (2), weed (2), weeds, withered (2), wolf, wood (2), worms, wormwood, yew, younglings; and it further implies basilisk (poisoned view, shoot poison), cattle (beef, yoke stubborn necks), donkey (bray), falcon (fly it a pitch, soar), horse (pricking, riders, gallop), peacock (borrowed plumes), sheep (flock).

The Hunsdon Froissart

An important recent article (Prior 1993–4) cogently contends that the British Library copy (596.h.24, 25) of Froissart's *Chroniques*, once owned and annotated by Henry Carey, Lord Hunsdon, was studied and used by the author of *Edward III*. So that author 'must have known Hunsdon personally, had access to his library, and used his privileged knowledge in the writing of the play', which furthermore 'contains specific references to Hunsdon's interests; it flatters him by referring more or less directly to his achievements and by providing support for his views' (ibid., 243). Now, Hunsdon was the Lord Chamberlain whose theatre company Shakespeare joined in 1594, the year of its inception, and stayed with for the rest of his life; and no other dramatist is known to have had any such connection. The date of 1594 is of course only a *terminus ad quem* for the composition of the play, which may just as well have served to secure as to celebrate Hunsdon's patronage; he had been Lord Chamberlain, and hence responsible for his sovereign's theatrical entertainment, since 1585. But these new discoveries certainly enhance the evidence for a Shakespearean *Edward III*. Further, the lines instanced by Prior in support of his thesis preponderate in the so-called 'Part B' often denied to Shakespeare (e.g. 64, 128, 134–5, 161, 1240–2, 1335, 1410, 1494–8, 1528–9, 1534–5, 1587–8, 1594–5, 1658, 1662–9); so the argument strongly supports single authorship.

Ideas about War

Any Tudor war drama might mention drums, noise, soldiers or swords; but the dozens of separate and often surprising ideas on those subjects shared by Shakespeare with *Edward III* are surely significant. Examples are as follows.

DRUMS

King Edward has a solo drum speech full of special effects (869–82) as if the theatre company concerned had a virtuoso drummer who could improvise an accompaniment. The Bastard in *King John* also declaims lines about, and through, drumming. The situations are utterly diverse; Edward would far rather make love than war, while the Bastard is bent on battle. Yet the tones and tunings are the same for Venus as for Mars. So are the insistent thumpings on the same word or idea, thus:

Edward III	*King John* (V.ii.)
drum . . . drum . . . drummer . . . drum (869, 876, 879–80)	drums . . . drum . . . drum . . . (166, 168–9)
thunders (869), thundering (872)	thunder (173)
start (870)	start (167–9)
beateth (871)	beaten (166–7)
braces (880)	braced (169)
trouble heaven (882)	rattle the welkin's ear (172)

The crowd-pleasing simplicity of direction-finding by drums is equally analogous: cf. 'But soft, I hear the music of their drums/by which I guess that their approach is near' (1080–1) and 'Hark by the sound of drum you may perceive/their powers are marching unto Paris-ward' (*1 Henry VI*, III.iii.29–30).

NOISE

As Caroline Spurgeon says, 'the action of war is clearly associated in [Shakespeare's] mind chiefly with noise, whether he wants to convey dislike of it or delight in it on the part of his characters' (1935, 76); cf. the cannons' 'hideous noise' *Edward III*, 1207) which however was 'sweet harmony' to a French prince (ibid., 1171). Other parallels between *Edward III* and Spurgeon's further examples of abhorrent-sounding war are:

[drum's] . . . harsh resounds (882)	harsh-resounding trumpets (*Richard II*, I.ii.134)
uncivil [drumming] (881)	churlish drums (*King John*, II.i.76, III.i.303)
groaning cries of dying men (2525)	dying men did groan (*Julius Caesar*, II.ii.23)

SOLDIERS

The *Edward III* soldiers march in step with Shakespeare's men, in four separate respects. They fight or fly, a deliberate antithesis (237–8) often found in the early histories, also in the same line or successive lines (*1 Henry VI*, I.i.98–9, IV.v.44–5, *2 Henry VI*, V.ii.74, *3 Henry VI*, I.i.117–18). They suffer from lack of beef: 'scant [English soldiers] of their chines of beef . . . and presently they are . . . resty-stiff' (1481, 1483); thus jeers King John of France. Similarly the Dauphin compares 'the famished English' to 'pale ghosts'; 'they want their . . . fat bull-beeves', a duke explains (*1 Henry VI*, I.ii.89); cf. also the same jibe in 'shrewdly out of beef' (*Henry V*, III.vii.152) and the same phrase, 'chines of beef', in *2 Henry VI*, IV.x.57. Next, the French soldiers 'stand like metamorphosed images/bloodless and pale, one gazing on another' (2119–20); so the citizens 'like dumb statues or breathing stones/stared each on other, and looked deadly pale' (*Richard III*, III.vii.25–6), in the same memorably marmoreal tableau. Finally the same Bible story is applied to English soldiers in France. When they fight with stones and defeat a numerically far superior force, 'one poor David/hath with a stone foiled twenty stout Goliahs' (2249–50). In the canon it is the English who are 'Goliases' (a plural form imposed by the metre, in *1 Henry VI*, I.ii.33).

SWORDS

The *Edward III* sword is impressively versatile. In imagination, it serves for decapitation (523–4) or suicide (677). It is symbolically sheathed or sharp. It inspires such trenchant phrases as 'by dint of sword', 'fire and sword' or 'threatening swords'. All this can be matched in the canon. More individually, swords are used as arboricultural implements for cutting down, cropping or lopping people and their parts (2307, an idea elaborated in e.g. *3 Henry VI*, II.vi.47ff.). Other *Edward III* swords, again as in the canon, have teeth, tongues and speaking roles. The 'biting whinyards' (211) hang in the same armoury as Lear's 'biting falchion' (V.iii.277; cf. also 'my sword . . . shall bite', *The Merry Wives of Windsor*, II.i.130–1). The swords that shall 'plead for us and our affairs' (1423), namely 'the crown/which . . . I vow to have' (1416–17) are of the same profession and persuasion as the swords that 'shall plead it in the field', namely 'our title to the crown' (*3 Henry VI*, I.i.101–2).

Imagery

HOOPING

'The hooping of a barrel with bands of metal is a favourite image with Shakespeare and serves him to express vividly various ideas of binding' (Spurgeon 1935, 127); cf. the Black Prince among the foe, 'hooped with a bond of iron round about' (2204).

NIPPING

Caroline Spurgeon states categorically: 'I do not find, in all my search of the other dramatists, any single image of frosts and sharp winds nipping buds, which is so common with Shakespeare' (1935, 91). This exemplifies his keen awareness of 'the disastrous effect of spring winds and frosts on tender buds and flowers' (ibid., 88) as in many of his best-known lines, such as 'rough winds do shake the darling buds of May' (Sonnet 18.3). Miss Spurgeon recorded no special study of *Edward III*, which strikingly conforms with her findings *passim*. Thus it contains both the unique specimens she describes; the ill-fated grasshopper of the fable is nipped by frost ('frozen cold hath nipped his careless head', 1258), and the captive Countess's beauty by sharp winds ('a May blossom . . . pernicious winds . . . withered', 279–80).

BEAR-BAITING

Spurgeon also states (1935, 110) that 'I have not found a single bear-baiting image except in Shakespeare. . . . It is noticeable that in every one of Shakespeare's bear-baiting similes, his sympathy is wholly on the side of the bear, and he accentuates the bravery and horror of his position.' On the evidence, the dramatist was himself a spectator; and no doubt the commentator's own sympathies are engaged here. Nevertheless her words well describe the intention of the image in lines 2496–8, where a heroic figure is encircled by enemies.

ORNAMENTS

Shakespeare calls parts of the body 'ornaments', an idiosyncratic image of attire not found in the *OED*. Hair is the 'ornament of his cheek' (*Much Ado*

About Nothing, III.ii.46), hands are 'sweet ornaments' (*Titus Andronicus*, II.iv.18), a woman's lips are 'scarlet ornaments' (Sonnet 142.6). That same last phrase is used in *Edward III* to describe blushing cheeks (359).

SANDS

In *Edward III* the singular form signifies one single grain of sand, in 'the sea by drops ... the massy earth by sands/and sand by sand' (486–8) and 'my handful of so many sands ... count them sand by sand' (1958ff.). This meaning is first recorded by the *OED* from these passages. But on the *OED*'s own dating *3 Henry VI* (I.iv.25) is earlier. The image of infinity in sea and land is also Shakespearean; cf. 'numbering sands and drinking oceans dry' (*Richard II*, II.ii.146). The second *Edward III* passage offers further variations on the theme of infinite subdivision, one of which (counting distance by steps instead of miles) also appears in *Love's Labour's Lost* (V.ii. 194ff.).

TREASURY

The chaste Countess, assailed by Edward, is compared to Roman Lucrece 'whose ransacked treasury has tasked ... so many pens' (1021–2), notably Shakespeare's own; in his *The Rape of Lucrece*, her treasure (1056) was ransacked (838). This frankly physical image is characteristic; thus Ophelia's virginity is called 'your chaste treasure' (*Hamlet*, I.iii.31), Isabella's 'the treasures of your body' (*Measure for Measure*, II.iv.96) and Imogen's 'the treasure of her honour' (*Cymbeline*, II.ii.42). Compare also 'your wives will be abused/your treasure shared' (*Edward III*, 1311–12).

The Image-Cluster

Midway between ideas and imagery, drawing strength from both sources, stands the image-cluster, a convenient name for whole interlocking patterns of association which are arguably so individual as necessarily to have derived from one mind alone. This is the basis for the only demonstration of Shakespearean authorship that has ever been generally accepted, namely the attribution by R. Chambers (1923, 1939) of the insurrection scene in the manuscript play of *Sir Thomas More*. An analogous attempt was made by Professor Kenneth Muir on behalf of certain scenes in *Edward III*. One of his discoveries is here selected as an example well worth further study both in its own right and as a base for further exploration. This is the so-called blot-cluster, described thus:

> The key-word *blot* is accompanied by *heaven, night, moon, constancy, disguise (mask), sovereign, eye, winter* and *sun*. All these words, except *constancy* and *disguise*, appear also in a passage in *Love's Labour's Lost* (IV.iii.220ff.); five of them, including *inconstancy, constant,* and *disguise*, appear in *The Two Gentle-*

men of Verona (V.iv.107ff.), seven of them in *Richard II* (I.iii.202ff.), six of them in *Venus and Adonis* (773–816) and five in another passage in the same poem (154–93). There are traces of the same cluster in ten other plays and in *Lucrece*. (Muir 1960, 22–3)

The clear corollary is that a comparable passage in *Edward III* (495–525) is equally a series of Shakespearean signature-motifs.

The suggestion is not developed in any depth. It might have helped for example to add that *blot, disguise* and *mask* whether as nouns or verbs are rather rare in the canon, occurring only 44, 45 and 39 times respectively, in any form (including *unmask*), among 884, 647 instances of 29,066 different words (Spevack 1973, v). The cluster's components and contexts could also have been more ostensively defined. But there is at least no doubt that a definite and definable compound has been isolated, which might well have sufficed on its own to canonise *Edward III*, had it not been for the devil's advocacy later described (see pp. 209–12 below).

Another image-cluster was defined by its discoverer (Spurgeon 1935, 192–4) as belonging to the category of 'ideas which recur together, but some of them – though they undoubtedly and definitely follow one another in Shakespeare's mind – are so apparently unrelated that it is difficult to trace more than a thread of meaning in them. Such a group is the association of death, cannon, eye-ball, eye-socket of skull (a hollow thing), tears, vault, mouth (sometimes teeth), womb and back to death again.' Such associations are apparent in *Edward III*, where the Black Prince in his speech at Poitiers (1915–23) begins by saying that 'the arms of *death* embrace us round', imagined as a skeleton, 'and comfort have we none'. At Crécy, the prince explains, 'clouds of warlike smoke', i.e. the discharge from *cannon*, had choked up French *mouths*, whereas now their multitudes mask the sun (i.e. in the *vault* of heaven) leaving the English to the 'eyeless terror of all-ending night'. With this second vivid image of a skull's eyeless sockets the thought indeed moves back to death again.

The Law

This is the recurrent theme of the play, which dilates *passim* upon oath-taking and -breaking. These topics are of central concern to Shakespeare, alone among Tudor dramatists; they have been the subject of a special monograph (Shirley 1979, 74) which draws attention to 'technicalities' such as whether prior allegiance nullifies a vow. Such comments as ''tis deadly sin to keep that oath . . . and sin to break it' (*Love's Labour's Lost*, II.i.105–6) or '[thou] mak'st an oath the surety for thy truth against an oath' (*King John*, III.i.282–3) sound like quotations from *Edward III*; so do the following lines from *2 Henry VI*, V.i.182ff.:

> It is great sin to swear unto a sin
> But greater sin to keep the sinful oath,
> Who can be bound by any solemn vow
> To do a murderous deed, to rob a man . . .
> And have no other reason for this wrong
> But that he was bound by a solemn oath?

Like the *Sonnets* and *Love's Labour's Lost, Edward III* also contains constant but usually unobtrusive allusion to legal topics, e.g. inheritor (19), contempt (29), call to record (35), entailed (63), sworn . . . liegeman (68), title (69), repossess (70), penalty (74), liable (224), abstract . . . brief (433), convicted (439), gild . . . paper (477), inherit . . . dispossess (582, 585), sacred law (615), penalty . . . statutes . . . enacted . . . sealed (622–5), warrant (686), cancel . . . bonds (694), attorney . . . court (738), sentences . . . answer . . . suit (767–8), solicitor (774), strict forbidding . . . law . . . cancel (781–2), canon . . . prescribes (782), faults . . . give evidence (913), unlawful (938), title in (969), beyond our law (971), law . . . execute (972–3), guilty . . . gives in evidence . . . verdict . . . judge condemn . . . perjured . . . Star-Chamber . . . universal sessions (986–91), possession . . . surest point of all the law (1156–7), in this manner following (1372), plead for . . . our affairs (1423), covenant . . . lawless (1860–1), lawfully permitted (1866), date expired (2020, 2365), texted (2047), dispense (2317), public law at arms (2424). All this is in addition to 'swear' and its derivates 19 times, oath 15 and vow 5, with 'keep' or 'break (violate, infringe)' to match. Practically the entire cast of *Edward III* seems to have attended law school. The King, the Countess and her father debate like the Inns of Court; French and Scottish kings and princes, an ambassador, an esquire and even a herald all talk naturally in such terms. Further, the misprints 'testomie' (340) for 'testimony' and 'disposse' (585) for 'dispossess' suggest authorial abbreviations of the kind that a law clerk would use. In general, *res ipsa loquitur*.

Marriage

The association of marriage with a special linguistic and conceptual solemnity of ritual and oath-taking is characteristic of the young Shakespeare (Sams 1995a, 49–54, 152–3). Even in this exalted context the *Edward III* examples (lines 609–26, 1009) are transcendent; the language and ideals could not be more lordly. Marriage is a 'sacred law . . . the holy act/made by the mouth of God, sealed with his hand', because the first such ceremony was performed by God himself, imagined by the inventive visualising student of Genesis 2:22 as literally bringing Eve unto the man, leading her along and giving her away like one's heavenly father-in-law. The Countess thence draws the further remarkable inference, unlikely to have impressed her sovereign, that marriage outranks kingship.

'Memorial Reconstruction'

As already noted above (p. 154) and documented below (pp. 209–12), Professor MacDonald Jackson (1963) inadvertently undermined his own identification of *Edward III* as Shakespearean because of his unargued assumption that *Edmund Ironside* could not possibly be by Shakespeare. But this latter belief is baseless, as further analysis has confirmed (Sams 1995a *passim*, and Appendices A and B below). Only two years later Jackson made the same unargued assumption about two other early plays: those commonly short-titled *Contention* and *True Tragedy*, first published in 1594 and 1595 respectively. But this pair are at last gradually and grudgingly being acknowledged as Shakespeare's own first versions of *2–3 Henry VI* (Sams 1995a, e.g. 154–62), just as earlier commentators (e.g. Courthope 1903) once knew and explained, not so-called 'memorial reconstructions by actors' of the supposedly pre-existing *2–3 Henry VI*, which in fact remained unknown until 1623.

For this 'reconstruction' theory, no evidence of any kind has ever existed; yet it has reigned unchallenged for most of this century, ever since it was first propounded (Alexander 1929) and accepted by influential authorities (notably Chambers 1930, i. 281ff.). Indeed, it is still being freely asserted as a famous and well-attested fact (e.g. by Jackson 1986 *passim*, Schoenbaum 1987, 164, and Boyce 1990, 46), despite a dozen definitive disproofs (e.g. Greer 1933, 1956, 1957, Craig 1961, Sams 1983, 1995a, Urkowitz 1988). Under its spell, Professor Jackson assumed that all parallels between *Edward III* (1596) and the earlier *Contention* or *True Tragedy* 'must' derive from the fallible 'memories' of incompetent 'actors' acting as 'reporters', whose subconscious minds muddled up bits of *Edward III* as well as *2–3 Henry VI* in their supposed 'memorial reconstruction' of the latter pair as *Contention* and *True Tragedy*. So the professional Tudor speakers of Shakespeare's lines (as Jackson classifies *Edward III*) 'sometimes confused a passage in the play they were attempting to reproduce with a similar passage in some other play in their repertory' (Jackson 1965, 329). In other words 'they' could not tell one play from another; and this serious handicap allegedly explains all the parallels among all three plays, which are accordingly written off as 'confusions'.

Here (Jackson 1965) are some of the samples offered. 'Clearly the reporters had only a vague knowledge of [the scene in both *Contention* and *2 Henry VI* where Alexander Iden is knighted for killing Jack Cade]', so 'they therefore pieced out their account of it with their recollection of the very similar scene in *Edward III*, as the following quotations will make clear.' The excerpts cited from *Edward III* are these:

> 'Lo, to repair thy life, I give to thee
> three thousand marks a year in English land.' (2331–2).
> 'I took the king myself in single fight' (2425)
> 'Kneel therefore down, now rise King Edward's knight

and to maintain thy state I freely give
five hundred marks a year to thee and thine.' (2446–8).

These lines are then compared with

        'Lo, I present your grace a traitor's head,
        the head of Cade, whom I in combat slew . . .
        Iden, kneel down. Rise up a knight.
        We give thee for reward a thousand marks
        and will that thou henceforth attend on us.'
              (*2 Henry VI*, V.i.66–7, 78–80)

and

        'Lo here my Lord upon my bended knees,
        I here present the traitorous head of Cade
        that hand to hand in single fight I slew ...
        Then rise up sir Alexander Eyden knight
        and for thy maintenance I freely give
        a thousand marks a year to maintain thee . . .'
             (*Contention*,* 2093–5, 2109–11)

The reader is thereupon assured that 'the dependence of *The Contention* upon *Edward III*, as well as upon *2 Henry VI*, is unmistakable.'

What is in fact unmistakable is the inertial force of the *idée fixe* in favour of Alexander's 'generally accepted' 1929 theory of 'memorial reconstruction', without any evidence or argument. Successive further close parallels are similarly underscored with such serene assurances as 'it is almost certain . . . that the reporters were recollecting *Edward III*' (Jackson 1965, 331). On the contrary; all unprejudiced readers, especially those who are also aware that *Contention* and *True Tragedy* were jointly published as 'written by William Shakespeare, Gent.', will soon see the simple and obvious explanation of these close parallels, namely that certain passages in all three plays were written by the same hand at about the same time. Within Academia, however, such needless abstract entities as actors' memories and reporters' repertoires have hardened into concrete certainties, even in the context of *Edward III*, thus; 'MacDonald Jackson has demonstrated that the reporter of the *Henry VI* plays distorted several passages under the influence of his knowledge of *Edward III*' (Proudfoot 1986a, 181). Again, 'MacDonald Jackson . . . demonstrates that there are echoes of *Edward III* in two reported plays . . . I accept Jackson's evidence that the reporters knew *Edward III*' (Prior 1993–94, 264). But there is no such demonstration, and no such

---

* Throughout this section, the *Contention* and *True Tragedy* references are cited from Ule 1987.

evidence. On the contrary, the rules of reasoning require the solution of shared Shakespearean authorship, because that authorship is a well-known unitary fact and reportership is a baseless and multi-entitied theory. So the latter should at last be turned the right way round again, to face the facts, and enunciated thus: *Contention* and *True Tragedy* (*TT*) are Shakespeare's own first versions, and the copious parallels between them and *Edward III* set forth by MacDonald Jackson simply show that the same dramatist wrote all three.

In that context, Jackson's additional parallels are well worth citing, together with his own comments, verbatim, as follows.

(a) 'to maintain thy state' (*E3*, 2447, in the knighting scene already cited above) is matched by 'to maintain your state' (*TT*, 1468); neither phrase 'is used elsewhere by Shakespeare, Marlowe or Kyd' (Jackson 1965, 330);

(b) when the sun lifts up his head (*E3*, 496), the morning sun/ lifts up his beams above this horizon (*TT*, 1836–7);

(c) issue of their loins (*E3*, 12 and *TT* 1345–6);

(d) my soul was much perplexed (*E3*, 2545), my perplexéd soul (*Cont*, 46). As Jackson says, 'there is no other passage in the works of Shakespeare, or in the various plays served by the Marlowe and Kyd concordances, in which the sun is said to "lift up" either his head or his beams, or in which the phrase "issue of his loins" occurs'; nor is there any reference to a "soul" being "perplexed"' (ibid., 331);

(e) seditious Catilines (*E3*, 1056), the aspiring Catiline (*TT*, 1366); 'the context is similar' (ibid.).

Setting aside 'memorial reconstruction' theory, these are all Shakespearean ideas and phrases, especially to those who agree with Jackson that 'there are excellent reasons for believing that he wrote' the whole of *Edward III*. Caroline Spurgeon helps to confirm the (b) example; Shakespeare above all is the poet who sees the sun as a head or face and enlivens his personifications with active verbs of motion (1935, 51–2, 60–3). And Professor Jackson has missed the significant parallel 'when the gracious light [i.e. the sun] lifts up his burning head' (Sonnet 7. 1–2).

Other resemblances may be added. Thus the interjection '*via*', as an incitement to action, *prima facie* invented by Shakespeare in all its *OED* senses (1, 2a, 2b), appears in parallel contexts as an exhortation to take the road of conquest, thus: '*via* for the spacious bounds of France' (*E3*, 830) '*via* to London we will march amain' (*TT*, 710). Again, 'the rancour of their high-swoll'n hearts' (*E3*, 1178) sounds the same tones and overtones as 'the big-swoll'n venom of thy hateful heart' (*Contention*, 117). These and other such examples are surely more like one actual author than a multiplicity of imaginary memories.

New Parts of Speech

Throughout *Edward III* there is a deliberate attempt to extend the bounds of language by using known words as unexpected parts of speech, for example neighbour (adj., 202), compare (n., 559), sot (vb., 432), soar (n., 438), vassal (adj., 754), besiege (n., 769), resound (n., 882), delineate (adj., 910), aid (n., 1146), cranny (quasi-adj., 1212), guide (n. = guidance, 1319), impotent (n., 1446), patronage (vb., 1538), often (adj., 1654), begirt (vb., 1682), fresh (vb., 1773), text (vb., 2047), under (adj., 2097), retire (n., 2244), bemoaning (adj., 2309), bequeath (n. = bequest, 2338), quittance (vb., 2477), hereafter (adj., 2585), resolve (n., 2587). Such neologistic adaptations are typical of Tudor times, when the language was in flux; but Shakespeare was the most verbally inventive of all writers for the stage.

New Vocabulary

In every Shakespeare play there are certain words not found elsewhere in the canon. From the following list of *Edward III* words unknown to the Spevack 1973 concordance, common geographical or historical names and variant forms of known words have been omitted unless they are clearly intended as coinages (e.g. 'hugey'); but the very considerable residue, as follows, testifies to powers of verbal usage and invention unmatched by any other known Tudor playwright.

accomplements (2253), Almaine (158), animates (1531), attirement (1500), Bayard-like (1104), bed-blotting (814), begirt (135, 1682), belly-god (1477), Boheme (1649), boisterous-boasting (255), burgesses (1803), Catilines (1056), cheerful-sounding (166), chess (400), cleftures (1212), commonplace (2033), concept (1152), cornered (2112), counsel-bearer (877), counsel-giver (2295), day-stars (316), death-procuring (2499), delineate (910), discouragement (2243, 2301), emmets (1600), encouch (420), envired (771), ever-bibbing (1067), faceless (258), fear-possessed (2234), fire-containing (2225), flankers (540), flint-heart (423), foragement (753), forefront (1561), francs (1714), gaudiness (1935), glaives (1652), good-presaging (1533), haggard-like (1619), heretofore (49, 1062), herewithal (2553), high-vaunting (2285), honey-gathering (637), hugey (759), immovable (1451), impall (1504), inner (327), iron-hearted (1192), just-dooming (1574), light-borne (206), likened (507), lineage (21, 1455), lion-like (1601), love-lays (449), low-brought (2378), misdo (751), modelled (900), *Mortdieu* (2254), never-broken (2159), new-replenished (1934), nimble-jointed (2007), o'erspent (2412), oriental (360), over-ridden (1484), packing (992), parcelling (1955), piecemeal (104), poison-sucking (639), Polonian (1076), pretty-coloured (2226), quadrant (2490), resty-stiff (1483), scarce-appearing (1532), silkworm (466), snaily (144), sole-reigning (619), sots (vb) (432), stiff-grown (1451), stronger-battled (1928), subjugate (1267), summer-leaping (459), sweet-flowering (1287), swift-starting (2231), texted (2047), thorny-pricking (115), thrice-dread (572), thrice-loving (967), through-shot (1212), triangles (2112), undecked (333), under-garnished (342), unended (490), unfertile (334), unheard-of (2518), unreputed (793), untaméd (1352), ure (165), vastures (759), *vos* (1690), wheretofore (1876), whinyards (211), Xerxes (1102).

Noun-Verb Discord

This idiosyncrasy has been featured (Abbott 1869, 235) as typical Shakespearean grammar, with such examples as 'storms makes' (*Richard III*, II.iii.35), which has survived into the 1973 Spevack concordance although, as Abbott says, the form 'is generally altered by modern editors, so that its commonness has not been duly recognised'. Abbott adds that Shakespeare's general predilection for it 'may well have arisen from the Northern English third person plural in -s'. *Edward III* 1596 offers e.g. day-stars steals (316–17), perfections emulates (509), sessions calls (991), wedding-knives doth hang (998), words tends (1018), exhalations breaks (1175), envy and destruction is (1251), winds struggles (1935–6) hand, foot, head hath (1967), strength and number makes (2041).

Ovid and Plutarch

The dramatist who drew nine-tenths of his classical mythology from Ovid, mainly the *Metamorphoses*, and who in doing so showed no trace of classical learning, has been named as Shakespeare (Thompson 1952, 42). The same authority also identified certain typical allusions. Of one in particular '[Shakespeare] never seems to be weary' (ibid., 58). He likes to record the main names; 'Leander . . . Hellespont . . . Hellespont' (*The Two Gentleman of Verona*, I.i.21, 26), 'Hero . . . Leander' (ibid., III.i.119–20), 'Leander . . . Hero . . . Hellespont . . . Hero of Sestos' (*As You Like It*, IV.i.100, 101, 103, 106). The first context concerns deep love, the other two are about dying for love. So it seems unsurprising that the infatuated King Edward has no sooner told his adored Countess that 'thy husband and the queen shall die' than the names 'Hero . . . Leander . . . Hellespont . . . Sestos . . . Hero' spring to his mind, within five lines (978–82). The source of this story was Ovid's *Heroides*, 17–18; but all the other copious Ovidian allusions in *Edward III* are duly drawn from the *Metamorphoses*. Thus 'the touch of sweet concordant strings' that 'could force attendance in the ears of hell' (427–8) recalls Book X and the Orpheus legend that Shakespeare loved and often cited; so does the King's disappointment when he like Orpheus embraced the air instead of the Countess (643–5) or Eurydice. Similarly the nightingale that sings of 'adulterate wrong' (462) is the transformed Philomela in Book VI; Achilles' spear (749) of which 'poets write,' notably Shakespeare himself in *2 Henry VI*, V.i.100, appears in Book XIII. Perseus and his shield (1524) are in Books IV and V, the Hesperides (1943) in Book XI, the winds and their caves (2081) in Book I, the sun and his golden coach (2094–5) in Book II, the centaur's feast (2271) in Book XII. That last tale is told by Nestor, to whom 'Shakespeare is constantly alluding' as typifying 'the wisdom and gravity of old age' (Thompson 1952, 75); cf. King Edward's reference to 'Nestor's years on earth' (1609). No doubt the word 'metamorphosed' (2119) is equally allusive. 'The sweete wittie soule of *Ouid* lives in mellifluous and hony-tongued *Shakespeare*' (Meres 1598), and one such reincarnation suffices, especially one who like Shakespeare sometimes seems to misunderstand that source, as in the Hesperides and Perseus allusions.

Shakespeare's other main classical source was Plutarch, in translation; and *Edward III* duly obliges with references to Julius Caesar traceable to the Plutarch *Life*; see for example the notes to lines 170, 388–9, 865 and 2321.

Parallels with Later-published Canonical Works

RICHARD II, 1597

1. the . . . bosom of the earth (1117) . . . ocean crop the fleur de luce . . . spider . . . suck . . . deadly venom (1125–9)

    seas . . . earth . . . earth . . . earth spiders . . . suck . . . venom . . . [earth's] bosom pluck a flower . . . death (III.ii.3, 6, 10, 12, 14, 19, 22)

2. castle . . . flesh . . . little breach (2324, 2328)

    flesh . . . little pin . . . castle wall (III.ii.167, 169–70)

LOVE'S LABOUR'S LOST, 1598

3. far to go . . . tells [= measures] . . . miles . . . tell . . . steps . . . infinite (1971–3)

    measured many miles . . . weary steps measured many a mile . . . inches [etc.] . . . weary steps . . . weary miles . . . infinite (V.ii. 184–199)

ROMEO AND JULIET, 1599

4. his ear . . . drink her . . . tongue's utterance (351)

    my ears . . . drunk . . . thy tongue's uttering (II.ii.58–9)

HAMLET, 1604–5, 1623

5. blood . . . vile . . . branches . . . poison . . . root . . . leprous . . .

    orchard . . . hebona [= poison] . . . leperous . . . blood . . . milk

die . . . dug [= teat] . . . sin   . . . vile . . . blossoms . . . sin
(773–9)   (I.v.59, 62, 64–5, 69, 72, 76)

6. (see also 24), summer's day . . .   sun . . . maggots . . . kissing
   taint . . . carrion . . . kiss (795–6)   carrion (II.ii.181–2)

SONNETS, 1609

7. their scarlet ornaments (359)   their scarlet ornaments (142.6)

8. when the sun lifts up his head   when the [sun] lifts up
   (496)   his . . . head (7.1–2)

9. the basest weed . . .   the basest weed (94.12)
   the fragrant rose (516–17)   the fragrant rose (95.2)

10. lilies that fester smell far   lilies that fester smell far
    worse than weeds (808)   worse than weeds (94.14)

11. soul . . . yield this castle of my   soul . . . earth . . . rebel powers
    flesh . . . worms . . . soul . . . city   that thee array . . . outward
    . . . earthly (2324, 2326–9)   walls . . . mansion . . . worms
                                      . . . soul (146. 1–2, 4, 6–7, 9)

HENRY V, 1623

12. drone crept up by stealth . . .   eagle England . . . nest . . .
    eagle's nest [England] . . . shake   sneaking . . . tame [break into]
    . . . storm . . . harm (98–101)   havoc (I.ii.169–171, 173)

13. the tyrant [King of Scots]   [the Scot] girding with. . . .
    . . . begirt with siege . . . castle   siege . . . castles (I.ii.152)
    (135–6)

14. riders rest . . . rust . . . eat . . .   rusty . . . horsemen sit . . . staves
    snaffles [bits] . . . gimmaled   . . . gimmaled [jymould]
    [gymould] . . . staves (204–8)   bit . . . chewed . . . still
                                      and motionless (IV.ii.44–6,
                                      49–50)

15. spring . . . ordure . . . within . . .   outside . . . covering . . . with a
    like a cloak doth hide (338, 341)   coat . . . ordure hide . . . spring
                                      (II. iv. 37–40)

16. write I to a woman? . . . love-   I once writ a sonnet in
    lays . . . praise a horse? (447,   his praise . . . my horse is my
    449–50)   mistress (III.vii.39, 44)

17. sweets . . . sun . . . thaw cold . . .   freshly . . . cheerful . . . sweet
    . . . like the sun . . . cheer   . . . largess universal like the sun
    fresh . . . free and general as   . . . liberal . . . thawing cold . . .
    the sun (510–12, 515)   (IV. Chorus 39–40, 43–5)

18. glorious bright . . . streaming   silken streamers . . . Phoebus
    ensigns . . . silk . . . majestical . . .   . . . order . . . furrowed sea . . .
    order . . . course . . . plough the   majestical . . . course
    ocean (1114–15, 1118, 1125)   (III. Chorus 6, 9, 12, 16–17)

3 HENRY VI, 1623

19. tis impossible that he should
    scape (1585)

    tis impossible he should
    escape (II.vi.38)

20. fear . . . buzzed . . . fear . . .
    prophecy (2231–2, 2234, 2236)

    buzz . . . prophecies . . .
    fearful . . . fear (V.vi.86–9)

KING JOHN, 1623

21. citizens . . . peace . . . constraining
    . . . havoc . . . eyes . . . cities . . .
    fire . . . burning like an oven . . .
    leaking vapour [smoke] . . . wrath
    . . . tread . . . march . . . right
    hand . . . king . . . son . . . hear
    . . . France . . . shaketh like a
    tottering wall (1286–7, 1289,
    1292, 1295–8, 1302–5,
    1314–16)

    hear . . . France . . . eye . . .
    marched . . . wrath . . . walls . . .
    city's eyes . . . havoc . . . peace
    . . . king . . . march . . . city's . . .
    fire . . . shaking . . . walls . . .
    smoke . . . citizens . . . king . . .
    city . . . walls . . . right hand . . .
    son . . . tread . . . march . . .
    constraint (II.i.206–10, 212,
    215, 220–3, 227–9, 231–2,
    234, 236, 239, 241–2, 244)

MEASURE FOR MEASURE, 1623

22. a king . . . joyful clamours
    of the people . . . *Ave* (168–70)

    [the ruler] . . . the people loud
    applause . . . *Aves* (I.i.67, 70)

23. counterfeit . . . stamp . . . King
    of heaven . . . image . . .
    forbidden metal (610, 612–13)

    coin [counterfeit] heaven's
    image . . . stamps . . . forbid . . .
    metal . . . heaven (II.iv.45–6,
    48, 50)

24. (see also 6). summer's day . . .
    taint . . . carrion . . . kiss (795–6)

    sun . . . carrion . . . corrupt
    (II.ii.165–7)

25. holy place . . . authority . . .
    deck an ape . . . robe . . .
    scorn (799–803)

    dressed . . . authority . . . ape
    . . . high heaven . . . laugh
    (II.ii.118, 120–1, 123)

26. die . . . live . . . chase . . . live ...
    pursue . . . die (2051–4) . . .
    idiot . . . life . . . to seek [death]
    (2069–70)

    die . . . life . . . life . . . death's
    fool . . . runn'st toward
    [death] . . . seek to die
    (III.i.4–6, 11–12, 42)

As soon as these parallels are compared in detail their congruence will become even more apparent; and there are some 800 other cross-references to the canon (see the Index, p. 232 below, under association of ideas), all in publications postdating *Edward III*.

Proverbs

This well-documented feature of the early Shakespeare style is represented throughout *Edward III*, both generally and in each of its special aspects, as follows:

(a) a proverb is quoted and applied, as in *The Two Gentlemen of Verona*, III.i.304, 'and thereof comes the proverb'; *The Merry Wives of Windsor*, III.v.151, 'let the proverb go with me'; *The Comedy of Errors*, III.i.51, 'have at you with a proverb'; *A Midsummer Night's Dream*, III.ii.458, 'the country proverb known'; *The Merchant of Venice*, II.ii.149, 'the old proverb is very well parted', etc., with many similar instances of 'the saying is' and also 'the moral . . . is' (*Troilus and Cressida*, IV.iv.107). Compare 'now is the proverb verified in you' (2298) or 'the moral is' (750).

(b) Shakespeare's proverbs often refer to the weather, especially in battle scenes; cf. the former *Edward III* example above; 'too bright a morning breeds a lowring day' (2299), and more generally 'the sun that withers hay doth nourish grass' (747).

(c) Shakespeare often quotes from the Book of Proverbs, in allusions that seem to assume a knowledge of that source, as in *1 Henry IV*, I.ii.88; cf. 'made the wicked stumble at themselves' (1578).

Pun, Quibble, Word-play

Shakespeare is the master of the pun and quibble. No other Tudor playwright comes close to his delight and dexterity in word-play, which often deals deftly with serious subjects. This trait is manifest throughout *Edward III* in over fifty examples, such as:

ground . . . ground . . . sand (29, 31–2), lion . . . pride (102–4), wary . . . war (151–2), well . . . welcome . . . com'st well (265–6), excelled . . . excellence (286), contemplative . . . contemplation (318–19), attend . . . attend on (348), green . . . green (414), direct my style (431), descant . . . voluntary ground (473–4), chased . . . chaste (505), passing passing (528), ground (552), power . . . power (573), weed (642), duty (671), apparelled . . . suit (767–8), solicitor (774), wish . . . witch (842–3), all but one is none (849), charge . . . discharge (851, 853), foot trudge . . . horse (852), arms (883), light (915), colours (924), black (932), yield (949–50), respect respected (956), resolute . . . dissolved (993–4), stain . . . stain (1012), power . . . power (1015–16), handmaids . . . train (1121), quarter . . . quartering (1244), look . . . look for (1264), mould (1350), engraved . . . grave (1449–50), pen . . . draw forth (1518–19), profane (1536), travail . . . big with child (1784–5), therefore . . . therefore (1869–70), loss . . . less (1910), beast . . . beast (2011), expired (2020), pray . . . prayer . . . prayers . . . prayer . . . pray . . . prayer (2031, 2033, 2036–8), time . . .

time's . . . time (2043–4), choice . . . chase (2052), sleep . . . waking (2093), flight . . .flight . . . flight (2103–5), ravenous . . . ravens (2129, 2131), top . . . topless (2198), arm . . . army (2249), bravery (2276), temper (2330), fast- . . . fasten (2496, 2498).

Comparison with the canon exemplifies the same serious word-play, indeed often on the same words. Thus when a watchman stumbles over corpses he helpfully explains that we 'see the ground whereon these woes do lie' but cannot tell their true ground (*Rom*, V.iii.179–80). When a reference to the son of Edward III as a 'lion's whelp' is oddly introduced into the later history of a successor and contrasted with 'the full pride of France' (*H5*, I.ii.109, 112) it is hard not to see an allusion to the earlier pun as well as the earlier play. 'Come, death, and welcome' (*Rom*, III.v.24) is surely an intentional chime. 'Green' was a favourite word for punning on; thus in 'o'er-green my bad' (*Sonnet*, 112.4) that unique invented verb invites instructed readers to recall the recently published attack on Shakespeare by Robert Greene (1592), and the triple 'green' in *Love's Labour's Lost* (I.ii.82, 86, 89) is still eliciting editorial explanation. 'Descant' and 'ground' (*R3*, III.viii.49), 'passed' and 'passing' (*Rom*, I.i.234, 236) are equally typical, while 'apparel' and 'suit' (*AYLI*, IV.1.87) was duly noted in the eighteenth century, and occasioned the significant and insightful comment that 'it is observable that our Poet often falls into *apparent* quibbling or *involuntary* associations . . . when on other occasions the same subject has supplied him with a vein of *intentional* quibbling' (Whiter 1794, 83). No attempt is made here to draw any such distinction; the practice itself is already idiosyncratic enough without further subdivision or illustration.

Rhyme

The author of *Edward III* is a born rhymester, or 'rhyming mother-wit', as Marlowe contemptuously called that low-class category. Rhymes and assonances rise unbidden in his mind, even when there is no clear call for cues. But perhaps that is always their unobtrusive function, as in the canonical plays (Sams 1995a, 57). Thus France/whence (53–4) and storm/harm (100–1) occur at the end of a speech; so does the true rhyme scorn/borne (107–8); the scene closes with way/delay (174–5), and the Countess thus alerted passes the baton to King David with aside/pride (194–5). Similarly arms/comes (260–1) announces a new arrival on stage. No doubt, then, the deliberate change to rhymed couplets at 306–49 also has a dramatic function. Here the verse form itself announces a heightened utterance, like an operatic duet. The end of the scene is signalled when the couplets stop (349). Similarly the cue prove/love (371–2) is followed by an unrhymed line that gives the King time to make a slow and dignified entrance. Thereafter, the poetry relies on the internal word-music of each line rather than on chimes at the end. Later however the cuing resumes; thee/me, would/could (596–9) and thine/mine (602–3) introduces a new sequence of indicators, such as stay/away (630–1) for the Countess, you/too (680–1) for Warwick, reply/die (701–2) and advance/France for the King, and had/bad (724–5) and name/shame (813–14) for Warwick again. Despite inconsistencies, the pattern is perceptible; it permits the inference that swear/here (1013–14) and sky/harmony (1036–7) are intended as rhymes. In the next act (1043–690) the rhymes are rarer, but the basic pattern remains; new entrances, or the ends of scenes (e.g. 1236–7) or of unusually long speeches such as the Mariner's (1189–232), are sometimes signposted with a clinching or alerting rhyme. These were always Shakespeare's unpredictable but recognisable practices, from his first published play, *Titus Andronicus*; cf. for example days/praise before the entries at I.i.167–8, ground/hound at II.ii.25–6, and so forth.

Shakespearisms

In 1911, C.T. Onions published *A Shakespeare Glossary*, which drew upon the unrivalled knowledge he had acquired in his fifteen years of work for the *Oxford English Dictionary*. Eight years later the *Glossary* was issued in a revised second edition, which was reprinted with further corrections seventeen times up to 1980. Its invaluable achievement was to identify certain words or phrases as peculiar to Shakespeare. This signal scholarly service created an unrivalled instrument of identification. Of course it was not infallible; but it offered a clearer and more complete guide than any other such source, the parent *Dictionary* not excluded.

In 1986 a new edition appeared, 'enlarged and revised throughout by Robert Eagleton', *from which all the original references to Shakespeare's innovation had been silently removed*. Not only was this emasculation performed without a word of authority, explanation or apology; the new edition actually claimed that 'the original conception of the *Glossary* has been assiduously preserved'! Protest (Sams 1991) proved useless. But students of *Edward III* may wish to know and reflect on what the Onions *Glossary* said about certain words which occur in that play. These verdicts, cited below from the 1980 edition, have never been disproved or indeed discussed; they have simply been suppressed. Some have already been cited in the notes above; here is a fuller list. In each case the *Edward III* 1596 usage (identified by line number) precedes the publication data of the relevant canonical references given in the *Glossary*, except that 'accents' occurs in *The Rape of Lucrece* and 'bandy' and 'beguile' in *Titus Andronicus*, both 1594.

abstract (n.), in the sense of inventory (433), 'peculiar to Shakespeare'; accents (n.), meaning either language in general or a peculiar mode of utterance (380), 'first in Shakespeare'; bandy (vb.), to contend, strive, fight (2221), 'first in Shakespeare'; beguile (vb.), divert attention in some pleasant way (430), 'first in Shakespeare'; bury (vb.), to consign to oblivion (2261), a 'figurative use, not pre-Shakespeare'; character (vb.), to engrave, inscribe (663, 2160), 'not pre-Shakespeare'; characters (n.), in collective singular use = writing, printing (1449), 'not pre-Shakespeare'; clangour (n.), a loud resonant ringing sound (2502), 'not pre-Shakespeare'; constrain (vb.), to violate (1289), 'peculiar to Shakespeare'; content (vb.), used imperatively and elliptically to mean 'be calm' (1605), 'recorded only from Shakespeare'; cope (vb.), match with an equivalent (1383), 'only Shakespeare'; dear (adj.), important, significant (877), 'peculiar to Shakespeare'; defiance (n.), declaration of aversion, rejection (385), 'only Shakespeare'; in despite (prepositional use), in defiance of another's wish (1660), 'not pre-Shakespeare'; draw (vb.), receive (money), win (a stake) (2066), 'not pre-Shakespeare'; embrace (vb.), to welcome as a friend, companion, or the like (714), 'not recorded before Shakespeare'; engage (vb.), to pledge, pawn, mortgage (561), a 'Shakespearean use'; epithet (n.), term, phrase, expression (380), 'Shakespeare'; expedient (adj.), speedy, expeditious (1924), 'rare sense outside Shakespeare'; fairly (adv.), courteously, respectfully (216), 'recorded only from Shakespeare'; flattery (n.), in the sense of 'gratifying delusion' (657), is a Shakespearean usage; form (n.), order, military formation (546), 'not pre-Shakespeare'; form (n.), image, likeness (739), 'a peculiarly Shakespearean use of an old sense'; fruitful (adj.), abundant, copious (45, 1378), 'rare outside Shakespeare'; gone (adj.), dead (1003), 'not pre-Shakespeare' in this sense; health (n.), a toast (2316) 'recorded first from Shakespeare'; homely (adj.), not beautiful, plain, uncomely (307), 'not pre-Shakespeare in this sense'; honourable (adj.), upright, honest (1872), 'not pre-Shakespeare'; lottery (n.), what falls to one by lot (2066), 'Shakespeare only'; master (vb.), to rule as a master (319, 919), 'not pre-Shakespeare'; metal (n.), precious metal, gold (613), 'peculiar to Shakespeare'; opposition (n.), antagonism, hostility (971), 'not pre-Shakespeare'; out- (prefix), as in outscold (2223), i.e. 'compounds of the type exemplified in *outfrown*', etc. 'are very numerous in Shakespeare and are first exemplified in his works'; pawn (vb.), part with something valuable (744), 'apparently peculiar to Shakespeare'; present (adj.), this present time (1454), '"the present time" not before Shakespeare'; profit (n.), something advantageous or profitable (1838), 'only Shakespeare'; reflect (vb.), to shine (230), 'not pre-Shakespeare'; range (vb.), stretch out in a line (1543), 'not pre-Shakespeare'; rash (adj.), operating quickly (674), 'peculiar to Shakespeare'; return (vb.), give or send (an answer) (76), 'not recorded before Shakespeare'; round (vb.), hem in (1946), 'peculiar to Shakespeare'.

Perhaps some of these identifications were over-sanguine, or even refutable. The original *Glossary* of 1911 becomes less confident in its assertions later in the alphabet; by the time S and T are reached, hardly any words are announced as solely Shakespearean. It may be that Onions himself feared he had gone too far. But which is more likely – that a Shakespeare specialist was wrong about some forty examples of his chosen lifelong specialisation, or that such Shakespearisms occur throughout *Edward III*, as in *Edmund Ironside* (Sams 1985d, 1986d) for the good reason that each is in fact a Shakespeare play in its entirety?

Sir Thomas More *and Other Manuscript Characteristics*

This section starts from the standpoint that the so-called Hand D in three pages of the *More* manuscript, first described in 1728 (Hearne 1914), is indeed Shakespeare's – as first proposed 125 years ago (Simpson 1871), corroborated by detailed evidence half a century later (Pollard et al., 1923) and clinched by cogent argumentation a decade later still (R. Chambers 1939). This slow advance has been recalled by modern Academia. Thus Samuel Schoenbaum has grown less assured each time he tackled the topic: (a) 'Shakespeare's hand is now universally recognised to be present in *Sir Thomas More*' (1966, xix); (b) 'the cumulative evidence . . . may not be sufficient to sweep away all doubts' (1975, 157–8); (c) 'the ascription to Shakespeare remains a theory, not a fact' (1981, 112). The same spanner is thrown into the Oxford *Works*, e.g. in the face-saving clause 'if indeed Shakespeare wrote the scene' (Wells 1986b, 18).

On massive evidence, he did. The proofs include (Wilson, in Pollard 1923) many demonstrable resemblances between the habits of Hand D and the manuscripts behind the so-called 'Good Quartos', which by equally valid inference were printed from Shakespeare's holograph. Before long, the so-called 'Bad Quartos', as well as certain Folio texts, will also be recognised as authentically Shakespearean (Sams 1995a), which will make much more material available for analysis. Meanwhile the same procedure of detailed comparison with *More* Hand D can also be applied to *Edward III* 1596, which was also *prima facie* printed from authorial manuscript.

Hand D is notable for 'excessive carelessness' (Pollard 1923, 117) in its minim errors, e.g. writing the wrong number of downstrokes in forming such letters as *i*, *m*, *n* or *u* whether singly or in combination (ibid., 15). This also applies to the Good Quartos (ibid., 117–18). The same strange failing characterises the author of *Edward III*, whose way of writing 'sand' was twice reproduced by the printer as 'said' at line 488, where the previous phrase 'drop the massy earth by sands' continues 'and said by said print them in memory'. This is exactly the quirk of Hand D, where *n* is twice written with one minim only (ibid., 231). Similarly 'giulty' (630) for 'guilty', 'inploy' (575) for 'imploy', 'spout' (981) for ['Helle]spont', 'game' for 'gaine' (1098) and 'Nom' for 'Non' (1225) are all readily explicable as misreadings of a hand prone to minim errors.

Hand D uses a superscribed horizontal stroke to indicate contraction, but this is twice omitted (ibid., 102). 'Sone' for 'Somme' in *Edward III* (1320) suggests not only that the m̲ had been written or misread as n̲ (as above) but also that the abbreviation sign was omitted.

Hand D, and the Good Quartos, often evince 'the frequent and whimsical appearance of an initial capital C, in a way which shows that Shakespeare's pen was fond of using this letter in place of the minuscule' (Pollard 1923, 115). The same characteristic recurs in the *Sonnets* (e.g. the verb 'Commend' at the end of 69.4), which also give every indication of being printed from authorial copy (Sams 1995a, 195). *Edward III* has 'their Citie wals' (209), 'this Castle' (214), 'my Cosin' (262), 'a Country swaine' (328), '[like] Corrall' (361), 'letters Capitall' (476) and so on.

Hand D also introduces other gratuitous majuscules, e.g. in Bushell, Dvng, Iustice, Leade, Wisdom. So does *Edward III*, often with the same letters, e.g. Battailes (1543), Dug (778), Decke (801), Iacks (207), Lyon (103), Woodman (1655).

Hand D uses an italic instead of a secretary form for what seems to be an initial capital letter (*S*eriant, line 17). Such variation is common throughout *Edward III* (e.g. italic initial capital *A*h 180, *A*las 178, *A*nd 189, *A*rmors 165, *A*s 168, *D*ost 1353, *M*artialists 1496, *T*his 1034, 1094 *T*o 1575) within an otherwise Roman font.

As the following conspectus shows, Shakespeare's *More* and Good Quarto spellings, as analysed and listed by J. Wilson (Pollard, 132–41) exactly match those of *Edward III* 1596 whenever comparisons are available. For convenience, Wilson's numbered categories are cited here, although they are neither exhaustive nor entirely consistent. Where relevant, his comments are also included. Then an illustrative *Edward III* spelling in the given category is listed, together with its line reference – usually each time it occurs, unless it is very frequent, like 'Countes' or 'gratious'. Verbatim correspondences with Wilson's account of the Quarto and Folio spellings are denoted,* and with the *More* pages† (for this purpose otiose word-endings such as mute *e* are discounted).

'i. Doubled final consonant (generally after a short vowel) . . . the double consonant without *e* was apparently also common in manuscript, though rare in print after 1590.'
  doggs† (2498), giggs* [= jigs] (189), sinnes† (2035), wonn* (1411), lippes* (604), topps (1290), farre* (115, 1971), scarre* (2272), spurre* (206, 1409), starre* (990), warre*† (124, 146), sett† (82).

'ii. Absence of final *e* mute. after *c, m, n, s, t,* etc.'
. . . Misprints [such as] 'instant' for 'instance' can best be explained by Shakespeare's habit of omitting *e* after *c*.'
  recompenc (1327), cam (1559), som* (1310), begon* (1150), don (527), gon* (746), els* (562), contemplat (443), emulats (509), byt (1603), infinit (481), not (20), passionat (444), priuat* (36), respit (2365), requisit (452), tribut (607, 2347). Cf also the misprints 'aboundant' for 'aboundance' (859) and 'present' for 'presence' (364), which like the analogous examples cited by Wilson from Shakespeare can best be explained by the writer's

habit of omitting *e* after *c* and the compositor's misreading of the latter as *t*.

'iii. Doubled medial consonant . . . very frequent in Qq.'

cannon (782), collours (118, 650), comming (1800, 2380), coullours (924), courrage (1474), ennemie (1829), forrage (1909), hazzard (2335), limmit (917), linnen (1816), meddow (1116), mettel (613), morrall (750), pallace (592), pellican (1686), pennance (783), pennalty (622), pittie (2362), pollicy (1709), schollers (1450), shaddow (587), sollemnly (1061), trebble (1098), uppon* (74), vallor (1221).

'iv. Single medial consonant . . . frequent in Qq.'

abey (594), aray (824), ariue (2599), cherie (357), comaundt† (699), comence (151), comit (612), comixt (1838), dazle (513, 893), litel (566), litle (527, 578), mariage (615), maried (618), profered* (1991), puisant (2252), quarell (1427), shalow (1320), sodenly (325), stirop (2535), stragling (1160), tyranous (1370).

'v. Final -s for -ss. Writers and printers of the period had the choice between -s and -sse, and it seems certain that Shakespeare generally preferred the former, which had come in early in the 16th century and was going out at the end of it.'

beardles (979), boldnes (543), busines (2137), careles (2304), Countes (553, 562, etc.), darknes* (2081, 2326), endles (953), fatherles (1538), foolishnes (390), fructles (334), glas* (467, 468, 470), greatnes (719), haples (1899), heavines (2483), helples (675), highnes (57, 292, 729, 962 etc.), kindnes (2408), mightines (957), mistres (700), numberles (1301), quietnes (2398), readines (1046), remorseles (1422), saples (1541), senceles (1850), sharpnes (113), sollitarines (1343), stubbornnes (1774), sweetnes (532), unwillingnes (955), wildernes (90), wilfulnes (1613), willingnes (2325, 2366), worthles (1398).

'vi. *ck* for *k* after *n*.'

banckes*† (1421), drancke (1103), francks* [= francs] (1714), incke* (398), rancke* (234), thancket† (527), thinck*† (555).

'vii. *c* and *t* interchangeable, before -ion, ient, ial, etc. *c* was the early form, which *t* was superseding even in words in which it did not ultimately prevail'.

artifitiall (1403), condicion* (451), delitious (763), gratious* (18, 282, 343, 1338, 1530, etc.), pernitious* (279, 1382), spatious (804, 830), vitious* (1404).

'viii. *ct* for *t*.'

fruictfull (45), fructles (334), Poyctiers (1679).

'ix. *c*, *s* and *z* interchangeable. Frequent in Qq.'

brasen (1518), cowardize* (1222), defast* [= defaced] (2081), disgrast (2070), dispence (2317), disserne (1299), expence (1760), fenst [= fenced] (1512, 2253), forst [= forced] (186), horison (2493), orizons (1993), persing

[= piercing] (288), perst* [= pierced] (1237), scarse (1532), senceles (1850), twise [= twice] (2340, 2490).

'x. *sc* for *s.*'
No *Edward III* examples.

'xi. *a* and *ai* interchangeable.'
acquant (556), glaves (1652), prophaine (709), rainge (1235), Romaine* (1020), wast* (2178).

'xii. *a* for *e.*'
currant (2153).

'xiii. *ar* and *er* interchangeable (medial and initial).'
No *Edward III* examples (but see xiv below). One reason, unmentioned by Wilson, for this indifference is that Hand D uses the legal abbreviation *p* for both par (as in *p*snyps) and per (as in *p*ceaves), which could explain why the Quartos sometimes misprint 'parson' as 'person' or conversely.

'xiv. *-ar, er,* [*or*], *-our, ur, ure,* interchangeable.'
arber (412), armor (165), atturnie (738), conspiratours (1457), emperour (158, 844), flankars (540), fryer (1278), honor (171, 304, 616, 745), neighbor (202), pillers* (2523), progenitour (618), rancor (20), schollers* (1450), soliciter (774), timerous* (1408), tortering (2367), trayterous (161), treasory (1096), vigor* (47), vulger (670).

'xv. *au* for *aw.*'
braules* (871)

'xvi. *ay* for *-ey.*'
pray* [= prey] (1772).

'xvii. *ai* for *ei.*'
soueraignc (179, 302, 321, 402, 500, 545, 555, etc.), unfaignedly (1734).

'xviii. *e, ei* and *ie* interchangeable.'
feild* (1342), greif* (673), leige* (631), persing [= piercing] (288), perst* [= pierced] (1237), receue (1430), theis [= these] (1476).

'xix. *ea* for *ei* or *ie.*'
perceaue* (1296), receaude* (1865).

'xx. *ea* for *e.*'
alleageance (614), alleageaunce (2438, 2454), eare [= ere] (1702), hearb (1378), least* [= lest] (103, 1265), repleat* (26), shepheard* (44, 1441), tearmes* (343).

'xxi. *e* for *ea.*'
brest* (1349), ech* (174, 434, 1208), esterne (1036), fethered* (1896), leue (589), meger (1526), perle (1389), stelth (99), spred* (1227, 1488), swere* (598), thred* (2475), welthiest* (1815).

'xxii. -*ey* and -*y* interchangeable.'
hony* (1127).

'xxiii. *o* for *oa*.'
approcht* (1128), approching* (1461), bemoning (2309), cloke (904), cost† [= coast] (1148), croke* (2111), grone* (419, 885), groning* (2525), lothed* (796), othe* (132, 687, 697, 715), reproch* (108, 762), rods* [= roads] (203).

'xxiv. *oo* for *o*.'
belooued (2512), foorth* (190), loose (757, 760, 2266, 2426), moouing* (424), prooued* (1279), smoothered* (2206), woon* (134).

'xxv. *oo* for *ou*.'
No examples.

'xxvi. *ow* for *ou*.'
fowle* [= foul] (1406), howres* (233), howse† (554), rowse* (1281).

'xxvii. *ow* for -*o*, -*oo*, -*oe*.'
No examples.

'xxviii. *ew* for *ue*, *ieu* or *u*.'
No examples.

'xxix. Miscellaneous.'
'bin*† [= been]' (1414, 2434, 2569, 2573), 'to*† [= too]' (339, 463, 469, 681, 983, 1592).

'xxx. Abbreviations and colloquialisms.'
'ore*† [= o'er]' (501, 990, 2014), 'tane*† [= taken]' (1959), 'tis*†' (86, etc.), 'twere*†' (75, 452 etc.).

Edward III also contains certain spelling habits not itemised by Wilson, though surely just as idiosyncratic. In the following list of examples, actual Hand D spellings are added in brackets for comparison.

  i. a for ea: hart, harten, harty (hart).
 ii. au for a: alleagaunce, braunches, circumstaunce, chaunce, commaund, exchaunge, faulter, Fraunce, Flaunders, graunt, inchaunted, pursuivaunt, vauntage (advauntage, Fraunc, graunt).
iii. ee for ie: breefe, breefly, cheefest, feeld, peecemeale, releeve, seege, theevish, yeelded, yeelding (shreeve).
 iv. im- or in- for em- or en-: imbattled, imbost, imbracement, imbracing, imploy, incamp, inchaunting, inclose, incroach, indevor, indure, ingage, ingirt, ingrave, inkindled, inlarge, inow, insnared, inthrone, intombed, intreat, intrenched, inviered (Ingland).

One such example is worth special consideration, namely Hand D's persistent use of *y* for *i* (e.g. 'nyne', 'lyst', 'yt' and 'yf' in its first four lines), which as Pollard points out (1923, 17) identifies Shakespeare as an old-fashioned speller. *Edward III* abounds in evident examples, including 'yf' and 'yt'.

Similarly Shakespeare often writes the old-fashioned 'vild' for 'vile'; so in Sonnet 71.4 and in *Edward III* (188).

Again, the hand of the *Sonnets* manuscript wrote 'thy' in a way that could easily be misread as 'their', as for example in 70.6, where the manifest error 'Their worth' is regularly and rightly amended to 'Thy worth' in modern editions. The same idiosyncrasy is inferable from *Edward III* (442, 556, 761, 1152).

Sources

FROISSART 1513, TRANS. BERNERS 1523-5

As we have seen (p. 149), the Duke of Alençon (*1 Henry VI*, I.ii.29) quotes Froissart's *Chroniques*, which Shakespeare may have known in the original French (Prior 1993-4); the reference is to Chapter LXXVI, where during the campaign of 1367 every Englishman was reckoned to be 'worth a Rowland or an Oliver', the two knights of Charlemagne. So presumably this thoughtful dramatist had studied other pages too, for example in writing *Richard II* (Bullough 1957, i.367; Halliday 1964, 177). He had also researched, perhaps from the same convenient source, the pedigree and general history of King Edward III; cf. *1 Henry VI*, I.ii.31, II.iv.84, II.v.66, 76; *2 Henry VI*, II.ii.10, 20, 46; *Richard II*, I.ii.11, 17, II.i.121, 124, 125; *2 Henry IV*, IV.v.128; *Henry V*, I.i.89, I.ii.108, 162, 248, II.iv.93. The *Henry V* allusions in particular look and sound like deliberate authorial references to a previous work, a typical Shakespeare touch (see Personal Cross-Reference, pp. 164-5 above). The main canonical correspondences consist in the genealogical justification of claims to the English or French throne; their styles and significances are strikingly varied, yet their common authorship is manifest. So their close kinship with the opening scene of *Edward III* is most readily explicable on the same ground.

PAINTER 1566-7

Shakespeare turned to Painter's *Palace of Pleasure* for the Boccaccio plot of *All's Well that Ends Well* and also probably used it for *Romeo and Juliet*; as various verbal echoes clearly confirm, it certainly served as the source for the Countess sub-plot and hence also for the characters of her father Warwick and the King's secretary Lodowick.

STOW 1580

Shakespeare is also said to have studied Stow's *Annales* for special details in *1 Henry VI* (Sanders 1981, 13); so did the author of *Edward III* (Proudfoot 1986a, 168-9).

HOLINSHED 1577 AND 1587

Shakespeare's chief historical source seems to have supplied *Edward III* with the names of certain French towns and the presence of the commander Chatillon.

GENERAL

Edward III 'is as remarkable for the quantity of authentic detail it packs in as for its cavalier way with sources' (Proudfoot 1986a, 169), exactly as everyone has always noted about Shakespeare; thus *1 Henry VI*, one version of which also dates from *c.* 1590, derives details from four main and two subsidiary sources yet remains 'a strange mixture of fact and fiction which demonstrates no real sense of accurate historical chronology' (Sanders 1981, 13).

Tautology

GENERAL

The influential Edmund Chambers was disposed to acknowledge Shakespeare's hand in *Edward III* because 'the ringing of changes is like him', and the 'Shakespearean' scenes are marked by 'a constant habit of ringing the changes on individual words, which often run through longish speeches or sections of dialogue', a feature allegedly not apparent in the rest of the play (1930, i.516–17). But in fact it appears *passim*, for the purpose of hammering home a dramatic or verbal point (such as 'next succeeded . . . successfully' in lines 9–10 or 'ground', 29 and 31, as well as the constant antithesis in every scene).

REFLEXIVE

An editor who can identify 'few mannerisms' in Shakespeare (Kerrigan 1986b, 26) is confident that one of them is identificatory, and offers the following examples: 'Narcissus so himself himself forsook' (*Ven*, 161), 'In thyself thyself art made away' (ibid., 763), 'When he himself himself confounds' (*Luc*, 160), 'Myself myself confound' (*R3*, IV.iv.399). Compare 'fair is she not at all/if that herself were by to stain herself/as I have seen her when she was herself' (282–4), or 'but if himself himself redeem from thence' (1622).

DICTION

The play often piles up three, four or even five near-synonyms in one line, e.g. 'barren, bleak and fruitless' (191). Further examples occur in lines 280, 334, 594, 595, 763, 943, 1786, 1809, 1911, 1924, 1933–4, 1964, 2098 and 2326. This idiosyncrasy characterises the young Shakespeare, where in *Titus*

Andronicus fore example the rulers of Rome are notable for their 'virtue
. . . justice, continence and nobility' (I.i.14–15) but the environing woods are
'ruthless, dreadful, deaf and dull' (II.i.128). It is no mere stylistic trick,
however; the outburst of epithets expresses an intensity of positive or negative
thought, as in those two *Titus* examples and throughout *Edward III*. In later
plays the effect is used more sparingly, as in Hamlet's 'weary, stale, flat and
unprofitable' (I.ii.133). But there too the generative process is the same;
compare the first *Edward III* example above, or the next two: 'sullied,
withered, overcast and done' and 'barren, sere, unfertile, fruitless, dry'. The
same words or ideas often seem to spark off similar powder-trains within
the canon, e.g. 'barren, barren, barren' (*2H4*, V.iii.7), 'barren, lean and
lacking juice' (*Ven*, 136), 'deformed, crooked, old and sere' (*Err*, IV.ii.19)
etc.

IMPERATIVE-VOCATIVE CONSTRUCTION

The trick of enclosing a vocative within repeated imperatives, also familiar in
the canon from *Titus Andronicus* on, is evidenced in lines 477a ('read, lord,
read'), 1013 ('swear, Edward, swear'), 1165 ('fight, Frenchmen, fight'), 1580
('rescue, King Edward, rescue'), 1769 ('go, Derby, go'), 2227 ('away, Artois,
away'), and 2241 ('fly, father, fly').

REPETITIONS

In *Edward III*, as also in the canon from *Titus Andronicus* onward, the
same word or idea is often insistently reiterated, e.g. for the thundering
drums of lines 869–82 or the emphasis on 'break' in lines 686–8, 691, 694
and 702.

Turns of Speech

Wilson (1948, xxiii) lists a dozen turns of phrase in *Titus Andronicus* 1594
which all seem to him typical of, and some (though he does not say which)
peculiar, to Shakespeare. Half of them are readily identifiable in *Edward III*,
as follows. The cumulative succession of phrases beginning with 'this' or
'that' – 'this sacrifice, this first fruit of my sword' (1647); 'Even' (generally
used for emphasis) at the beginning of a line – 'even to the bottom of thy
master's throat' (94), 'even in the barren bleak and fruitless air' (191), 'even
when we had that yielded to our hands' (215), 'even she, my liege' (278),
'even by that power I swear' (1015); 'Now' (as introductory flourish to a mild
oath) 'now God forbid' (554); 'But, soft' – 'but soft, here comes' (538), 'but
soft, I hear' (1080), 'but soft, methinks I hear' (1629); 'Why, there's a . . .'
(Fr. *voilà*) – 'why, there it goes' (928); 'What a . . . !' – 'what a strange
discourse' (377), 'what a world of descant' (473).

Types and Classes

Edward III is remarkable for its intense and constant yet unobtrusive concern with human types and classes, trades and professions. Here is a sample list of those named (omitting ranks, nationalities and classical allusions, which would yield dozens more): actor, advocate, ambassador, author, babe, burgess, chaplain, child, citizen, cockney, conspirator, countryman, coward, cynic, emperor, epicures, esquires, fool, footmen, foreigner, fowler, governor, guardian, handmaid, herald, hermit, idiot, imperator, infant, judge, lover, maid, mariner, married man, martialist, master, messenger, minister, mistress, mourner, nurse, nymph, peer, pirate, playfellow, poet, prisoner, prophet, rebel, reporter, rider, robber, sailor, scholar, servitor, shepherd, slave, soldier, solicitor, spendthrift, starveling, strumpet, thief, traitor, treasurer, tyrant, vassal, villain, warrior, watchman, witch, woodman.

There are also less specific but unmistakable allusions to other trades and pursuits: beggar (begged a gift, needy mate), blacksmith (anvil), butcher (slaughter-house), cooper (hooped with a bond of iron), horseman (reins you with a mild and gentle bit), hunter (the game's afoot), labourers (labouring for a knighthood), ostler (saddle my bonny black), teacher and pupil (Nestor, teach me), tinker (soldered), and writer or clerk (charactered, engraved, ink, paper, pen, print, register, text).

Even to the analytical eye, such references often pass unnoticed. But Caroline Spurgeon patiently counted and classified their use in imagery, and her summary of 'the people of Shakespeare's world as he saw it' is well worth citing and comparing; those noted in *Edward III* are italicised. 'Pilgrims and *hermits*; *beggars*, *thieves* and *prisoners*; *pirates*, *sailors* and *serving-men*; pedlars, gipsies, *madmen* and *fools*; *shepherds*, *labourers* and *peasants*; *schoolmasters* and *pupils*; *heralds*, *ambassadors*, *messengers*, *officers of state*, spies, *traitors* and *rebels*; *burghers*, *courtiers*, *kings* and *princes*. Mingling here and there with these are the members of definite trades and professions, *tinkers* and tailors, tapsters and *ostlers*, as well as *nurses* and *babes*, *women* and *children*, *mothers*, *lovers*, *parents* and *schoolboys*. Thus we find similes drawn from every sort and type of person, but as we should expect, Shakespeare is particularly fond of the humblest and least respectable: *beggars*, *thieves*, *prisoners* and *servants*' (1935, 142–3). These examples, and their close correspondence, are found throughout *Edward III*; in particular that monarch himself is the beggar, his son the servitor, another English hero the thief, and the prisoner in 'dark immured constraint' is an image of concern.

Another character-image has been specially noticed: 'paint, used in the sense of make-up, is mentioned with such distaste . . . and is so constantly brought into connection with certain unpleasant ideas that it can hardly be doubted that it had an intense emotional significance for [Shakespeare]' (Armstrong 1946, 66–7). So it had for Edward of England also, in his address to John of France, whose intention 'with a strumpet's artificial line/to paint thy vicious and deforméd cause' would fail because 'the counterfeit will fade/

and in the end thy foul defects be seen' (1403–6). So Hamlet told the skull: 'let her paint an inch thick, to this favour must she come' (V.i.194); so Claudius calls 'the harlot's cheek, beautied with plastering art' just as 'ugly' as 'my deed to my most painted word'. Such associations with paint, duplicity, whoredom and foulness are, as Armstrong observes, unlikely to be fortuitous.

Words Beginning with 'un-'

Minds that move electively along avenues of antithesis might be expected to use and indeed to coin 'un-' words in profusion. For reasons already given (pp. 171–2), dating and other difficulties impede the progress of research into attribution by way of such an approach; but a list of all such words in *Edward III* is appended in anticipation of better times. The numbers in brackets are those of appearances in the Spevack concordance; the words are often extremely rare or unknown within the canon, as might be expected if they were Shakespearean idiosyncrasies. Those first recorded by the *OED* from this play are marked*, and from the canon†.

unadvised (3), unbridled (2), uncivil (8), uncomfortable† (1), uncouple (3), undecked* [the *OED*'s 1570 citation has a different meaning] (0), undone (61), undoubtedly (1), unended (0), unfeignedly (4), unfertile* (0), unfolded (4), unfought* (1), unhappy (41), unheard-of (0), unholy (4), unlawful (11), unmasked (0), unnatural (38), unnecessary (3), unpolished*† [the two senses are not readily distinguishable] (2), unrelenting† (3), unreputed* (0), unrestrained* (0), unsay (3), unseen (22), unspotted (7), unswear† (1), untamed (0), untimely (27), untouched (2), untuned (0), unwillingness† (3).

Closer comparisons with the canon are also rewarding, as the following selection suggests. First the *Edward III* and then the canonical contexts are considered.

King Edward's 'hot unbridled son', as a Frenchman describes the Black Prince (1305), is clearly conceived as a mettlesome colt much disposed to dangerous kicking. In the canon, 'unbridled' occurs only twice, each time applied to mettlesome youth; the scapegrace Bertram is a 'rash and unbridled boy' (*AWEW*, III.ii.28), and Cressida's unruly thoughts are 'like unbridled children, grown/too headstrong for their mother' (*Tro*, III.ii.122–3). The *Edward III* link of 'hot' with a colt, furthermore, and the canon's of 'unbridled' with youthful wildness, resurface in 'young hot colts being raged do rage the more' (*R2*, II.i.70). The same hand seems to be holding both pen and rein.

The Countess castigates what she calls the 'skipping jigs' of the barbarous invading Scots as 'uncivil' (189); her sovereign applies the latter epithet to overloud drumming (881). In one canonical context (*2H6*, III.i.310), a cardinal speaks contemptuously of the 'uncivil kerns of Ireland'; in another

(*Mac*, I.ii.30), Norwegian invaders are called 'skipping kerns'. It seems that their primitive music and dances, bagpipe and drum, are rated especially revolting; the loud drum is often called 'churlish' (*Ven*, 107, *JN*, II.i.76, III.i.303).

The word 'uncomfortable' occurs only once in *Edward III* and throughout the canon. Both its basic meaning and its shared associations will surely sound surprising to modern ears. In both contexts, it is intended as an unusually strong expression, denoting no mere absence of comfort but the menacing presence of doom and death. A supernatural night falls on the battlefield, so that 'the under earth is as a grave, /dark, deadly, silent and uncomfortable' (2097–8); that last word is intended as climax not anticlimax. Just so in a canonical play; there too the epithets pile up, the sunlight fails ('never was seen so black a day'), death holds dominion, and this moment of time is called 'uncomfortable' by Juliet's agonised father (*Rom*, IV.v.53,59–60, etc.)

Villiers will 'unfeignedly perform' the action of returning into captivity (1734); his adverb means that to do so is his duty, with which he is truly willing to comply, however uncongenial he may find it. Just so in the canon; Queen Elizabeth is instructed to hold out her hand for the hated Hastings to kiss, 'and what you do, do it unfeignedly' (*R3*, II.i.22).

The Countess implores her royal would-be seducer to abandon his 'most unholy suit' (1009). The epithet, carefully chosen to connote evil intent, as contrasted with the holy sanctity of lawful marriage, occurs only four times in the canon, and thrice with that same special meaning. The link is clearest when Polonius denounces 'unholy suits' to Ophelia, warning her that she (like the Countess) will be Hamlet's mistress, not a queen (*Ham*, I.iii.129); but 'unholy match' (*TGV*, IV.iii.30) and 'unholy service' (*Per*, IV.iv.50) carry the same implications.

So does 'unlawful'. Even King Edward admits that he aims at an 'unlawful bed' (938, as also in *R3*, III.vii.190): and that adjective, or its adverb 'unlawfully', continues to connote and condemn sexual sin, not crime, for most of the respective eleven or three canonical usages.

Appendix A:
Edward III *and* Edmund Ironside

General

The acceptance of *Edward III* as Shakespearean should entail the same conclusion about *Ironside*, since both plays are plainly from the same hand (Everitt 1954). The same conclusion will be found to follow from a detailed comparison between the characteristics analysed above (pp. 163–202) and those of *Ironside* (Sams 1985d, 1986d). But this identification has been ignored or rejected, over the last half-century, for no reason except built-in bias (e.g. Jackson 1963 and Schoenbaum 1966, as refuted at pp. 209–12 below). Unsurprisingly, a proposed reappraisal of *Ironside* (Sams 1982a) was met by a misstatement of all the salient facts, and an invented date which supposedly permitted the explanation of 'plagiarism' for all the scores of detailed parallels between *Ironside* and the canon (Proudfoot 1982). The errors were soon refuted, and the inventions exposed (Sams 1982b). But when the play was published (Sams 1985d, 1986d) academic commentators continued to feel that their own rejection was a conclusive criterion. Further, such noted authorities as Samuel Schoenbaum, American Adviser to the Oxford Shakespeare, and Richard Proudfoot, Textual Adviser to the Oxford Shakespeare, had given a lead and set the tone. The chorus soon swelled. *Ironside*, however Shakespearean, was not good enough for Shakespeare, even in his youth; so 'plagiarism' with its necessary but unevidenced 'late date' caught on. No published commentary (as summarised in Sams 1986d, ix–xv) ever mentioned the evidence for early composition *c.* 1588, or ever sought to justify the necessary notion of '1595–1600' (designed solely to give time for the 'plagiarist' to consult and copy a few published Shakespeare texts), or ever wondered why, how or when (let alone whether) the 'plagiarism' had taken place. Such non-stop invention had already become second nature to a profession which relies on it for the current theories of 'collaboration', 'memorial reconstruction', 'source plays' and so forth (Sams 1995a, 173–88).

These academic fantasies have now infested the supposedly scientific study of 'stylometry' (Sams 1995a, 189–92), that is, deciding authorship by computations. Thus one academic statistician has announced that '*Ironside* is not by Shakespeare' (Smith 1993, 204; 1995, 296), on the sole ground that its use of certain 'function words', *c.* 1588, such as 'that' or 'it', is differentiable from the pattern found in *2 Henry VI* 1623 or *Richard III* 1623. The sole defence offered for this bizarre inference is that those two texts 'in fact . . . by scholarly consensus seem to be contemporaneous with *Ironside*' (Smith 1995, 298). In other words, let us assume that the literary consensus must be right. But if that were so, 'stylometry' would never be needed. And in fact the admired consensus, however widespread and however long-lasting, is demonstrably and indefensibly wrong, and so is the 'stylometry' based upon it (Sams 1994c, 1995a, 1996b).

The Shakespeare establishment has remained unimpressed by *Ironside* (so say Honigmann 1987, Schoenbaum 1991 and Smith 1993, 1995). The case contra is often reckoned to be clear-cut (Nunn 1986, Taylor 1986, Ewbank 1986) and the play continues to be dismissed out of hand: *Ironside* is a 'truly execrable' play (Bate 1995a). Even so, it allegedly impressed Shakespeare so profoundly that he stole its ideas and phrases by the dozen for decades afterwards; so he himself was the imaginary 'plagiarist' (D. Foster 1988a, 1988b). Similar fantasies are still being asserted as facts, such as the notion that the Shakespearean authorship of *Ironside* has been 'convincingly' refuted (Seymour-Smith 1995). This echoes the baseless claim that *Ironside*, 'scholars have convincingly argued, was not a juvenile work by [Shakespeare] but rather a second-rate imitation of him' (Bate 1995a). Or again, '*Ironside* seems to date from the later 1590s, so the parallels are more likely to be imitations of *Titus* than marks of the same authorial hand' (Bate 1995b, 81). In reality, *no* scholars have *ever* argued (though a few have assumed, in defiance of textual and historical facts) that *Ironside* is either later than, or a plagiarism of, or by, Shakespeare.

Outside Academia, writers (Burgess 1986, Arden 1995) and a documents expert (Hamilton 1986) as well as actors and directors (Heath 1986, Keatley 1986) were entirely content to accept *Ironside* as an early Shakespeare play, in accordance with the copious evidence. Even an Oxford editor conceded that its author might well have been among the supposed 'contributors' to *1–3 Henry VI* (Taylor 1983), and could almost be identified as Shakespeare 'on stylistic grounds' (Sams 1986b). So 'the whole subject merits further investigation' despite self-induced difficulties such as 'uncertainty over Shakespeare's sole authorship of the three *Henry VI* plays and *Edward III*' (Taylor 1988, 138), i.e. four texts that displayed profound and profuse parallelism with *Ironside* and with each other.

In fact, nobody but Taylor disputes the *Henry VI* trilogy's authenticity; and even he himself (1990) has now accepted *Edward III* as Shakespearean. So have other opponents of *Ironside* (such as Jackson 1965, Proudfoot 1986b, Kerrigan 1986a, Wells 1990). But none of them has ever published any serious investigation of the subject.

Such an investigation now follows. It seeks to show that *Ironside* is from the same hand as *Edward III*; so all who accept the latter as partly or wholly Shakespearean should also in equity accept the former, 'execrable' or not, in its entirety. Further, the evidence, as exemplified by some 120 references in the notes above and summarised in the following pages, relates to the whole of *Edward III* and not to any particular section of it; so the integrity of that play is again validated.

Parallel Ideas

The first Shakespearean to see and state this clear connection was Professor E.B. Everitt (1954, 74): 'Though I believe that *Edward III*, written about two years after *Ironside* [1590–91], and possibly revised in the Countess of Salisbury scenes at even a later date [1593–4], is a much better play in fluency of poetry, and perhaps in dramatic construction (but by no means exemplary in either), I am convinced that the same author wrote both of them in their entirety. Elements of style would persuade me without more objective evidence, but the latter is also forthcoming.' Everitt then sets forth his evidence, which consists of several deep and strong parallels between the two texts, which he cites verbatim. He adds that these are only samples, and that exigencies of space have inhibited a complete conspectus; but 'with so much similarity in style and construction generally, they carry a considerable assurance' (1954, 74–8). So they surely do. Of course both plays should be studied and compared in full detail; the following summary, which includes (marked *) the passages to which Everitt drew attention, is perforce much condensed from the canonical passages concerned and the comparisons drawn in the notes above.

1. Climbing to kingship: 'John of Valois indirectly climbs' (*E3*, 40); 'the ladder upon which your father climbed to get and you to hold this gotten kingdom' (*EI*, 76–8); cf. 'thou ladder wherewithal the mounting Bolingbroke ascends my throne' (*R2*, V.i.55–6).

2. How to treat rebels: 'yoke their stubborn necks' (*E3*, 52); 'yoke . . . their stubborn necks' (*EI*, 114–15); cf. 'stop their mouths with stubborn bits' (*H8*, V.ii.58).

3. Desirable subjects: 'sworn true liegeman' (*E3*, 68); 'sworn . . . liegemen' (*EI*, 890–1); cf. 'true liegemen' (*1H6*, V.iv.128).

4. Unmasking a double-dealer: 'truth hath pulled the vizard from his face' (*E3*, 81); 'he pulls the velvet patch off his face . . . truth . . . truth' (*EI*, 1312, 1314, 1316); cf. 'unmask . . . truth' (*Luc*, 940).

5. Rival kings: 'tell him the crown that he usurps is mine/and where he sets his foot he ought to kneel' (*E3*, 84–5); 'feet . . . Thou standst upon my ground . . . this land is mine . . . usurpation . . . crown' (*EI*, 1807, 1815–17, 1822); cf. 'my earth . . . feet . . . usurping steps do trample thee' (*R2*, III.ii.12, 16–17).

6. How to discredit someone: 'take away those borrowed plumes of his' (*E3*, 89); 'make thy peacock's plumes fall down' (*EI*, 283); cf. 'We'll pull his plumes and take away his train' (*1H6*, III.iii.7).

7. Speaking up to a king: 'I do pronounce defiance to thy face' . . . 'return him my defiance in his face' (*E3*, 92, 2001); 'we do return defiance in thy face' (*EI*,

719); cf. 'defiance in King Henry's teeth' (*1H4*, V.ii.42), 'even to the eyes of Richard/gave him defiance' (*2H4*, III.i.65).

8. Traitors to the realm = matricidal vipers: 'regenerate traitor, viper to the place/where thou wast fostered in thine infancy' (*E3*, 109–10); 'foul mother-killing viper, traitor' (*EI*, 167); cf. 'civil dissension is a viperous worm/that gnaws the bowels of the commonwealth' (*1H6*, III.i.72–3).

9. Traitors = vipers and basilisks: Artois, the viper in (8) above, instantly becomes a basilisk with a 'poisoned view' (*E3*, 121), while the traitor Edricus, also the viper in (8) above, exerts the same fatal effect on the beholder: 'his sight . . . is venomer than is the basilisk's' (*EI*, 1651–2).

10. Colonising: 'the planting of Lord Mountford [in France]' (*E3*, 140); 'I plant you [Danes in England]' (*EI*, 135); cf. 'plant . . . accord [between England and France]' (*H5*, V.ii.353).

11. Defeat in battle = dishonour = blot: 'dishonour's blot' (*E3*, 150); 'dishonourable blot' (*EI*, 748); cf. 'dishonour . . . blot' (*2H6*, IV.i.39–40).

12. Subordination of nobility to their inferiors: 'what a grief it is' (*E3*, 183) [for a Countess to be captive to rough Scots]; 'what a grief it is' (*EI*, 234) [for nobles to see the base-born promoted].

13. A messenger announces an approaching enemy army: 'marching hitherward . . . a mighty host' (*E3*, 228–9); 'coming hitherward with a . . . company of arméd men' (*EI*, 916–17) . . . 'he is coming with a mighty host' (*EI*, 1765); cf. 'with a . . . mighty power is marching hitherward' (*2H6*, IV.ix.26–7).

14. A messenger offers poetic descriptions of the hostile force's weaponry: like 'a wood of pikes' (*E3*, 231) or 'as it were a grove of. . . . pines' (*E3*, 1113), because as Audley later explains, 'upright pikes do seem/straight trees' (*E3*, 1939–40); 'like a . . . grove of ashes' (*EI*, 1340) or with 'spears . . . upright . . . like . . . a wood of pines' (*EI*, 1339–41); cf. 'the thorny wood' (*3H6*, V.iv.67), i.e. an enemy army bristling with weapons.

*15. A messenger offers poetic descriptions of seaborne invaders' banners: 'their streaming ensigns wrought of coloured silk/like to a meadow full of sundry flowers' (*E3*, 1115–16); 'their flags and banners, yellow, blue and red/resembles much the weeds in ripened corn' (*EI*, 1342–3); cf. the analogous associations that begin *Lr*, IV.iv., where an invading army from France enters 'with drum and colours' when Lear is 'mad as the vexed sea' and crowned with coloured 'weeds that grow in our . . . corn'.

16. Soldiers' alternatives: 'fight . . . fly' (*E3*, 237–8); 'fight . . . flight' (*EI*, 182); cf. 'We will not fly but . . . fight' (*1H6*, I.i.98–9).

17. Kneeling and standing: a kneeling subject speaks six or seven lines and is commanded by the sovereign to stand (*E3*, 290–5; *EI*, 360–7); cf. *2H6*, I.i.11–17.

18. A writing scene: ink and paper are called for and appear after a few lines' delay (*E3*, 398, 410–39/*EI*, 1137, 1149, 1159–203), with shared words and ideas – ink (410/1171), ease/easy (415/1169), golden (416/1160, 1189), Muse/s (416/1174), enchanted/ing (417/1189), pen (417/1173, 1188), thou writest (420/1159), word/words (420, 436/1176), sweet/sugared (421, 427/1185), raise/d (422/1180), drops (422/1188 and dew 1172), eye (422/1198), poet/Parnassus (425, 429/1172), love (426/1179), concordant/melodious harmony (427/1175), strings . . . hell/Cerberus (covert allusions to the Orpheus legend, 427–8/1189), ears (428/1164), wit/s (429/1159, 1165), world (434/1184), flattery (439/1181, flatter 1191, 1203).

*19. Drums: they are 'scolding', 'uncivil' (*E3*, 876, 881) 'churlish' and 'rude' (*EI*, 956); they announce arrivals: 'I hear . . . their drums' (*E3*, 1080, 1314; 'what drum . . . tis Edmund!' (*EI*, 956, 959); they can convey bad news: 'our drums strike nothing but discouragement' (*E3*, 2243); 'drum . . . hollow voice . . . mourn' (*EI*, 1561–3). In such disparate respects they are singularly Shakespearean: 'churlish drum(s)' *JN*, II.i.76, III.i.303, (*Ven*, 107), 'Clarence . . . I hear his drum' (*3H6*, V.i.10–11), 'beat thou the drum, that it speak mournfully' (*Cor*, V.vi.149).

*20. Shared sources: 'with Xerxes we compare of strength/ whose soldiers drank up rivers in their thirst' (*E3*, 1102–3); 'we compelled by thirst to suck the stream of this fair river dry' [like the army of Xerxes] (*EI*, 884–5).

21. The enemy and their commander encountered: 'to their cost' (*E3*, 1253), 'he shall be welcome' (*E3*, 1365); 'he is welcome, though I hope unto his cost' (*EI*, 919); cf. 'we'll meet thee to thy cost' (*1H6*, I.iii.82), 'I'll meet thee to thy cost' (ibid., III.iv.43).

22. The demeanour attributed to enemies: 'disdainful pride' (*E3*, 1351), 'haughty courage' (*E3*, 1474); 'haughty courage and disdainful pride' (*EI*, 905); cf. 'haughty courage' (*1H6*, IV.i.35), 'proud and disdainful' (*Ant*, III.xiii,142).

23. Idleness on active service: 'there have . . . securely slept' (*E3*, 1413); 'Canute . . . securely sleeps' (*EI*, 309); cf. 'in dangerous wars, whilst you securely slept' (*Titus*, III.i.3).

24. Swords plead like tongues, for thrones: 'swords . . . shall plead' [for the crown] (*E3*, 1422–3); 'plead your coronation with my sword' (*EI*, 43); cf. 'title to the crown . . . swords shall plead it' (*3H6*, I.i.102–3).

25. Choice of kings: 'true-born sovereign' (*E3*, 1447), '[not a] foreigner [but] mild and gentle' (*E3*, 1466, 1468); 'king . . . true-born [not a] foreigner' (*EI*, 854–5), 'English-born . . . I will be mild and gentle' (*EI*, 213–14); cf. 'I will be mild and gentle' (*R3*, IV.iv.161).

26. National troop defections: '[Genoese] . . . straight retiring' (*E3*, 1562); 'Danes . . . straight retire' (*EI*, 1051); cf. 'our English troops retire' (*1H6*, I.v.2).

*27. Callous fathers: 'if [he dies], what remedy, we have more sons/than one, to comfort our declining age' (*E3*, 1594–5); 'if [our sons] die, they die' (*EI*, 271); cf. 'what remedy? I am . . . unapt to weep' [Reignier, when his daughter is captured] (*1H6*, V.iii.132–3 and V.iv.33).

28. Wounded adversaries: 'sword . . . reeking . . . with blood of those that fought' (*E3*, 1665–6); 'I won with blood, blood of myself and proudest Dane that fought . . . my falchion' (*EI*, 1657–8, 1664).

29. Favoured dukes: 'I . . . am . . . possessed in [my] dukedom [thanks to the] king' (*E3*, 1695–7); 'possess my dukedom and Canutus' grace', (*EI*, 286).

30. Kings at a siege: 'they refuse our proffered league' (*E3*, 1738), 'it will repent them of their stubborn will' (*E3*, 1747), 'when we proffered truce it was refused' (*E3*, 1765); 'dare they thus refuse my proffered grace?' (*EI*, 908), 'your wills . . . you repent it' (*EI*, 899–900), 'stubborn . . . wills' (*EI*, 146–7); cf. 'frown upon this proffered peace' (*1H6*, IV.ii.9).

31. Wrongs redressed: 'enter six poor Frenchmen' (*E3*, 1744); 'enter' [the poor Danes], (*EI*, 105, 137). They recite their grievances to a clement king, who appoints one of his followers to look after them: 'Go, Derby, go and see they be relieved' (*E3*, 1769); 'Swetho, look to them, they shall be your care' (*EI*, 136).

32. Binding oaths: 'mine oath . . . which I . . . may not violate' (*E3*, 1853–4); 'what tis to violate a lawful oath' (*EI*, 677); cf. 'thou makest the vestal violate her oath' (*Luc*, 883).

33. Battle plan: 'then thus it stands' (*E3*, 1949); 'for thus I think it stands' (*EI*, 1403).

34. Associative links: 'married man. . . . blushing. . . . perilous . . . bud' (*E3*, 2048–50, 2055); 'married men. . . . blushing. . . . perilous. . . . buds' (*EI*, 1153–4).

*35. An imagined eclipse: 'fog . . . hath hid the airy flower of heaven [i.e. the sun]/and made at noon a night unnatural' (*E3*, 2114–16); 'the sun looks pale . . . not twelve o'clock . . . tis night' (*EI*, 785, 787, 792).

*36. Weather proverbs after the battle: 'too bright a morning breeds a lowring day' (*E3*, 2299); 'a louring morning proves a fairer day' (*EI*, 1059).

37. Self-slaughter: 'the French do kill the French' (*E3*, 2241); 'English gainst English fight' (*EI*, 1080).

38. Each play and its wars end with a rueful speech about how casualties might have been avoided: 'But had you at first done as now you do' (*E3*, 2558ff.); 'Oh had this day been but a year ago' (*EI*, 1922ff.). The fighting stops: 'sheath up your swords' (*E3*, 2594); 'sheathe up thy . . . sword' (*EI*, 1864). Peace brings respite: 'refresh your weary limbs' (*E3*, 2594); 'refreshing ointments to my wearied limbs' (*EI*, 2015). There will be a short seaside holiday: 'after we have

breathed/a day or two within this haven town' (*E3*, 2595–6); 'go we unto our coasts and feast us there' (*EI*, 2052).

39. Revenge is sweet: 'unheard-of dire revenge' (*E3*, 2518); 'vengeance . . . some unlicard . . . death' (*EI*, 709–10), 'never-heard-of torturing pain' (*EI*, 1276); cf. 'some never-heard-of torturing pain' (*Titus*, II.iii.285).

40. Little England: 'that little isle' (*E3*, 2577); 'this little isle' (*EI*, 1897); cf. 'This sceptred isle . . . this little plot' (*R2*, II.i.40, 45).

41. Flattery is condemned *passim*, in all its forms; each play contains the words flatter, flatterer, flattering and flattery, with six such references in *Edward III* and no fewer than fifteen in *Ironside*; cf. the copious canonical parallels.

42. Finally there is the blot-cluster, as already adumbrated at pp. 177–8 above and now to be discussed in detail.

The Blot-Cluster

Many commentators have recognised Shakespeare's hand in *Edward III*, but few have defined any of its fingerprints. Much credit is due to Professor Kenneth Muir (1960) for his discovery in that play of a particular image-cluster character-istic of the canonical Shakespeare. This strong new link was tested by Professor MacDonald Jackson (1963), who inadvertently destroyed it in the process (p. 156 above). This was doubly unfortunate, because he repeatedly concluded in further articles (1965, 1971) that *Edward III* was indeed Shakespearean, which on any rational assessment helps to validate this image-cluster as an authentic example of subconscious association, and hence a mark of individual identity. Professor Jackson, furthermore, was able to augment the already powerful evi-dence by further discoveries of his own. His actual words are worth recording. He explains (1963, 331) how 'E. A. Armstrong, in *Shakespeare's Imagination* (1946), has shown how certain ideas, words and images tend to become associ-ated one with another in the dramatist's subconscious mind, so that they are likely to appear together in his pages even though there may be no immediate logical connection between them. The presence of peculiarly Shakespearean image-clusters in *Edward III* and *The Two Noble Kinsmen* is one of the criteria by which Shakespeare's hand in these plays is demonstrated by Kenneth Muir', whose definition of the *Edward III* blot-cluster (pp. 117–8 above) is then cited verbatim. Jackson next proceeds to extend that definition further, very insightfully, as follows:*

> '*Disguise* is the only element lacking in a *blot*-cluster appearing in *Edmund Ironside*: *blot* (748), *heaven(s)* (784, 786), *night* (792), *moon* (785), *eye* (782), *frost* (743) for *winter*, *sun* (785), *forsaken* (754) and *fickle* (769) for

---

* Save that the *Ironside* line references have been changed to conform with the latest edition (Sams 1985d, 1986d).

(in)constancy, monarchs (776) for *sovereign*. It will be noted that the main body
of this cluster is somewhat separated from the keyword, while the juxtaposi-
tion of such words as *heaven, sun, eye, moon* and night is not likely to have been
a habit peculiar to Shakespeare; thus the appearance of a *star* in the *Venus and
Adonis* (773–816), *Love's Labour's Lost* and *Edmund Ironside* contexts is not
surprising. But between the *Edmund Ironside* passages and the two passages in
Venus and Adonis there exist less predictable links. In the poem at line 163 are
the words *Torches are made to light* and Canutus tells Edricus *go, fetch a torch
to light me to my tent*, while the expression *misty vapours* is common to poem
(184) and play (796); *midday* in *Venus and Adonis* might be compared with
twelve o'clock in *Edmund Ironside* (787). The number *twenty thousand* provides
an additional link between the play (741) and the other *Venus and Adonis*
cluster (745). An *Ethiopian* follows the cluster in *Edmund Ironside* (811) and
an *Ethiope* in *Love's Labour's Lost* (IV.iii.262). Everitt (1954, 134–5) notes that
the words *blot* and *twenty thousand* occur in a passage in *Richard II* (III.iii.62–
90), which is closely paralleled in this portion of *Edmund Ironside*. There is a
speech in *The Two Gentlemen of Verona* (II.vi) which, although it does not
contain the word *blot*, is related to the *blot*-cluster in that play and includes the
words *star, sun, sovereign, heaven, constant* and *disguising*, and there too the
word *Ethiope* and the number *twenty thousand* appear.'

For many readers, that analysis might well have sufficed to show the presence
of Shakespeare's hand in *Ironside*. Professor Jackson went on to reinforce that
inference by examining contexts in which the word 'blot' appears in work by
other Elizabethans. He 'traced fifty-odd examples in the concordances to
Spenser, Kyd, and Marlowe, and found that in no case did more than a few
components of the Shakespearean cluster occur within comparable distance of
the keyword, while the tautology *misty vapours* was not used by the three authors
at all'.

To recapitulate: Jackson, thirty years ago, accepted Muir's image-cluster technique as showing Shakespeare's presence in *Edward III*: indeed, only two years
later (Jackson 1965, 330) 'It is now virtually certain that Shakespeare had at
least a share in the writing of *Edward III*, and there are excellent reasons for
believing that he wrote it all.' Jackson had already also agreed (1963, 331)
that one reviewer (Reese 1955) had not only paid detailed tribute to the work
of E.B. Everitt on *Edmund Ironside* but found it 'an impressive statement in
favour of Shakespeare's authorship' which was not only 'interesting' but 'persuasive'.

So the conclusion follows as day night; not only *Edward III* but *Edmund
Ironside* is authentically Shakespearean. Some of the new evidence, furthermore,
was added by Jackson himself. His analysis of the blot-cluster contains various
inaccuracies and lacunae, for example his failure to stipulate *king* (767) as well as
monarchs in *Ironside*, or to explain that the protagonist Edricus will soon be
literally disguised and unmasked, so that 'disguise', so far from being a missing
element, is actually a main theme. Nor should Shakespeare's phrase *misty vapours*

have been dismissed as mere tautology; the epithet (however surprisingly) connotes darkness here as elsewhere in the works. Again, it would have been helpful to point out that *misty vapours* is unique in the canon – and that each of its components, like *torch*, is a rarity. Further, *Ethiopian* in any form is found only eleven times all told, while 'midday' (or any synonym, including 'noon'), like 'twenty thousand', occurs only some thirty times. And since an admittedly genuine but hitherto unobserved Shakespearean image-cluster is under discussion, some thoughts on the associative interconnection of its components might not have come amiss.

But all such carping is eclipsed by the illuminating presence of this same cluster in both *Edward III* and *Edmund Ironside*, given also the accepted Shakespearean origins of the former. Yet no such inference was drawn; quite the contrary. Professor Jackson accepted the method as identificatory; he accepted this particular image-cluster as valid for *Edward III*; he documented its appearance in ten words from fifty *Ironside* lines; he even added half a dozen new links of his own. Yet his conclusion (1963, 332) was not only that all this 'may be thought of either as supporting Everitt's [*Ironside*] theory or as raising doubts as to the validity of this kind of evidence' but indeed that such doubts must prevail – ostensibly because a quite different image-cluster, the validity of which remains entirely undiscussed, arguably occurs in a poem by Shelley. And these same illogical reservations were still being explicitly avowed and defended twenty years later (Jackson 1982).

The only possible explanation for such a *non sequitur* is the underlying and unstated assumption that *Ironside cannot possibly be by Shakespeare*, so the shared cluster *must* be mere coincidence. And this has remained the accredited attitude throughout academia. It was duly admired and applauded by one authority in particular, again without evidence or discussion, as follows: 'The blot-cluster that Muir cites as evidence for Shakespeare's hand in *Edward III* has recently been discovered in the anonymous *Edmund Ironside* which, *pace* Everitt, Shakespeare is most unlikely to have written' (Schoenbaum 1966, 147). Again the investigator rates his personal opinions about *Ironside* as vastly more significant than any objective evidence and indeed even considers them an argument for the rejection of *Edward III* itself. Yet these opinions appeared in Professor Schoenbaum's *Internal Evidence and Elizabethan Dramatic Authorship*, still the only book on its subject, and the source of Schoenbaum's Law, already cited (p. 152), namely that opinions are of no account, 'no matter how learned, respected or confident the authority'.

No doubt there is no infallible Rorschach test for the blot-cluster. But its train of thought runs on lines paralleled so often and so closely in the canon that the route looks recognisably Shakespearean. The right way to explore it proceeds through the canonical texts cited by the two pioneers Muir and Jackson, which lead directly to other such discoveries. This same Shakespearean essence can be seen, distilled and crystallised, in Sonnet 33, which begins with a large number: 'Full many a glorious morning'. The implied 'sun' soon emerges as 'sun (heavenly, celestial, suns, heaven's sun)' via 'flatter', 'sovereign', 'eye', 'face (visage, brow)', in stark contrast with 'basest clouds', 'region cloud', 'ugly rack', 'unseen', 'disgrace' and 'masked', to close in the final chilling discord 'stains . . . staineth'. Inconstancy is the theme; 'noon' is implied in the transit from east to west. The whole picture is painted from the blot-cluster palette. And if 'every word doth almost tell my name', as Shakespeare said in and of his sonnet-writing (76.7), the parallel passage in *Edward III* (495–525) is hardly less identificatory.

Further, two similar contrasts in analogous language occur elsewhere in *Edward III*. At lines 282–93 the words 'her dim decline hath power to draw/my subject eyes from piercing majesty/to gaze on her' are preceded by *king, stain* and *eyes* and followed by *many millions*, while lines 1918–23 contain *clouds, smoke, multitudes of millions, masking, sun, dark, eyeless, night*. The whole question of such associations in the canon merits closer investigation. In particular, it is time to release the blot-cluster argument from its present undignified position of having been summarily stood on its head for the last thirty years and more. As soon as it is set to rights it will be heard clamouring that what makes sense for the Shakespearean attribution of *Edward III* must also apply to *Edmund Ironside*, because both those plays, and the canon, identifiably contain the same 'blot' image-cluster.

Vocabulary and Diction

Similarly both those plays, and the canon, contain the same vocabulary and diction. Those are the grounds on which *Edward III* was first identified as Shakespearean (Hart 1934, 219–41). *Ironside* strongly resembles *Edward III* in such respects also, as first expounded twenty years later (Everitt 1954, 158–67). But again, as already adumbrated (pp. 203–4 above), *Ironside* aroused resistance and misrepresentation (e.g. Schoenbaum 1966, 126), no doubt quite unconsciously. Certainly deliberate, however, was the concomitant dismissal of Everitt's work as eccentric folly (Schoenbaum 1966, 143, 188). Those tones and attitudes have continued for a quarter of a century (Schoenbaum 1991, 552), without any trace of objective argument.

The record should surely be set straight, and posthumous amends made to E.B. Everitt, who read Hart carefully and interpreted him correctly. Here is what the latter actually said. First '*Edward III* has in proportion to its length the largest vocabulary of any play belonging to the last decade of the sixteenth century that I have examined; in this respect only *King John* is the only play that may challenge comparison with it. . . . If we must pick from known dramatists one literary parent for this nameless waif, Shakespeare is the man. Each of his plays on English history, not alone those written prior to 1596, has a vocabulary comparable in size to that of *Edward III*.' Hart adds that this vocabulary size makes the play 'a misfit' if placed alongside 'Marlowe's, Greene's, Peele's or Kyd's', all of which he had analysed in depth and detail. He concedes the possibility that 'the author of *Edward III*' may be an unknown man, but 'the possession of an unusually large stock of words is a rare and well-marked literary characteristic, unlikely to be common to two dramatic authors of this short period' (1934, 222–3).

So the conclusion thus far is not an unknown Anon. but Shakespeare. The Ule concordance (1987) permits a direct comparison between *Edward III* and *Ironside*. The former (Ule 1987 I, 195) has a total vocabulary of 3,724 different words (counting each inflexion separately) in 2,646 lines (including stage directions); the latter (ibid., 469), on the same basis, has 3,036 different words in 2,157 lines. Thus the unusually large word stock of *Edward III* works out at 1.41 per line; and this is exactly matched by the word-stock of *Ironside*, which is also 1.41 per line. This precise correspondence plainly points to the same playwright at about the same period; and Hart in effect identifies him as Shakespeare.

Further, those who are content to read and ponder what Everitt himself actually says will come ineluctably to the same conclusion. His words are these: 'Does the vocabulary of *Edmund Ironside* conform with the idiosyncrasies of *Edward III* and Shakespeare's early plays? Surprisingly, we find that its attributes are precisely those discerned and described by Alfred Hart, and that they are even more marked than in *Edward III* and *1 Henry VI*, the two plays chronologically closest to it among the five to ten he variously uses for his data on diction' (Everitt 1954, 159). Further, *Ironside* exceeds even the accepted Shakespearean plays in its use of compound words. It has 'a compound for every 20 lines; *Edward III*, one for every 18' (ibid., 162), while Marlowe, Greene and Peele each average one compound for every 32 lines.

The only other vocabulary analyst to have investigated *Edward III* comes to the same conclusions; the results are 'compatible with authorship by Shakespeare at an early stage in his dramatic career' (Slater 1988, 135), while a similar analysis of *Ironside* 'can be regarded as providing evidence which tends to support the hypothesis' that it too is an early Shakespeare play (ibid., 258).

It should be said that Slater's rare-word approach to attribution problems has been rejected on technical grounds by a mathematician (Smith 1986, 1988b), whose own methods have also been called into question (Sams 1994c, 1996b). But so-called 'stylometry' is a young and unproven discipline, which is no doubt capable of further development (Sams 1995a, 189–92). Meanwhile it can at least be said that Slater's work 1975–88 has escaped the criticism of Schoenbaum (1991); and that the latest stylometric methods for determining the authorship of Renaissance plays either allocate *Edward III* to Shakespeare (Matthews and Merriam 1993) or find no serious challenge to its status as 'the best candidate from the apocryphal plays for inclusion in the canon' (Hope 1994, 137) while *Ironside*, by the latter criteria, 'looks a very strong candidate for further investigation' (ibid., 140, 154).

Meanwhile other vocabulary evidence can be deployed, such as the remarkable affinities between *Edward III* and *Ironside* at the level of single words. Thus the former play was documented under the heading 'New Vocabulary' above (pp. 183–4) as containing many words which do not occur in the canon. But several of these occur verbatim, or are closely matched, in *Ironside*, in the same or analogous contexts. Thus 'discouragement' (*E3*, 2243, 2301) is paralleled by

Ironside's 'discourage' (1106, 1754) and 'discouraging' (1000), which are also unknown in the canon. All five usages refer to the literal military sense of rendering a force unfit to fight by depriving soldiers of their courage. Similarly the unknown 'forefront' (*E3*, 1561) means the van of a battle in *Ironside* also (998, 1704). 'Heretofore' for 'hitherto' is found in both sources (twice in *E3*, 49, 1062, once in *Ironside*, 1482); so is 'immovable' (1451 and 2001 respectively). In both plays, 'likened' is used to introduce a long and elaborate image (507, 606); 'masterships' is applied ironically *de haut en bas* (1820, 1253); 'piecemeal' (104, and thrice in *Ironside*, 611, 696, 738) refers in all four contexts to physical dissolution, and in both plays (104, 696) to dismemberment. Similarly the uncanonical 'unheard-of' in *Edward III* (2518) matches the rare 'unheard' (710) in *Ironside*; the former threatens 'sharp unheard-of dire revenge' and the latter 'vengeance . . . some unheard monstrous death'.

Again, both plays use uncommon words beginning with 'un-' in the same special sense, which make the negative particle no mere denial but a passionate affirmation of the opposite; thus 'uncivil' (*E3*, 189, *Ironside* 1805) means hatefully foreign and barbaric, and 'unrelenting' (1505, 1434) merciless in battle.

Some of *Edward III*'s many Shakespearisms (listed under that heading above, pp. 190–2) as specified in Onions 1980 also occur verbatim in *Ironside*, namely bury (*E3*, 2261, *Ironside*, 1725), content (1252/1605/2515, 1951/1991), defiance (92/2001, 719), embrace (41, 365), flattery (657, 1464) homely (307, 1847), honourable (1872, 634) and return (2001, 719), among many other such correspondences. The manifest inference is again that the same writer has coined or is using the same vocabulary in the same contexts.

Manuscript Characteristics

Other qualities common to both plays also impose the inference of shared authorship. Thus the first edition of *Edward III* was *prima facie* printed from authorial holograph fair copy including corrections; there is every reason to accept, and none to doubt, that its many endemic errors and eccentricities, which appear constantly and consistently, reflect the idiosyncrasies of the manuscript, not the whim of the printers. So these characteristics should be analysed with care, and carefully compared by expert specialists with each play that can be reasonably attributed to the young Shakespeare. Several samples have been suggested (e.g. in Everitt 1954 or Sams 1995a). The following items relate to *Edward III*. Those marked * have already been discussed in detail (pp. 192–9); they are repeated here in abbreviated form for convenience of comparison with *Ironside*.

1. The stage directions are centred and italicised.
2. On occasion these directions are printed in much larger type (e.g. at 1038ff.), as if they had been written in a different style.
3. The word 'FINIS' is added at the end, in large letters.

4. The use of different styles may suggest legal training or experience.
5. Latin citations are italicised (e.g. 'when *Ave Caesar* they pronounce aloud', 170, or '*sic et vos*', 1690).
*6. The writer's hand was liable to minim errors.
*7. The writer used a horizontal stroke over *n* or *m* to indicate that the consonant was doubled.
8. The first letter of a line or word is often printed as italic (168, 178, 180, etc.).
*9. Initial letters, especially *C*, are capitalised for clarity.
*10. The same applies to other capitals of almost every letter-form, which are also used on occasion, quite arbitrarily, instead of their lower-case equivalents.
*11. Much of the orthography was old-fashioned for 1596 or indeed earlier.
*12. In particular, *y* was often used for *i*, (Boswell 1928, xvi).
13. The writer's 'thy' was sometimes misread as 'their' (442, 556, 761, 1152).
*14. The spellings are Shakespearean in the verifiable particulars of some thirty separate categories, as analysed by Wilson (Pollard 1923, 113–41).
15. In addition, there are certain *Edward III* spellings not itemised by Wilson (yet just as idiosyncratic as his examples), such as *a* for *ea* (hart, harten, harty); *aine* for *-en* (barraine, suddaine); *au* for *a* (alleagaunce, braunches, circumstaunce, chaunce, commaund, exchaunge, faulter, Fraunce, Flaunders, graunt, inchaunted, pursuivaunt, vauntage); *ee* for *ie* (breefe, breefly, cheefest, feeld, peecemeale, releeve, seege, theevish, yeelded, yeelding); *im-* or *in-* for *em-* or *en-* (imbattled, imbost [embossed], imbracement, imbracing, imploy, incamp, inchaunting, inclose, incroach, indevor, indure, ingage, ingirt, ingrave, inkindled, inlarge, inow, insnared, inthrone, intombed, intreat, intrenched, inviered); *o* for *ou* (cosin, yonger, mornefull); *oa* for *o* (choake, droane, smoake, stroake, throane, yoake); *ou* for *o* (aboundance, coullors, coult, gould, Mountague, scoulding, souldered, wounder); past participles in *-t* (e.g. comixt, curst, disperst, past, stept); 'these' spelt 'theis', and the leaving of spaces in the middle of words, e.g. 'a misse' (amiss).

The extant manuscript of *Edmund Ironside*, as any ticket-holder can verify in the Students' Room of the British Library, contains all the above-mentioned characteristics including most of the idiosyncratic spellings identified by Wilson.

1. The stage directions are centred and sometimes italicised.
2. The writer is well versed in various styles, including 'a beautiful Text hand' and 'Roman capitals' (Everitt 1954, 48) as well as italic, two kinds of secretary (cursive and formal), and imitations of black-letter type.
3. The final 'Finis' is in large italics.
4. 'The hand . . . is of a very formal and distinctly legal type'; the possible slips of 'messuage' for 'message' and '*eos*' for '*oes*', i.e. *omnes* 'would certainly suggest the scribe's familiarity with legal phraseology' and contractions (Boswell 1928, vii).

5. A Latin quotation is italicised (1555–6).
6. Inadvertent minim errors abound, e.g. 'Comquest' (12) 'emough' (174), 'esteened' (237), 'exclaine' (1648), 'tyneles' (1928); Boswell (1928) draws attention to a score of such examples.
7. Double *m* is commonly indicated by a tittle over the *m*.
8. 'An Italian capital at the beginning of a word in English script is frequent' (Boswell 1928, vii).
9. The use of large for small *C* is conspicuous throughout, even in verbs. Furthermore, these otiose capitals often begin the same words in the *Ironside* MS as in the *Edward III* Quarto, e.g. Cannot, Captain, Castle, Children, City, Cloak, Conquest, Coronation, Cousin, Country, Courage, Court, Crown. The inference is that each writer was aware that his way of writing a small *c* lacked clarity.
10. Almost every other letter is occasionally capitalised, very often in the same actual words as in *Edward III*, e.g. Art, Arms, Axe, Banners, Battles, Dominions, Duke, Earl, Herald, Isle, Lady, Law, Navy, North, Northen [*sic*], Orator[y], Queen, Realm, Royal, Son, Summer, Sun, Town, Traitor, Trumpet, Warlike.
11. 'We find . . . forms . . . current in the fifteenth century but antiquated in the days of Elizabeth' (Boswell 1928, viii).
12. Among old-fashioned forms, *y* for *i* appears *passim*, in frequent examples including *yf* and *yt*.
13. 'Thy' is consistently spelt 'thie' (see for example the Boswell reproduction of the last page, Fol. 118: 'thie selfe' and 'thie enimies'). Whenever terminal *e* was written with an added flourish, as often in *Ironside*, the ending could readily be misread as *r*; and 'their' was often spelt 'thier' in Tudor times.
14. There are evident hazards in comparing manuscript spellings *c.* 1588 with those of a printed text dated 1596. Each source contains wide variation; and the latter would no doubt be normalised in accordance with the house style. Nevertheless the authorial orthography of *Ironside* can be matched in *Edward III* in almost all the categories identified by Wilson as typically Shakespearean. Examples are copious; the following list, again numbered as in Pollard 1923, 132–41, is confined to exact correspondences between the two texts:
    i. dogg, farre, scarre, sinne, starre, sunne, warre.
    ii. els, gon, privat, welcom.
    iii. collour, pittie, pollecy, uppon, vallor.
    iv. arive, comaund, lytle, marie.
    v. busnes, healples, highnes, kindnes.
    vi. incke, thancke, thincke.
    ix. expence.
    xiv. armor, honor, tortering.
    xvii. soueraigne.
    xviii. feild, leige[men], theis.

  xix. perceave, receave.
   xx. eare [ere], tearmes.
  xxi. brest, spred.
  xxiii. approch, costs, othe.
  xxiv. loose, woone,
  xxvi. hower, howse.
  xxix. bin [= been], to [= too].
  xxx. ore [o'er], tis, twere.

15. *Ironside* shares these same characteristics, often in the same words or stems, thus: hartes; barraine, suddaine; chaunce, comaund, faulter; breefe, peecemeale, releeve, theeves; imbrace, imploye, inchaunting, indevor, indured, intreat; morne; stroakes, yoake; gould, skould; past participles in -*t* (mixt, curst, disperst, past, stept); 'these' spelt 'theis'; and the leaving of spaces in the middle of words, e.g. 'su ch' for such.

Many Shakespeareans might have thought such questions worth investigating further. The professional editor, as typified by Taylor (1988, 138), simply says that Sisson (1955) was unconvinced by Everitt, and Hamilton (as cited in Corathers 1986) is 'controversial' and 'too recent to have been subjected to thorough scholarly scrutiny'. Indeed, one commentator has recently made the claim that Hamilton later withdrew his support for 'the rather second-rate' *Ironside* (Fleissner 1995), which is entirely untrue; but as Shakespeare says, 'a staff is quickly found to beat a dog'. The rest is silence, and may well remain so for ever. Palaeography is a dying art, if not a dead letter, and its practitioners prefer to keep their own counsel on such subjects. Meanwhile stylometrists as well as stylists have accepted or rejected *Ironside* and each other (as discussed in Sams 1986d, vii–xv, 1994c and 1995a), and will no doubt continue to do so. But even some of the rejectors (Taylor 1988, 138, Hope 1994, 141) prudently concede that there is quite a good case, which is well worth further investigation. In academia the *Ironside* jury is still out. But its current recorded *Edward III* verdict is Shakespeare, *nem. con.* So if those two plays are demonstrably from the same hand, then all the massive *Ironside* evidence so far overlooked or dismissed should at last be given its full due by stylometrists and palaeographers as well as commentators in general. More than ever, *pace* Dr Smith (1993, 204) it is indeed 'just irrational to canonise one of [these two plays] while anathematising the other' (Sams 1986f, 2), like Professors Kerrigan (1986a, 1986b), Muir (1960, 1982), Proudfoot (1982, 1986b), Taylor (1986, 1990) and Wells (1986b, 1990). Palaeographers as well as stylometrists should reconsider all the relevant facts, including *yt*, *yf* and other such *prima facie* identificatory formulations in the *Thomas More* manuscript *c.* 1600, Shakespeare's will and elsewhere.

  Finally the components of Shakespeare's early style should be rethought and reanalysed, as already suggested (Sams 1995a). It will be found that the only corresponding item missing from *Edward III*, out of a long list, is bawdry, and even that is represented by the King's cheery quip about how he would rather have the Countess 'chased than chaste'. If a reason is sought for that omission, it is that this play was written more for the gentry than the groundlings; and the impressive inferences drawn from an analysis of annotations on Lord Hunsdon's own copy of Froissart's *Chroniques* affirm the probability that *Edward III* was performed before him and his family by the company formed under his patronage as Lord Chamberlain in 1594, of which Shakespeare was an early and leading member (Prior 1993–4).

Appendix B: Edmund Ironside *and* Sir Thomas More *Hand D*

The self-evident explanation for all the multifarious correspondences listed in Appendix A is that *Ironside c.* 1588 was a Shakespeare play (Everitt 1954, Sams 1982a, 1982b, 1985d, 1986d), and that its British Library manuscript is a holograph (as first proposed by Everitt 1954, and independently avouched by the documents expert Charles Hamilton, 1986). Thus all the many resemblances would have stemmed from Shakespeare's own hand, in every sense. In theory, this thesis could be confirmed or falsified from a comparison with Hand D of *Sir Thomas More*, an accredited Shakespeare manuscript, generally attributed to 1603–4 (Taylor 1988, 124–5). At least the identifications of both playscripts as by Shakespeare have never been seriously challenged, let alone refuted. But nor have they been generally accepted. The requisite expertise is rare. Handwriting identification is difficult and time-consuming; the hazards (such as error and eye-strain) are high, and the rewards low. Access to the two documents is restricted to British Library pass-holders; *Ironside* is over 2,000 lines long and Hand D often illegible; reproductions are unsatisfactory and copying is expensive.

Further, the occasional differences of writing, spelling, abbreviation and so on are sometimes more evident than the deep and consistent similarities. But hands and their habits can change overnight, and here the hiatus spans some fifteen years. For all these reasons, the present analysis concentrates on character-istics and claims that can be considered without detailed investigation of the original documents (though interested readers can find facsimile pages of *Ironside* in Boswell 1928 and Everitt 1954, and of all three Hand D pages in Pollard 1923).

First, each of these playscripts is itself vastly variable in its own internal letter-formation and spelling, from page to page, from line to line, and even from word to word. Indeed, this is a prime shared quality. Its evidential value may not be instantly apparent; the argument 'that's Proteus; I'd know him anywhere' has not impressed the profession. Nevertheless it is worth asking how many dramatists habitually wrote thus. One certainly did, namely Shakespeare, as a study of his signatures shows; they deploy *forty-three* distinct letter-forms, although a mere fifteen would have sufficed for what he wished to write (Everitt 1954, 93). Hand D also uses twice as many letter-forms as letters; the *Ironside* proportion is higher still. But each of those sources shares the same divergence, e.g. the same five varieties of letter *a* and so forth.

Next, Shakespeare's spelling is equally variable, on the evidence of the Quartos (Wilson in Pollard 1923, 132–41) and the works in general; so is that of Hand D and of *Ironside*. But here too there is plentiful overlap. Again, both those playscripts show signs of legal skills, including what is called a scrivener style (Boswell 1928, vi–vii; Thompson in Pollard 1923, 70ff.). Both exemplify two different and distinguishable modes of penmanship – one light and fast, the other heavier and more deliberate (Everitt 1954, 48–9; Thompson in Pollard 1923, 68–9); these correspond to the ordinary Tudor secretary hand written at speed and the more formal and deliberate legal script. Both use spellings and vocabulary which are old-fashioned for the later Elizabethan age (Boswell 1928, vii; Pollard 1923, 17), as if each scribe had first learned his letters decades earlier, perhaps in the provinces. The constant use of *y* for *i*, e.g. in *yt* or *yf*, is one typical example among very many.

Each of these playscripts averages some 50 lines per page. Hand D's speech-prefixes are very variable; thus the very first speaker is variously Lincolne, Linco, Linc and Lin within the first dozen lines. The *Ironside* penman exhibits a parallel impatience when working at speed; thus in Act III the Archbishop of Canterbury is first Caunterb, then Canter and finally Cant'.

But this is just a beginning. Both hands very often employ an initial capital *C* instead of a small *c*, not only on nouns but even on verbs – which very few other Elizabethan or Jacobean sources, written or printed, ever deliberately capitalised. Of course all such claims rely on personal experience, which is both variable and fallible. Nevertheless, it is extremely rare for any writer to capitalise the verbs 'Command', 'Cannot' or 'Come'; and *all three of those certainly rare and perhaps unique expressions appear in both sources*. Indeed, the only other comparable formation that comes to mind may be one that in fact exemplifies the rule; the verb 'Commend', so spelt, occurs in the 1609 *Sonnets* (69.4), which were *prima facie* printed from Shakespeare's autograph (Sams 1995a, 195). No doubt the writer realised in each case that his minuscule *c* could be confused with other letters, whereas the capital equivalent could not. But then the practice should be consistent, and it is not, in either playscript. Thus Hand D uses 15 initial *c*s of which 10 are capitalised and 5 left as minuscule. The treatment in the *Ironside* MS, which is a fair copy intended for performance and later printing (as shown by the many italicised words) is predictably more consistent. But there are still irregularities; thus of some 500 words beginning with *c*, some 400 are capitalised and the rest (though often beginning the selfsame words) are not. The inference is surely manifest; each writer intended to capitalise for clarity but often omitted to do so, whether through haste or inadvertence or both. How many playwrights in these years wrote thus?

Of those playwrights, how many replaced other initial minuscules by their capital forms, for no ascertainable grammatical reason, and also on verbs as well as nouns? The 147 lines of Hand D contain (in modernised spelling) Beef, Brother (twice), Bushell, Dung, German, Justice, Lead (vb.), Let (vb.), Peace, Sergeant, Sheriff (thrice), Wisdom (twice), while other countries ('spain', 'portugal') offices ('magistrate', 'mayor', 'sheriff') or abstract nouns ('law', 'inhumanity') remain uncapitalised. *Ironside* uses those capitals too, among others, just as arbitrarily. Yet the total picture stays constant. Setting aside the *C*- or *c*- words already discussed, some other arbitrary capital letter occurs once in every ten lines set down by Hand D; the 2,000 lines of *Ironside* exhibit exactly the same proportion.

Of the playwrights who needlessly capitalised verbs as well as nouns beginning with *C* and other letters, how many abbreviated the prefix 'par' to '*p*'? This quirk has become strangely habitual in both sources. Thus the *Ironside* hand thrice writes 'parte' as '*pte*', and once 'partners' as '*ptners*'. The same syllable is expressed thus even within the middle of a word, where it has no prefixal function; 'departe' is 'de*pte*'. Hand D is deeply steeped in the same dye; it amusingly uses the same symbol for the first syllables of 'parsnip', 'parsnips' and 'partly', within the same six lines. The same abbreviation also stands for 'per' in both playscripts, in each of which 'perceive' is written as '*pceave*'. Only one playwright is known to have adopted this rather confusing use of the same symbol for two quite different syllables, namely Shakespeare, on the independent evidence that 'person' is misprinted as 'parson', and conversely, in undisputedly authentic Quarto texts (Wilson, in Pollard 1923, 137). And that habit came so naturally to his hand that he even wrote the syllable 'per' or 'pear' in his own name with the same symbol, at the foot of his testimony in the Belott lawsuit of 1612. A similar (but not identical) symbol, another variant of the letter *p*, does duty for the prefix 'pro', again in Hand D (p[ro]clamation) as well as *Ironside* (p[ro]nounce). Curiously, Wilson (in Pollard 1923, 141) omits to mention these abbreviations, which surely have some evidential value. He does however include the overhead loop that stands for 'er' in Hand D's 'euer' (= ever); and this too is equally idiosyncratically used in *Ironside* in the form 'Sou[er]aigne'. Many other abbreviations are common to both sources, though not common even singly, let alone in combination, in other playscripts of the period. Thus a superscribed tittle as a contraction-sign indicates the omission of a terminal or a doubled *n*, or a doubled *m*, and this sign itself is often inadvertently omitted. Similarly the contraction 'Matie' often appears for 'Majesty', again with the sign often omitted. 'L,' is used for 'Lord', 'ore' for 'o'er' and 'w^ch', 'yo^u', 'youle' or 'yor' for 'with', 'which', 'you', 'you'll' or 'your' respectively. 'Tis' and 'twere' are also frequent in both sources, and the *OED* (whose researchers did not collate either playscript) can find no instance of the latter before Shakespeare's *Macbeth* and *Coriolanus* dated 1605 and 1607 respectively. 'Tis' and 'twere' are also frequent in accredited Quarto texts; so are 'L', 'M^atie' and 'ore'.

The letter-formation is equally quirky. In the secretary hand of each playscript, only one letter is in the wrong fount, so to speak; this is a long italic *s*, which occurs in the middle of *Ironside*'s 'prosperitie' and at the beginning of Hand D's 'seriant' (= sergeant). It is also found in the middle of the otherwise secretary-style signature 'Shakespeare' as appended to his Blackfriars conveyance of 1613. The minim errors already defined (p. 192 above) seem especially identificatory, because of their profusion in both playscripts, as shown by the footnotes in Boswell 1928 *passim* or Pollard 1923, 228–43; their line-numbers are added to facilitate reference. Thus the *Ironside* hand sets down the n̲n̲ of 'tyranny' (194) as three minims only, i.e. one n̲ has only one minim. Similarly in Hand D, the n̲ in 'prenty' (22) – itself a false start for 'prentisses' (= apprentices) has only one minim. In 'conquest' (12), 'enough' (174) and 'number' (189) however the *Ironside* n̲ has three minims; so has the Hand D n̲ in 'and' (101). Again, u̲n̲ in *Ironside* 'daunte' (138) has only three minims instead of the required four; the same is true of the u̲n̲ in Hand D's 'sounde' (117). Letter m̲ is shorn of a minim in *Ironside*'s 'esteemed' (237), 'Comaunding' (875), 'my' (1392) and 'exclaime' (1648), so that they read 'esteened', 'Conaunding', 'ny' and 'exclaine', respectively; in Hand D, similarly, 'William' (10) appears as 'Willian'. In *Ironside*'s 'Canutus' (1569), conversely, n̲u̲ has an extra minim, making five in all; Hand D writes u̲n̲ in 'dung' (12) exactly thus. In *Ironside*, the 'mun' of 'Edmund' (1839) has six minims only, instead of seven; similarly in Hand D the u̲n̲ in 'found' has three minims only, instead of four. This latter error may incidentally shed some light on the mysterious 'momtanish' in Hand D's line 140; presumably 'mountanish' was intended. Again, *Ironside* has four minims for i̲n̲ (770) and six for i̲m̲u̲ in 'contimulious' (830); these have no Hand D equivalents. But the degree of correspondence elsewhere is surely beginning to extend beyond coincidence. Of those playwrights whose handwriting exhibited all the other characteristics listed above (such as the same capitals, mainly *C*, and the same abbreviations) how many made the same minim mistakes (also in the same proportions per line)? Furthermore, other mistakes proliferate, in profusion. There are dozens of alterations, omissions and false starts in the 147 lines of Hand D; in the 2,000 lines of *Ironside* there are hundreds – which makes it quite inconceivable (though frequently assumed and asserted, e.g. in Boswell 1928, vi) that the latter hand is that of a professional copyist. On the contrary, the difficulties it must have presented even to the most competent of compositors would serve to align it with Shakespeare's hand, which was notoriously hard to read, even without the positive identifications with Hand D.

There are however a few consistent differences among the topics accessible to amateurs, on which this Appendix concentrates. These concern spellings, and they consist in only two general categories. 'Self' in *Ironside* is always 'sealf' in Hand D; and the former's modal auxiliaries 'should' and 'would' become 'coold', 'shoold' and 'woold' in the latter. But Shakespeare's spelling was endlessly variable from line to line, let alone over a fifteen-year time-span. It was also very often phonetic, and *Ironside* writes e.g. 'help' as 'healpe'. The poor Danes are recorded as crying 'Healpe, healpe, Canutus, healpe and sccor [*sic*] vs', complete with gratuitous capital *H* and the inadvertent omission of a two-minim letter; 'ea' was a permissible way of writing the short e̲, and 'sealf' or 'sealves', was acceptable in *c.* 1588 as in *c.* 1603–4. But Shakespeare was a phonetic as well as a variable speller; and *Edward III*, like *Ironside* and the *Sonnets*, often represents modern o̲ as o̲u̲, e.g. by writing the syllable '-old' as '-ould' (gould, hould, etc.). Sooner or later, anyone with such a writing habit might well wish to distinguish the very different sound o̲o̲ in 'could', 'should' and 'would' by writing them as 'coold', 'shoold' and 'woold' respectively.

All in all, therefore, the general writing habits exemplified in *Ironside* and Hand D, as well as the more technical aspects of their letter formations as attested by the only two experts who have ever published the results of their analyses (Thompson 1923, Everitt 1954), confirm identity of penmanship and hence authorship. But Hand D, by common consent as well as detailed analysis, is Shakespeare's own. So, therefore, is *Ironside*. Thus the argument of Appendix A above (pp. 203–18) receives further corroboration; for, as it seeks to show, whoever wrote *Edward III* wrote *Ironside* too.

Bibliography

The following list, which includes sources consulted as well as those cited, is designed to aid further research and reflection. Selected rejections, refutations and recantations have been added in square brackets.

CHE	The Chronicle of Higher Education
ELN	English Language Notes
ELR	English Literary Renaissance
FT	Financial Times
HamS	Hamlet Studies
JEGP	Journal of English and German Philology
LLC	Literary and Linguistic Computing
LRB	London Review of Books
NYRB	New York Review of Books
N&Q	Notes and Queries
PBA	Proceedings of the British Academy
PMLA	Proceedings of the Modern Language Association
RES	Review of English Studies
SJ	Shakespeare Jahrbuch
SN	Shakespeare Newsletter
SQ	Shakespeare Quarterly
SS	Shakespeare Survey
ST	Sunday Times
TES	Times Educational Supplement
THES	Times Higher Education Supplement
TLS	Times Literary Supplement

Abbott, E. *A Shakespearean Grammar*, 1869.

Alexander, P. *Shakespeare's Henry VI and Richard III*, 1929 [Greer 1933, 1956, 1957; Craig 1961; Sams 1983, 1989a, 1995a, etc.; Urkowitz 1988; Bains (forthcoming)].

Anders, H. *Shakespeare's Books*, 1904.

Anon., 'Footnotes' in *CHE* 25/9, 27 Oct. 1982.

Arden, J. 'First Appointment', *TES*, 24 Feb. 1995, 13.

Armstrong, E. *Shakespeare's Imagination*, 1946, 2/1963.

Armstrong, R. ed., *Edward III*, in *Six Early Plays Related to the Shakespeare Canon*, ed. E. Everitt, 1965.

Bains, Y. *Making Sense of the First Quartos of Shakespeare's Romeo and Juliet, Henry V, The Merry Wives of Windsor and Hamlet*, 1995.

——— *The Contention and The True Tragedy: William Shakespeare's First Versions of Henry VI, Parts 2 and 3* (forthcoming).

Baldwin, T. *On the Literary Genetics of Shakespeare's Plays 1592–4*, 1959.

Baldwin, W. et al., *Mirror for Magistrates*, 1559.

Bandello, M. 'Oduardo terzo, re d'Inghilterra, ama la figliuola d'un suo soggetto e la piglia per moglie' in *Novelle* (ii.37), 1554.

Bartlett, H. *Mr. William Shakespeare: Original and Early Editions of his Quartos and Folios, his Source Books, and those containing Contemporary Notices*, 1922.

Barton, A. 'Leontes and the Spider: Language and the Speaker in Shakespeare's Last Plays', in *Shakespeare's Styles*, ed. P. Edwards et al., 1980.

Bate, J. 1995a. 'Shakespeare the Farmer's Boy', *Sunday Telegraph*, 15 Jan. 1995.

——— 1995b, ed., *Titus Andronicus*, 1995.

Bell, M. 'Concordance to the Shakespeare Apocrypha', diss., Liverpool, 1959.

Boswell, E. ed., *Edmund Ironside*, Malone Society, 1928.

Boyce, C. *Shakespeare A to Z*, 1990.

Bradbrook, M. *Shakespeare and Elizabethan Poetry*, 1951, 2/1964.

——— 'Shakespeare's Eleven Plus', *Guardian*, 13 Feb. 1986.

Broadbent, C. personal communication, 13 Feb. 1987.

Brooke, C. ed., *The Shakespeare Apocrypha*, 1908, 69–101.

Brown, T. '*Edward III*', *Guardian*, 3 July 1987.

Bullough, E. *Narrative and Dramatic Sources of Shakespeare*, 8 vols, 1957–75.

Burgess, A. 'Cygnet of Avon', *Observer*, 2 Feb. 1986.

Calvert, H. personal communication, 2 Jan. 1987.

Capell, E. *Prolusions*, 1760.

——— ed., *The Comedies, Histories and Tragedies*, 10 vols (1767–8).

Chambers, E. *The Elizabethan Stage*, 1923.

——— *William Shakespeare: A Study of Facts and Problems*, 2 vols, 1930, i.516–18.

Chambers, R. 'The Expression of Ideas – particularly Political Ideas – in the Three Pages and in Shakespeare', in *Shakespeare's Hand in the Play of Sir Thomas More*, ed. Pollard, 1923, 142–87.

——— 'Shakespeare and the Play of *More*', in *Man's Unconquerable Mind*, 1939, 204–49.

Collier, J. *King Edward the Third: A Historical Play attributed by Edward Capell to William Shakespeare and now proved to be his Work*, 1874.

Corathers, D. 'Much Ado', *Dramatics*, 88, 1986, 15–17.

Courthope, W. *A History of English Poetry*, iv, 1903, rev. 1911, 1916.

Craig, H. *A New Look at Shakespeare's Quartos*, 1961.

Crundell, H. 'Drayton and *Edward III*', *N&Q*, clxxvi, 1939, 258–60.

Curzon, L. *Law of Evidence*, 1978.

Deloney, T. 'Of King Edward the Third and the faire Countess of Salisbury, setting forth her constancy and endlesse glory', in *The Garden of Goodwill*, 1593.

Digges, L. 'Upon Master William Shakespeare, the deceased Author, and his Poems', in *Poems*, 1640.

Eagleson, R. ed., *A Shakespeare Glossary*, 1986 [Sams 1991].

Evans, G. ed., *The Riverside Shakespeare*, 1973.

Everitt, E. *The Young Shakespeare: Studies in Documentary Evidence, Anglistica II*, 1954.

——— *Six Early Plays Related to the Shakespeare Canon, Anglistica XIV*, 1965.

Ewbank, I. 'Shakespearean Constructs', *TLS*, 25 April 1986, 451 [Sams 1986e].

Ezard, J. 'Bard's Play Theory Backed', *Guardian*, 4 Sept. 1986.

Fabian, R. *New Chronicles of England and of France*, 1516.

Farmer, J. ed., *The Reign of King Edward III 1596*, in facsimile, 1910.

Fleissner, R. 'Edmund Ironside', *TLS*, 3 Sept. 1982, 947 [Sams 1982b].

—— 'Is the Handwriting in the *Cardenio* Ms the Same as That in Shakespeare's Will?', *SN*, 1995, 15.

Foster, D. review of *Edmund Ironside*, *SQ*, 39, 1989a, 118–23 [Sams 1988b].

—— 'Donald Foster replies', *SQ*, 39, 1988b, 253.

Froissart, J. *Chroniques*, 1513, trans. Lord Berners, 1523–5.

Godshalk, W. 'Dating Edward III', *N&Q*, ccxl, 1995, 299–300.

Golding, S. 'The Authorship of *Edward III*', *N&Q*, cliv, 1939, 313–15.

Greene, R. *A Groatsworth of Wit*, 1592.

Greer, C. 'The York and Lancaster Quarto–Folio Sequence', *PMLA*, 48, 1933, 655–705.

—— 'The Quarto–Folio Relationship in *2* and *3 Henry VI* once again', *N&Q*, cci, 1956, 420–1.

—— 'More about the Actor-Reporter Theory in *Contention* and *True Tragedy*', *N&Q*, ccii, 1957, 52–3.

Greg, W. *Dramatic Documents from the Elizabethan Playhouses*, 2 vols, 1931.

Halliday, F. *A Shakespeare Dictionary*, 1952, 2/1964.

Hamilton, C. *In Search of Shakespeare: A Survey into the Poet's Life and Handwriting*, 1985.

—— personal communication, 30 June 1986; and see Corathers, and Ezard.

Harbage, A. *Annals of English Drama*, rev. S. Schoenbaum, 1964.

Hart, A. 'The Vocabulary of *Edward III*', in *Shakespeare and the Homilies*, 1934, 219–41.

—— 'Vocabularies of Shakespeare's Plays', *RES*, 19, 1943, 128–40.

—— 'The Growth of Shakespeare's Vocabulary', *RES*, 19, 1943, 242–54.

Hattaway, M. ed., *1–3 Henry VI*, 1990–3 [Sams 1994b].

Hawkes, N. 'Play on Words Blanks Out the Bard's Drama', *Observer*, 12 Jan. 1986. [meaning T. Merriam's notion, called 'the pitiless scrutiny of science', that *Ironside* was 890 million million million times more likely to have been written by Greene than by Shakespeare; Sams 1995a, 190].

Hearne, T. *Remarks and Collections*, ix, Oxford Historical Society, 1914, 393–6.

Heath, T. personal communication, 5 Jan. 1986.

Herz, E. *Englische Schauspieler und englisches Schauspiel zur Zeit Shakespeares in Deutschland*, 1903.

Heywood, T. *Edward IV*, 1599.

—— *An Apology for Actors*, 1612.

Hill R. 'The Composition of *Titus Andronicus*', *SS*, 10, 1957, 60–70.

Hobday, C. 'Why the Sweets Melted: A Study in Shakespeare's Imagery', *SQ*, 16, 1965, 1–17.

—— *Shakespeare's Mind* (unpubl.), 1969.

Holderness, G. and Loughrey, B. 'The Real Shakespeare', *TLS* Letters, 5 May 1995.

Holinshed, R. *The Chronicles of England, Scotland and Ireland*, 1577, 2/1587.

Honigmann, E. *Shakespeare's Impact on his Contemporaries*, 1982.

—— *Shakespeare: the 'Lost Years'*, 1985.

—— 'Fingerprinting Shakespeare', *NYRB*, 12 Feb. 1987, 23–4 [Sams 1987a].

—— *Myriad-minded Shakespeare*, 1989.

Hope, J. *The Authorship of Shakespeare's Plays: A Sociolinguistic Study*, 1994 [Sams 1995e].

Horn, F. *'The Raigne of King Edward III*: a Critical Edition', diss, Delaware, 1969.

Housman, A. 'Cambridge Inaugural Lecture, 1911', in *Collected Poems and Selected Prose*, ed. C. Ricks, 1988.

Hoyle, M. *'Edward III'*, *FT*, 3 July 1987.

Jackson, M. 'Shakespeare and *Edmund Ironside*', *N&Q*, ccviii, 1963, 331–2 [Sams 1985d, 1986d].

——'Edward III, Shakespeare and Pembroke's Men', *N&Q*, ccx, 1965, 329–31.

——'A Note on the Text of Edward III', *N&Q*, ccxvi, 1971, 423–4.

——'Edmund Ironside', *TLS* Letters, 10 Sept. 1982, 973 [Sams 1982b].

——'The Transmission of Shakespeare's Text', in *The Cambridge Companion to Shakespeare Studies*, ed. Wells, 1986, 163–85.

Jenkins, H. 'Shakespeare's Bad Quarto', *TLS* Letters, 15 April 1994 [Sprinchorn 1994c].

Jones, J. 'Naming the Bard', *FT*, 1 Feb. 1986 [Sams 1986d, ix].

Keatley, C. personal communication, 8 Feb. 1986.

Kerrigan, J. ed., *Love's Labour's Lost*, 1982.

——1986a 'Diary', *LRB*, 6 Feb. 1986, 21 [Sams 1986c, 1986d, ix].

——1986b ed., *The Sonnets*, 1986.

——'*Henry IV* and the Death of Old Double', *Essays in Criticism*, 1990, 24–53.

Kingston, J. review of *Edward III*, *The Times*, 2 July 1987.

Koskenniemi, I. 'Themes and Imagery in *Edward III*', *Neuphilologische Mitteilungen*, 65, 1964, 466–80.

Lapides, F. ed., *Edward III*, 1966, 1980.

Lebrecht, N. 'Now, a New Play?', *ST*, 29 Dec. 1985, 1–2.

Levi, P. 'Something Useful in the New Shakespeare', *Literary Review*, May 1988, 5.

—— *The Life and Times of William Shakespeare*, 1988 [Sams 1989b].

Limon, J. *Gentlemen of a Company: English Players in Central and Eastern Europe, 1590–1660*, 1985.

Livy, T. *History of Rome*, 35 books.

Locke, J. *An Essay Concerning Human Understanding*, 1690.

MacDonald, M. *Brahms*, 1990.

Madden, D. *The Diary of Master William Silence*, 1897.

Mann, F. *The Works of Thomas Deloney*, 1912, 370–75, 581–4.

Marder, L. 'Eric Sams and *Edmund Ironside*', *SN*, 1986, 26.

Martin, R. 'Critical Editions of *Edmund Ironside* and Anthony Brewer's *The Lovesick King*', D.Phil. thesis, University of Oxford, 1986.

Matthews, R. and Merriam, T. 'Neural Computation in Stylometry: An Application to the Works of Shakespeare and Fletcher', *LLC*, vol. 8 no. 4, 1993, 203–9.

——'A bard by any other name', *New Scientist*, 22 Jan 1994, 23–7.

Melchiori, G. *Shakespeare's Garter Plays*, 1994.

Meres, F. *Palladis Tamia*, 1598.

Merriam, T. cited in Hawkes, 1986, q.v.

——'Marlowe's Hand in *Edward III*', *LLC*, vol. 8 no. 2, 1993, 60–72; see also Matthews and Merriam.

Metz, G. *Four Plays Ascribed to Shakespeare*, 1982.

Mills, J. personal communication, 28 Jan. 1987.

Milward, P. 'Edmund Ironside', *TLS* Letters, 19 Nov. 1982, 1273.

228   EDWARD III

Moorman, F. in *Cambridge History of English Literature*, 1910.
Muir, K. 'A Reconsideration of *Edward III*', *SS*, 6, 1953, 39–48.
—— *Shakespeare as Collaborator*, 1960.
—— cited in *CHE*, vol. 25 no. 9, 27 Oct. 1982, 19.
Nashe, T. Preface to Greene's *Menaphon*, 1589.
—— *Pierce Penniless*, 1592.
Noble, R. *Shakespeare's Biblical Knowledge*, 1935.
Nunn, T. in 'Chit Chat', *The Stage*, 1986.
O'Connor, F. *The Road to Stratford*, 1948, 24–33.
Onions, C. *A Shakespeare Glossary*, 1911, 2/1919 repr. with corrections 1980; see also Eagleson.
Østerberg, V. 'The Countess Scenes of *Edward III*', *SJ*, 65, 1929, 49–91.
Ovid, P. *Fasti*.
—— *Heroides*.
—— *Metamorphoses*.
Oxford English Dictionary [*OED*], 1897–1928, 2/1989, ed. J. Simpson and E. Wiener.
Painter, W. *The Palace of Pleasure*, 1566–7, 2/1575.
Parfitt, G. ed., *Edward III*, 1985.
Peter, J. review of *Ironside* performance, *ST*, 20 April 1986.
Phipson, E. in *Transactions of the New Shakespeare Society*, 1889.
Plutarch *Lives*, trans, North, 1579.
Pollard, A. ed., *Shakespeare's Hand in the Play of Sir Thomas More*, 1923.
—— Introduction, ibid., 1–32.
Potter, L. 'Shakespeare's Life, Times and Stage', *SS*, 36, 1983, 172.
—— review of *Edward III*, *Renaissance Drama Newsletter*, vol. 7 no. 2, 1987, 22–4.
—— 'Reconstructing Shakespeare', *TLS*, 7 April 1995, 21.
Prior, R. 'The Date of *Edward III*', *N&Q*, ccxxxv, 1990, 178–80.
—— 'Was *The Raigne of King Edward III* a Compliment to Lord Hunsdon?', *Connotations*, vol. 3 no. 3, 1993–94, 243–64.
Proudfoot, R. review of Schäfer 1980, in *ELN*, Sept. 1981, 60–62.
—— 'Edmund Ironside', *TLS* Letters, 17 Sept. and 8 Oct. 1982, 1102 [Sams 1982b and 1986d].
—— 1986a '*The Reign of King Edward III* and Shakespeare', British Academy Shakespeare Lecture, 1985, *PBA*, lxxi, 1986.
—— 1986b 'Canon Fodder', *THES*, 27 June 1986, 18 [Sams 1986f].
—— 'Commentary', *TLS*, 17 July 1987, 770.
—— 'King Edward III 1596, by . . .?', Cambridge Arts Theatre programme, 27 July–1 Aug. 1987.
—— preface to Slater 1988, xiii.
Puttenham, G. *The Arte of Poesie*, 1589.
Ranson, N. and Kneploy, J. '*Edmund Ironside*: A Reappraisal Appraised', *SN*, 1986, 16.
Ratcliffe, M. 'Well Done, by Anon', *Observer*, 4 July 1987.
Reese, M. review of Everitt 1954, *RES*, vi, 1955, 310–13.
Ribner, I., *The English History Play in the Age of Shakespeare*, 1957.
Riverside Shakespeare, see Evans, G.
Roe, J. ed., *The Poems*, 1992.
Rowse, A. 'Further Light on Shakespeare', *Spectator*, 26 April 1986 [Sams 1986g].

—— *Discovering Shakespeare*, 1989.

Sams, E. 1982a '*Edmund Ironside*: a Reappraisal', *TLS*, 13 Aug. 1982, 879.

—— 1982b 'Edmund Ironside', *TLS* Letters, 24 Sept. 1982, 1037 and 29 Oct. 1982, 1193.

—— 1983 'Viewpoint: Shakespeare's Text and Common Sense', *TLS*, 2 Sept. 1983, 933–4.

—— 1984 'Dating *The Shrew*', *TLS* Letters, 3 Aug. 1984, 869.

—— 1985a 'Editing Shakespeare', *TLS* Letters, 1 Feb. 1985, 119 and 22 Feb. 1985, 201.

—— 1985b 'Dramatically Different', *TLS*, 22 March 1985, 318.

—— 1985c 'Shakespeare's Lost Years', *TLS*, 17 May 1985, 549.

—— 1985d *Shakespeare's Lost Play Edmund Ironside*, 1985.

—— 1985e 'The Timing of the Shrews', *N&Q*, ccxxx, 1985, 33–45.

—— 1986a 'The "Lost" Shakespeare', *ST*, 2 Feb. 1986, 34.

—— 1986b 'The Bard's Play: Taylor's U-turn', *ST*, 16 Feb. 1986, 29.

—— 1986c 'Shakespeare Nods', *LRB*, 6 March 1986, 4.

—— 1986d *Shakespeare's Edmund Ironside: The Lost Play*, 2/1986.

—— 1986e 'Edmund Ironside', *TLS* Letters, 9 May 1986, 501.

—— 1986f 'Right Playwright', *THES*, 1 Aug. 1986, 1 and 22 Aug., 2.

—— 1986g 'Attrib. Shakespeare', *Spectator*, 21 June 1986.

—— 1987a 'Edmund Ironside', *NYRB*, 7 May 1987, 48.

—— 1987b 'Where There's a Will: the Oxford or the Stratford Shakespeare?', *Encounter*, lxix/1 June 1987, 54–7.

—— 1987c 'Revisionist Shakespeare', *Oxford Magazine*, 25, 1987, 7; 27, 1987, 15.

—— 1988a 'Oxford Shakespeare', *LRB* Letters, 18 May 1988.

—— 1988b 'To the Editor', *SQ*, 39, 1988, 25.

—— 1988c review of Ule, *A Concordance to the Shakespeare Apocrypha*, *N&Q*, ccxxxiii, 1988, 372–3.

—— 1988d 'William Shakespeare: A Textual Companion', *TLS*, 11–17 Nov. 1988, 1251.

—— 1989a 'Shakespeare, or Bottom? The Myth of "Memorial Reconstruction"', *Encounter*, lxxii/1, Jan. 1989, 41–5.

—— 1989b 'A Plague o' Both Your Houses', *Encounter*, lxxii/4, April 1989, 58–60.

—— 1989c 'Shakespeare Studies', *TLS*, 8–14 Sept. 1989, 973.

—— 1990a 'Fatal Fallacy', *Encounter*, lxxiv/1, Jan.–Feb. 1990, 62–4.

—— 1990b 'Mistaken Methodology', *LRB*, 14 June 1990, 4–5; 28 June 1990.

—— 1991 '"If you have tears . . .": Onions and Shakespeare', *Connotations*, 1, 1991, 181–6.

—— 1992a 'Shakespeare and the Oxford Imprint', *TLS*, 6 March 1992, 13.

—— 1992b 'The Play's the Thing', *THES* Letters, 3 July 1992.

—— 1993a 'A Documentary Life?', *TLS*, 12 Feb, 1993, 13.

—— 1993b 'The Hand of a Lawyer's Clerk?', *TLS*, 24 Dec. 1993, 14.

—— 1994a review of *Hamlet* 1603 and *The Taming of a Shrew* 1594, ed. Holderness and Loughrey, *N&Q*, ccxxxix, 1994, 93–4.

—— 1994b review of *1–3 Henry VI*, ed. M. Hattaway, *N&Q*, ccxxxix, 1994, 242–3.

—— 1994c 'Edmund Ironside and "Stylometry"', *N&Q*, ccxxxix, 1994, 469–72.

—— 1995a *The Real Shakespeare*, 1995.

—— 1995b 'Bard Barb', *THES*, 14 July 14, 1995.

—— 1995c 'Hamnet or Hamlet, That is the Question', *HamS*, 17, i–ii, Summer–

Winter 1995, 94–8.

—— 1995d 'Look Here upon this Picture', [published as ' "My Name's Hamlet, Revenge": Why Two Dutchmen have the Answer to the Riddle of Shakespeare's Early Hamlet'], *TLS*, 22 Sept. 1995, 18.

—— 1995e review of Hope, *The Authorship of Shakespeare's Plays*, *N&Q*, ccxl, 486–7.

—— 1996a, review of Irace, *Reforming the 'Bad' Quartos*, *N&Q*, ccxli, 211–12.

—— 1996b, rebuttal of Smith 1995, *N&Q*, ccxli [forthcoming].

Sanders, N. ed., *The Two Gentlemen of Verona*, 1958.

—— ed., *1–3 Henry VI*, 1981.

Schaar, C. *Elizabethan Sonnet Themes and the Dating of Shakespeare's Sonnets*, 1962.

Schäfer, J. *Documentation in the O.E.D.*, 1980 [Proudfoot 1981].

Schoenbaum, S. *Internal Evidence and Elizabethan Dramatic Authorship*, 1966.

—— *William Shakespeare: A Documentary Life*, 1975.

—— *A Compact Documentary Life*, 1977, 2/1987.

—— *Records and Images*, 1981.

—— *Shakespeare's Lives*, 1971, 2/1991.

Seymour-Smith, M. 'Beyond Necessity', *Scotland on Sunday*, 26 Feb. 1995.

Shirley, F. *Swearing and Perjury in Shakespeare's Plays*, 1979.

Shorter, E. 'A Robust Revival', *Daily Telegraph*, 4 July 1987.

Simpson, J. personal communication, 8 Nov. 1993.

Simpson, R. 'Are There Any Extant MSS in Shakespeare's Handwriting?' *N&Q*, viii (July 1871), 1–3.

Sisson, C. review of Everitt 1954, *SQ*, 6, 1955, 455–6.

Slater E. 'The Vocabulary of *Edward III*', diss, London University, 1982.

—— 'Edmund Ironside', *TLS*, 18 March 1983, 268.

—— *The Problem of the Reign of King Edward III: A Statistical Approach*, 1988.

Smith, M. 'Eric Sams and *Edmund Ironside*', *SN*, 36, 1986, 1, 19 [Smith, M. 1993].

—— '*Edmund Ironside* and Principles of Authorship Attribution', *SN*, 37, 1987, 50.

—— 1988a 'Word-links and Shakespearean Authorship and Chronology', *N&Q*, ccxxxiii, 1988, 57–9.

—— 1988b 'Word-links and the Authorship of *Edmund Ironside*', *N&Q*, ccxxxiii, 1988, 447–9.

—— 'Shakespearean Chronology: A New Approach to the Method of Word Links', *N&Q*, ccxxxv, 1990, 198–203.

—— 'The Authorship of *The Raigne of King Edward the Third*', *LLC*, 6, 1991, 166–74.

—— '*Edmund Ironside*', *N&Q*, ccxxxviii, 1993, 202–5 [Sams 1994c].

—— '*Edmund Ironside*: Scholarship versus Propaganda', *N&Q*, ccxl, 1995, 294–9 [Sams 1996b].

Smith, R. 'Edward III', *JEGP*, 10, 1911, 90–104.

—— *Froissart and the English Chronicle Play*, 1915.

Spenser, E. *The Faerie Queene*, books I–II, *c.* 1589.

Spevack, M. *The Harvard Concordance to Shakespeare*, 1973

Sprinchorn, E. 'Shakespeare's Bad Quarto', *TLS* Letters, (a) 21 Jan. 1994, (b) 1 April 1994, (c) 27 April 1994 unpublished (in Sams 1995a, 134–5).

Spurgeon, C. *Shakespeare's Imagery*, 1935, 2/1965.

Steffen, T. 'Modes of Iteration in Shakespeare's Plays: The *Hanging-Love* Cluster', *SJ*, 131, 1995, 128–37

Stow, J. *Annales*, 1580.

Swinburne, A. *A Study of Shakespeare*, 1880, 2/1918, 231–75.

—— *Essays and Studies*, 1897, 325.

Taylor, G. '*Edmund Ironside*', *TLS* Letters, 1 April 1983, 328.

—— 'Anticipating an Attack', *ST*, 9 Feb. 1986, 2 [Sams 1986b; 1986d, x–xi].

—— *A Textual Companion to the Oxford Shakespeare*, 1988 [not '1987' as printed], rejects *Edward III*, 136–7 [Taylor 1990].

—— *Reinventing Shakespeare*, 1989.

—— reported as accepting *Edward III*, *SN*, 1990, 28.

Tetzeli von Rosador, K. review of *Ironside* edn (Sams 1985d), *SJ*, 1988, 305–6.

Thompson, E. in Pollard 1923.

Thompson, J. *Shakespeare and the Classics*, 1952.

Tillyard, E. *Shakespeare's History Plays*, 1944.

Timberlake, P. *The Feminine Ending in English Blank Verse*, 1931.

Tyndale, W., trans. *The New Testament*, 1526.

Ubaldino, P. *A Discourse concerning the Spanish Fleet invading England, in the Yeare 1588 . . .*, trans. Anon., 1590.

Ule, L. '*Edmund Ironside*', *TLS* Letters, 15 April 1983.

—— *A Concordance to the Shakespeare Apocrypha*, 1987.

Urkowitz, S. ' "If I mistake in those foundations I do build upon": Peter Alexander's Textual Analysis of *2–3 Henry VI*', *ELR*, 18, 1988, 230–56.

Vickers, B. '*Hamlet* by Dogberry', *TLS*, 24 Dec. 1993 [Sprinchorn 1994b].

—— 'Shakespeare's Bad Quartos', *TLS* Letters, 4 Feb. 1994 [Sprinchorn 1994b] and 4 March 1994 [Sprinchorn 1994c, in Sams 1995a, 134–5].

Waimer, P. *Elisa: Ein Newe vnd lüstige Comoedia von Eduardo dem Dritten dieses Namens, Könige in Engellandt, Vnd Fraw Elisen einer geborenen Gräffin von Warwitz*, 1591.

Wells, S. 'The Failure of *The Two Gentlemen of Verona*', *SJ*, 99, 1963, 161–73.

—— 'Introduction: The Once and Future King Lear', in *The Division of the Kingdoms*, ed. G. Taylor and M. Warren, 1983, 1–22.

—— 'Editing Shakespeare', *TLS* Letters, 7 Feb. 1985.

—— 1986a BBC radio interview, 1 Jan. 1986 [Sams 1986d, ix–xi, xiv].

—— 1986b letter rejecting *Edward III*, *LRB*, 8 March 1986 [Wells 1990].

—— 1986c *William Shakespeare: The Complete Works*, 1986.

—— 'Revisionist Shakespeare', *Oxford Magazine*, 24, 1987, 10–13; 26, 1987, 15; 28, 1987, 12–13 [Sams 1987c].

—— contributions to *Textual Companion* (Taylor 1988, q.v.).

—— reported as accepting *Edward III*, *SN*, 1990, 28.

Wentersdorf, K. 'Shakespearean Chronology and the Metrical Tests', *Shakespeare-Studien*, 1951.

—— 'The Authorship of *Edward III*', diss., Cincinnati, 1960.

—— 'The Date of *Edward III*', *SQ*, 16, 1965, 227–31.

—— 'Imagery as a Criterion of Authenticity: A Reconsideration of the Problem', *SQ*, 23, 1972, 231–59.

Whiter, W. *A Specimen of a Commentary on Shakespeare*, 1794, ed. Bell, 1972.

Wilders, J. BBC radio interview, *Kaleidoscope*, 16 Feb. 1986 [Sams 1986d, ix–x].

Williams, I. 'Much Ado about Anon', *Independent*, 2 July 1987.

Wilson, J. 'Bibliographical Links between the Three [*More*] Pages and the Good Quartos', in Pollard 1923, 113–41.

—— ed., *Titus Andronicus*, 1948, 2/1968.

Xuereb, P. '*Edmund Ironside*', *TLS*, 3 Sept. 1982, 947 [Sams 1982b].

Index

This index is inevitably somewhat selective in its treatment of topics and themes. An asterisk* denotes a component of the 'blot-cluster', qv.; a dagger† denotes a component of another such 'association of ideas', qv. Main references are in **bold** type.